REFLECTIONS ON THE WAY TO THE GALLOWS

VOICES OF JAPANESE

REBEL WOMEN

Translated and Edited

with an Introduction

by MIKISO HANE

REFLECTIONS

ON THE WAY TO

THE GALLOWS

A Special Collaboration between
Pantheon Books and the University of California Press

Library of Congress Cataloging-in-Publication Data

Reflections on the way to the gallows : voices of Japanese rebel women /
translated and edited, with an introduction by Mikiso Hane.

p.   cm.

"A special collaboration between Pantheon Books and the University of California Press."

Includes bibliographical references.

Contents: People's right and national rights / Fukuda Hideko—
Reflections on the way to the gallows / Kanno Sugako—The road to nihilism / Kaneko Fumiko—The Sekirankai / Sakai Magara...[et al.] —From the factories and the rice paddies / Tanno Setsu—Tenant disputes in Kisaki village / Takizawa Mii, Ikeda Seki, Satō Tsugi— The world of the stars / Yamashiro Tomoe.

ISBN 0-679-72273-4

1. Women social reformers—Japan—Biography.   2. Radicalism— Japan—History—20th century.   3. Japan—Social conditions—1912–1945.   I. Hane, Mikiso.

[HN726.R44   1990]

303.48'4'0952—dc20   89-43217

CONTENTS

ACKNOWLEDGMENTS

I am indebted to countless friends and colleagues for their advice and assistance. I am especially grateful to Tom Engelhardt for initiating this project and for constantly supporting and guiding my efforts with astute observations and counsel. John W. Dower also helped to launch this project and has provided me with sagacious advice and encouragement. I wish to thank Patricia Tsurumi and other readers who examined the manuscript with discerning eyes and made many insightful suggestions. Dan Cullen of Pantheon went over the first draft with meticulous care, raising questions, pinpointing ambiguities, and tightening up the writing. Also Jeanne Sugiyama, Betsey Scheiner, and Pat Castor of the University of California Press provided me with thoughtful and incisive editorial assistance in their effort to make the translation accurate, smoother, and more concise. Needless to say, whatever shortcomings remain are entirely the result of my own inadequacies.

Michiko Tanaka has been invaluable in providing research assistance in Japan. I also called upon many others for assistance, including Tatsuro Tanabe, Sharon Sievers, and Danny Kwok. The staff members of the Library of Congress, Stanford University, University of Chicago, and University of Michigan, in particular Masaei Saito of Michigan, have facilitated my access to the necessary materials.

I wish to express my gratitude to the following persons for permission to translate their writings or writings to which they or their firms hold copyrights: Kondo Chinami, Makise Kikue, Yamakawa Shinsaku, Yamashiro Tomoe, Hashimoto Yasuo of Chikuma Shobō and Manabe Takashi of Heibonsha. I also wish to thank Asahi Shimbun for use of the photograph on the cover.

I am obligated to Knox College for assistance, financial and otherwise, in facilitating my work on this project. I also wish to express my appreciation to my Knox colleagues for patiently responding to my incessant questions about diction and style. My wife, Rose, has again typed and retyped the manuscript, and my daughters, Laurie and Jennifer, have given me constant moral support.

Japanese names in the introduction and translation are transcribed in the conventional Japanese fashion: family name first, given name second. The honorific *san* used by the writers or speakers in the original texts has been deleted in the translation.

REFLECTIONS ON THE WAY TO THE GALLOWS

ONE

INTRODUCTION

"In the beginning, women in truth were the sun. We were authentic human beings. Today, women are the moon. We live as dependents and simply reflect the light that emanates from another source. Our faces are pale blue, like the moon, like the sick." So wrote Hiratsuka Raichō (1886–1971) in the first issue of her magazine, *Seitō* (Bluestocking), in 1911.[1]

Indeed, it appears that women at the dawn of Japanese history were the "sun." The Sun Goddess (Amaterasu) was the founding deity of Japan and the ancestor of the imperial family. And yet Japan became a staunchly patriarchal society, with men compelling women to be subservient, submissive, self-effacing, and humble. Centuries of feudal rule by the warrior class had fixed the place of women in the society and in the family into a rigid mold.

With the end of the feudal Tokugawa rule and the advent of the new era following the Meiji Restoration in the mid-nineteenth century, significant social, political, economic, and cultural changes began to take place. But improving the status of women was not on the agenda of the new government, as will be seen in the discussion below. In fact, it may have worsened with the new legalistic concepts that were adopted. There were, however, a growing number of women who began to fight for their rights. Some followed the path of moderation and worked for reforms within the framework of the new sociopolitical order. But many soon became disillusioned with the prospect of gaining equal rights with men under the new regime, which retained numerous aspects of the old order while establishing a new political order under the new elite, who were consolidating their political authority by marshaling military, bureaucratic, capitalistic, and traditionalist forces. This situation drove a number of advocates of women's rights to embrace radical political philosophies, including socialism, anarchism, and communism.

The excerpts from memoirs, recollections, and essays translated and included here are from women who fought for equality and social justice from the early years of Meiji to the outbreak of the Pacific War. There were, of course, many others who fought for the feminine cause and also struggled to achieve social justice and economic well-being for the general populace. The memoirs included here were chosen not only because of the significant roles these women played in the reform movements in Japan before World War II but because they are especially candid and honest in revealing their innermost thoughts and feelings and in accounting for their personal actions and experiences. Traditional strictures and conventions would have required women to conceal their true thoughts and sentiments with a veneer of platitudes, clichés, and rhetoric, but these women discussed their thoughts and lives in a down-to-earth, unadorned manner, baring their souls without pretentiousness or cant. In this respect they present a refreshing contrast to the autobiographies and essays of the more traditional-minded women leaders who sought to provide moral guidance to women in the prewar years. These activist women were in a sense all iconoclasts who challenged the conventional customs and moral principles.

What they craved most were opportunities for self-fulfillment and the freedom and right to participate in the social, political, economic, and intellectual life of the society without being compelled to become "good wives and wise mothers." They generally rejected the traditional imperatives of the marital institution and believed that they should have the freedom to live with whomever they pleased without the sanction of society. In the course of their struggle to assert their individuality, achieve self-perfection, and win equality and justice for women, they, of necessity, gravitated toward men who were challenging the established order. Thus in the early Meiji years they joined hands with the advocates of "freedom and popular rights" (*jiyū minken*). But later when the early Meiji fighters for people's rights joined the ruling elite to build "a strong and rich nation" (*fukoku kyōhei*) at the expense of the well-being of the masses, many women activists joined the circle of budding socialists, communists, and anarchists to fight, not just for their personal fulfillment, but for social justice for the underprivileged members of the society as a whole. Thus, their struggle came to be fused with the general socialist-communist struggle against the ruling elites and the entrenched economic interests.

In the course of their struggles these women displayed a remarkable degree of courage, determination, and idealism. They willingly endured privation, physical beatings, imprisonment, humiliation, sickness (most often tuberculosis), and even death. The triumph of the spirit over the fear of death is most strikingly revealed in the image of Kanno Sugako, diligently studying English by herself almost to the very moment she mounted the scaffold (see chapter 3 below). And the fiery spirit of independence is demonstrated by Kaneko Fumiko in tearing up the imperial reprieve that commuted her death sentence (chapter 4).

Although they were all fighting for the same cause, they were distinctive personalities. Some, like Kanno and Kaneko, driven to the edge in their fanatical determination to stand up against the established authorities, seemed to court death. Then there was Yamakawa Kikue, who was a rationalist (chapter 5); Tanno Setsu, the good Communist soldier to the end (chapter 6); Fukuda Hideko, whose life mirrors the transition from "popular rights" to socialism (chapter 2); Yamashiro, the idealist studying mathematics behind prison walls (chapter 7); Kutsumi Fusako, who became involved in the Sorge spy affair (chapter 5); and the young activists, Sakai Magara, Hashiura Haruko, and others, who organized the Sekirankai (Red Wave Society) and defied the authorities in joining the May Day parade in 1921 (chapter 5).

Some were accused of being sexually loose; others of being difficult and abrasive; still others of being docile slaves to their men, falling into the very trap that they were trying to escape, that is, from being treated merely as mistresses and housekeepers. Many were drawn into the radical political circle through their male relations or friends, but they were predisposed toward pursuing such a course, and once they entered that road, they turned out to be more determined and steadfast than a number of their male counterparts.

Taken together these women constitute a strong current in the history of modern Japanese social and political life. Until recently little attention was paid to their lives and the roles they played. The spotlight had been focused on the male activists. Many women, however, actively and from behind the scenes in Japan before World War II, played roles as significant as those of the male activists in laying the groundwork for the continuing struggle to extend human rights and ensure social justice for all members of the society. So the stories they tell are more than accounts of their individual lives; they constitute an essential aspect of prewar Japanese social history, especially because they reveal the inner workings of the family, the social life, the economic life, the prison life of the turbulent century following the Meiji Restoration.

The Historical Background

The sociopolitical and cultural forces that these activists had to confront can be perceived by briefly surveying the historical background, which saw the status of women changing from that of relative equality with men to one of subordination and oppression. The practices and attitudes that developed in the feudal period persisted after the Meiji Restoration of 1868 and posed formidable difficulties for women who aspired to win equality with men and develop their individuality.

In the early years of Japanese history the imperial throne was occupied frequently by women. The *History of Wei*, written in the third century A.D. in China, states that Japan in the second century was ruled over by a queen, Pimiku or Himeko. Legend has it that an empress, Jingū Kōgō, led a military expedition to Korea in the third century. The family system tended to be matriarchal. The husband went to live with the wife's family, and their children remained with their mother. Expressions of love between men and women were expressed freely in the *Man'yōshū*, a collection of poems compiled in the eighth century. And yet by the Heian period (794–1185) women were evidently beginning to be regarded as inferior to men.

What accounts for this changing status of women? In part it may have been influenced by the advent of Chinese thought and Buddhism, which occurred in the fifth and sixth centuries. Confucian China taught the doctrine of a hierarchical social order, distinguishing between "superior" and "inferior" persons, men and women, elder and younger persons. Buddhism taught that salvation was not possible for women. Not until the Kamakura period (1185–1333) and the rise of popular Buddhist sects did the concept of salvation for both sexes come to be preached in Japan.

The changes in the perception of women's status by the Heian period can be discerned in the literary masterpiece of this period, *The Tale of Genji*, written in the early eleventh century by Murasaki Shikibu (978–1016?), a lady-in-waiting at the imperial court. In this novel the hero,

Prince Genji, remarks, "But what was the good of trying to please women? If they were not fundamentally evil, they would not have been born women at all."[2] Undoubtedly the author was reflecting the thinking of men of her age, at a time when women writers like her were creating the golden age of Japanese literature.

With the ascendancy of the samurai class in the twelfth and thirteenth centuries, the condition of women seemed to have worsened considerably. As the struggle for land and power intensified, physical strength and martial skill came to be valued above all. The practice of inheritance steadily changed from the custom of dividing property among all the children to primogeniture, although in the Kamakura period daughters still had the right of inheritance, and a widowed mother controlled the family property.[3] Distinctions in speech between male and female members of the society grew more pronounced, and eventually Japanese developed into a language with one of the most finely and minutely differentiated styles of speech between men and women, with intricate levels of distinction between humble and honorific words, phrases, and speech patterns.

When the Tokugawa shogunate was established in the early seventeenth century, the founder, Ieyasu, set out to freeze the social order and establish a rigid hierarchical system. This entailed maintaining rigid distinctions between men and women, especially among the warrior class. For the samurai class, primogeniture was mandatory, and women were deprived of property rights. In this class the head of the family had absolute authority, including the power of life and death over family members. In sexual relations, the husband could be as promiscuous as he pleased, but if there was the slightest hint of infidelity on the part of the wife, she could be executed by her husband. Chikamatsu Monzaemon (1653–1724), the most renowned of the Tokugawa playwrights, has a samurai's wife tell her daughter in one of his plays, "When you are alone with any other man— besides your husband—you are not to so much as lift your head and look at him."[4]

Marriages were arranged by the parents, and daughters were given no voice in the matter. The husband could readily divorce his wife, whereas the wife had to endure hardships and abuses with patience and self-abnegation, devoting herself to the well-being of her husband and her in-laws. The ideal behavior for the samurai woman was prescribed by a Confucian scholar, Kaibara Ekken (1630–1714), in his *Onna Daigaku* (Great Learning for Women). He asserted that "from her earliest youth, a girl should observe the line of demarcation separating women from men, and never, even for an instant, should she be allowed to see or hear the slightest impropriety." The wife must serve her husband as faithfully as her husband serves the feudal lord, Ekken argued, because "a woman has no particular lord. She must look to her husband as her lord, and must serve him with all worship and reverence." In her daily life she must "rise early in the morning, and at night go late to rest." As for the character of women, he averred that "the five worst maladies that afflict the female are indocility, discontent, slander, jealousy, and silliness. Without any doubt, these five maladies infest seven or eight out of every ten women, and it is from these that arises the inferiority of women to men. Such is the stupidity of her character that it is incumbent on her, in every particular, to distrust herself and to obey her husband."[5] A widow, of course, was not to remarry but to continue to serve her dead husband's parents. These ideas may not have been followed to the letter, even in the Tokugawa period, but they guided the thought and behavior of women to such an extent that they persisted into the twentieth century.

The Tokugawa townspeople did not subscribe to the rigid code of the samurai. Ihara Saikaku (1642–93), who wrote about the life of the townspeople, believed that it was natural for the husband and wife to show affection toward each other. He pointed out that among the townspeople a widow could remarry without any stigma being attached to her. Some townspeople believed that the relationship between husband and wife, not father and son, as the Confucians taught, was the cardinal human relationship. "The way of humanity originated with husband and wife," they asserted.[6] Primogeniture was not the norm among the townspeople. Parents could divide their property among their children as they pleased. Saikaku believed that the eldest son should get the largest share, but that the other children must also be given a share of the family property. In the later years of the Tokugawa period, the townspeople began to emulate the samurai, especially as the distinction between the wealthy merchants and the samurai was becoming blurred.[7]

The mores that influenced the peasants were not the more humane ways of the townspeople but those of the samurai, although the peasants' social relations were nowhere as rigid as those of the samurai. The wife worked just as hard as her husband in the field and harder at home, so her value as a partner was undisputed. Often authority in the household was shared by husband and wife. The family seal was seen as the emblem of the husband's authority while the rice scooper was the wife's symbol of authority. But publicly the husband's authority was regarded as supreme. A husband who was henpecked was an object of pity and ridicule. The ruling class exhorted the peasants to keep their women in line. The shogunate's injunction stated, "The husband must work in the fields, the wife must work at the loom. Both must do night work. However good-looking a wife may be, if she neglects her household duties by drinking tea or sightseeing or rambling on the hillsides, she must be divorced."[8] The peasantry, however, did not adhere strictly to the samurai class's practice of primogeniture.

Even after the Tokugawa era ended and Japan entered the "modern" age, feudalistic attitudes persisted. Nitobe Inazō, a Christian educator, wrote at about the turn of the twentieth century that feudal woman's "surrender of herself to the good of her husband, home and family was as willing and honorable as the man's self-surrender to the good of his lord and country. Self-renunciation, without which no life enigma can be solved, is the keynote of the loyalty of man as well as the domesticity of woman."[9]

Status of Women after the Meiji Restoration

With the arrival of the new era of Meiji there was an initial rush to adopt Western things and practices. But the status of women hardly changed. Even though traditional attitudes remained unchanged, however, for a brief period in early Meiji it appeared as if progressive ideas might change the mode of thinking and way of life of the society, because a number of people began advocating the adoption of Western liberal concepts and practices. A handful even championed the cause of women. Among the most influential "Westernizers" of Meiji Japan was Fukuzawa Yukichi (1835–1901). From the outset of his career as a publicist and proponent of Westernism he called for equality between the sexes. In one of his most influential works, *Gakumon no Susume* (Encouragement of Learning), he wrote, "Men are human beings, so are women." The family system, he asserted, should be built on the relationship between husband and wife, not on that of father and son as taught by the Confucians. "The great foundation of human relations," he argued, "consists of husband and wife. The relationship between husband and wife emerged before that of parents and children or brothers and sisters." "Marriage being a partnership of equals," he averred, "women should have the same rights as men to run the household, own property, get a divorce, remarry, and so on." Because women are just as intelligent as men, girls should be given the same up-bringing and education as boys, he asserted.[10]

In the circle of men interested in liberalizing Japan there were others who shared Fukuzawa's views on women. Among them was the first min-ister of education under the cabinet system established in 1885, Mori Arinori (1847–89). In one of the journals that the "Westernizers" pub-lished in the 1870s Mori wrote a series of articles condemning the practice of concubinage. "The relation between man and wife is the fundamental of human morals," he wrote. "Just relations between husband and wife," he observed, "are not in the least practiced under our national customs. In truth, the husband is entirely the master of the slave, and the wife is no different from a chattel."[11] He suggested that a marriage contract be signed defining the rights and obligations of both parties. When he mar-ried he followed his own proposal and did sign such a contract. A younger liberal thinker and prominent advocate of people's rights, Ueki Emori (1857–92), also advocated granting equal political rights to women and abolition of the public brothels. But regarding the latter, he seemed to see no contradiction in his call for banning the institution and his patronage of it.[12] Among other early advocates of women's rights were the converts to Christianity. They were particularly concerned about the practice of con-cubinage and the institution of public brothels.

In the 1870s a movement emerged to compel the Meiji government to share political power. This movement for "freedom and popular rights" was led by those who resented being locked out of the power structure by the new oligarchs; it was not meant to extend the franchise to the masses or to women. But it became something of a grass-roots movement, and a number of women joined the movement in hopes of gaining equal rights for women.

Granting suffrage to women was not remotely in the minds of the rul-ing elites. In fact they set out to prohibit women from taking part in any political activity. In 1882 the government forbade women to make political speeches and in 1890 made it illegal for women to participate in any politi-cal activities whatsoever. Women were even forbidden to listen to political speeches. The Police Security Regulations of 1900 reinforced these stric-tures. Article 5 of the regulations prohibited women from forming any political organization whatever.[13]

In 1871 the Meiji government began drafting a civil code. The men assigned the task turned to the French civil code for their model, and they invited a French jurist, Gustave Boissanade, to assist in drafting the code. This draft made the nuclear family the legal family unit, rather than the extended family. The rights of the wife were recognized, and no provisions were made to give legal authority to the head of the extended family. The opponents charged that it was patterned too closely after the French code and did not take into consideration traditional Japanese mores and institutions. Although the *genrōin* (council of elder statesmen) gave its approval, the opponents managed to prevent enactment of the code.[14] The government then drafted a code that was more conservative. This code was adopted and enacted in 1898.

This, the Meiji Civil Code, gave the head of the extended family (which included his married sons and their families, his unmarried sons and daughters, as well as his unmarried brothers and sisters) virtually absolute authority. Now that traditional class distinctions were no longer legally recognized, the legal provisions encompassed all classes. The rights of women of all social classes were restricted, in line with traditional samurai practice. The more liberal practices that prevailed among the Tokugawa townspeople were eliminated. For example, primogeniture was now mandated for all classes. The head of the extended household was given the right to control the family property, determine the place of residence of each household member, and approve or disapprove marriages and divorces.

The wife was treated as a minor and was placed under the absolute authority of the household head and of her own husband. One of the provisions held that "cripples and disabled persons and wives cannot undertake any legal action."[15] Needless to say, the wife was without any property rights. Before the Meiji period the wife retained her own family name even after marriage, but the Meiji civil code required her to take her husband's family name, unless she was the only or the eldest daughter of a family without sons. In this case the husband married into her family. A son could not marry without the consent of the father until he was thirty, and a daughter could not do so until she was twenty-five. But the consent of the household head was required regardless of age.[16]

Among the practices that the reformers, led by the Christians, sought to eliminate were de facto polygamy and public brothels. The legal code of 1870 had given legal recognition to concubines. Not until 1882 was the practice of including concubines in the family register ended. Husbands could commit adultery with impunity (unless the woman happened to be someone else's wife), whereas wives committing adultery were punished severely.

Brothel districts were a legacy from the Tokugawa period. The brothel quarters of the major cities, like the Yoshiwara in Tokyo, were touted as glamorous centers of hedonism, despite the fact that the inmates were hapless daughters of impoverished peasants who were forced to sell them to the brothels. As the urban population grew while agrarian poverty persisted, the number of girls being sent into the brothels increased steadily. In 1904 there were 43,134 inmates in public brothels; in 1924 there were 52,325.[17] Despite the "modernization" of Japan, the institution of public brothels survived until the end of World War II.

Among the early fighters against this institution was Yajima Kajiko (1833–1925), a Christian educator who formed the Fujin Kyōfūkai (Women's Moral Reform Society) in 1886 to carry out her campaign against public brothels and male promiscuity. In Gunma prefecture (in the Kantō region) anti-brothel reformers succeeded in getting the prefectural assembly to ban public brothels in 1882. The law was enacted in 1888, making Gunma the only prefecture without public brothels before 1947, when the national legislature banned them.[18]

The Salvation Army, led by Yamamuro Gumpei (1872–1940), played an active role in the movement to eliminate public brothels and free the inmates who had been sold to these houses. Despite occasional successes in helping some inmates to gain their freedom,[19] the movement to ban the practice proved futile, and thousands of young girls in their teens continued to be sent to the brothels. In the 1930s when there was a serious famine in northern Japan, of the 467 girls and women between the ages of fifteen and twenty-four in one village, 110 were sent to the urban brothels as indentured prostitutes. They were bound by contract to serve from four to six years in return for payments to their parents of about 150 yen (at that time the yen was worth about twenty to twenty-five cents in U.S. currency).[20] Many young girls from the southern regions of Japan were sold to serve in brothels in Southeast Asia. In Singapore alone it is estimated that in about 1910 there were from 3,500 to 5,000 Japanese women in the brothels.[21]

The move to provide educational opportunities for girls started simultaneously with the onset of the liberal reform movement, or the so-called movement to "enlighten and civilize" the country. Fukuzawa Yukichi was a forceful spokesman for this cause. "In matters of learning," he argued, "there should be no difference between men and women."[22] Prior to the proclamation of the Education Act of 1872 the Department of Education submitted to the Council of State a document advocating universal education and asserted that "in the way of mankind, there is no distinction between men and women. There is no reason why girls cannot be educated as well as boys. Girls are the mothers of tomorrow. They are to become the educators of children. For this reason the education of girls is of utmost importance."[23]

Although the ideal of equal education was proclaimed in 1872, its implementation progressed at a snail's pace. In 1876, 46 percent of the boys of school age, but only 16 percent of the girls, were in school.[24] The figure did not approach 50 percent until the end of the nineteenth century. (This at a time when compulsory elementary education was required for only three years. It was not extended to four years until 1900. Finally, in 1907 it was extended to six years and remained so until the end of World War II.) Girls in rural areas in particular were kept out of school because farm families saw female education as a waste of time. Such an attitude prevailed among members of the middle class too. Higuchi Ichiyō (1872–96), a prominent writer of the Meiji era, was a daughter of a low-level government official. She was not allowed to complete elementary school because her mother believed that "it is harmful for a girl to get too much education."[25] Not until the first decade of the twentieth century did the rate of attendance increase. By the end of that decade attendance had jumped to about 96 percent.[26]

Government officials were aware of the importance of universal education for nationalistic ends. The wars with China and Russia, and the rapid industrial expansion at the turn of the century, caused greater emphasis to be placed on education. But government leaders did not believe that boys and girls should get the same education. They adhered to the traditional notion of keeping the sexes apart. In 1879 the government decreed that boys and girls beyond the elementary school level must attend separate schools. The purpose of women's education was to prepare them, not to become professional women, but to become "good wives and wise mothers." That is, girls were to be educated primarily to perform their duties in the household. For that reason the education of girls beyond the elementary level was neglected. In 1895 there were only thirty-seven "higher"

schools for girls, that is, schools above the primary level. These were operated mainly by missionaries.[27] Not until 1911 was a college for women
established.

In defining the goals of high school education the Ministry of Education stated in 1899 that the purpose of higher education for girls was "to
foster characteristics that will make them develop into wise mothers and
good wives. For this reason elegant and refined manners, and docility and
modesty are qualities that must be fostered."[28]

The domestic arts were stressed in the education of girls. About 20 percent of the subjects taught fell in the category of home economics, sewing,
and handicrafts. Foreign languages and mathematics were only one-third
of what was taught in boys' schools, and science was one-half.[29] Also ideals
that were reminiscent of Kaibara Ekken's teachings were emphasized in
textbooks on moral education. One of the lessons in a morals text issued in
1900 said:

> Girls must be gentle and graceful in all things. In their conduct and
> manner of speech, they must not be harsh. While remaining gentle,
> however, they must have inner strength in order not to be easily
> swayed by others. Loquacity and jealousy are defects common
> among women, so care must be taken to guard against these faults.
> When a girl marries she must serve her husband and his parents
> faithfully, guide and educate her children, be kind to her servants, be
> frugal in all things, and work for the family's prosperity. Once she
> marries, she must look upon her husband's home as her own, rise
> early in the morning, go to bed late, and devote all her thoughts to
> household affairs. She must assist her husband, and whatever mis-
> fortune befalls the family she must not abandon it.[30]

These same ideals were inculcated into the girls at home. Ishimoto Shizue
(1897–), who was one of the first women to be elected to the Diet after the
end of World War II, wrote in her autobiography:

> Consciously or unconsciously, my mother taught her daughter to
> crush her desires and ambitions, and trained her to be ready to sub-
> merge her individuality in her husband's personality and his family's
> united temper. Girls were to study first of all how to please their
> husband's parents with absolute obedience. Mother never thought it
> possible that I should become a good companion, discussing social

problems or politics with my husband or reading books with him.
Marriage for the Japanese girl meant losing individual freedom.[31]

In the educational journals issued for teachers' reference traditional
Confucian ideals were emphasized. For instance, one article published in
1887 stated: "The difference between day and night results from the con-
cord of yin and yang. The four seasons are also the result of this con-
cord. . . . The male is yang and the female is yin. Consequently, it is only
natural that women should remain in the house and be docile. Who in the
world would doubt this truth?"[32]

Well-bred women were not expected to take employment outside the
home. Yamada Waka, who was regarded as a public counselor of women
in the 1920s and 1930s, remarked in 1919, "I am opposed to women's entering professional fields, because it is unnatural. Men and women have
deep-rooted relations. I do not approve of theories about women which
treat women separately from men."[33]

Lower-class girls were employed on a large scale in a host of menial
jobs, especially in the textile plants and other factories that sprang into
existence as Japan embarked on the road to industrialization. Large numbers of young girls were recruited from the rural areas and put to work in
these factories. At the turn of the twentieth century 90 percent of the
workers in weaving sheds and silk filatures and 80 percent of the opera-
tives in the cotton-spinning mills were women. In 1897, 49 percent of the
workers in these factories were girls less than twenty years of age, and
13 percent were younger than fourteen. Most were indentured servants
whose parents had been given a relatively insignificant sum of money in
return for their daughters' labor in these plants. The girls were housed in
dormitories under strict control. The pay was low, and working conditions were poor. The girls were required to work long hours, and often
they were punished physically if they violated the rules set by the employers. The poor food and living conditions and the harsh working conditions
contributed to the deterioration of the workers' health, and many contracted tuberculosis and beriberi.[34] Protests against these conditions began
to break out, but they proved to be futile. The first strike by women workers occurred in 1885 in a silk filature in Kōfu city in central Japan. Other
strikes followed, but any move to organize labor unions was swiftly suppressed by the authorities.[35] Union organizers, including women organizers, became more active in the twentieth century.

Hard as life was for the girls who were sent into the silk filatures and textile plants, the girls and women left behind in the rural villages had to labor long hours in backbreaking work. Unlike the women who went to work in the cities, farm women hardly got a glimpse of the tantalizing products of the West. Life for them was dull, arduous, and Spartan. The feudal mores of obedience and self-denial had deep roots in the villages and persisted well into the twentieth century.

Because they had to labor as hard as men on a meager diet, farm women aged early and ended up with bent backs, hands marked with deep cracks and calluses, and faces wrinkled and withered. One old woman who grew up in a mountain village in central Japan recalled, "In the old days we used to put a big pot of tea on the fire, and the whole family would ladle the tea out and pour it on sorghum powder. That was our staple."[36] One woman who, as a young girl, saw her friends leave for the factories remarked, "I stayed behind without friends and burned the hillside to open up farm-land to grow grass and millet. I used to walk five miles along a mountain road covered with snow up to my hips and with a sack of rice and a box of flour on my back. I worked beside six men and raised six children."[37]

For the farm women there was no escape, though a number of them were involved in tenant disputes that began to break out in the 1920s. But for the most part they endured the arduous work, poverty, and social im-peratives that prevented them from developing their minds and spirits, as some of the urban, middle-class women could do.

Although "good" families regarded sending their daughters out to work as demeaning, more women began to enter a variety of occupations and professions during the Taishō era (1912–26). Teaching at the elemen-tary school level was one profession open to women. But they were re-stricted primarily to teaching the lower grades. In fact, a resolution of the Japanese Educators' Association stipulated that women teachers be re-stricted to the first two years of elementary school.[38] Not until 1931 was a woman appointed principal of an elementary school.[39] Because teachers were held in high esteem by the society rooted in Confucianism, however, once women entered this field, even as elementary school teachers, they were held in high regard by the general populace. Here, unlike women in other occupations, women teachers who got married were not automati-cally dismissed from their jobs.

Medicine was the other profession in which Japanese women moved ahead more rapidly than women in America. The entry of women into the medical professional in Japan was a hard-won right, which a few determined pioneers captured in early Meiji. Takahashi Mizuko (1852–1927) was one of the first women to fight for the right to enter the medical profession. She wanted to become a doctor, but because the government did not grant medical licenses to women, she first became a midwife. Then in 1884, because of the petitions submitted by Takahashi and a few other women, government officials decided to recognize women doctors. She applied for admission to a medical school but was denied admission. She then stationed herself by the front gate of another school for three days and three nights to see the president and finally persuaded him to admit her. She literally worked her way through medical school, passed the licensing examination in 1887, and became one of the first female doctors in Japan. Other determined souls, like Yoshioka Yayoi (1871–1959), who established the first medical preparatory school for women in 1900, followed Takahashi's example. The graduates of Yoshioka's school, however, could not practice medicine until 1912, because only graduates of medical schools certified by the government were allowed to take the national medical examination. The government refused to certify her school until 1912. By 1928 over eight hundred students had enrolled in her college.[40] In the 1970s about 10 percent of the doctors and 10 percent of the dentists in Japan were women, a much higher percentage than in the United States.[41]

Women distinguished themselves also in literature and in the cultural fields, particularly in the theater and in motion pictures. More women came to be employed in modern stores and in business offices, but only in low-level positions. They were paid from one-half to two-thirds the salary that men received. The practice of dispensing with their services once they got married was the norm—a practice that persisted well past World War II.

More women in large cities began to wear Western garments, but in 1925 a survey taken in the heart of Tokyo showed that whereas 67 percent of the men wore Western suits, 99 percent of the women were clothed in traditional Japanese kimono.[42] But in the 1920s at the height of "Taishō democracy" young "swingers" of the big cities, known as *mobo* (modern boy) and *moga* (modern girl), emerged. They defied the traditional ways and embraced Western music, dance, and movies, and emulated the lifestyles of the young people of the West. But even though they were influenced by the romantic actions they encountered on the silver screen, they were not permitted to engage in romantic love themselves or marry boys and girls of their own choosing. As a result, double suicides by young lovers became almost a fad in the 1920s and 1930s.

The rising level of literacy among women, and their growing interest in cultural and social affairs, were reflected in the increase in the number of women's magazines that came to be published. Many of them were designed primarily to entertain the readers. Although the emphasis was on "good housekeeping" types of articles, others catered to the growing sophistication of the women whose social and political consciousness had been aroused.

The high point of the feminist movement in Japan in the years before World War II was reached during the 1920s, but its origin can be traced back to the early years of Meiji.

From Liberalism to Radicalism

The historically rooted inequities, the social, political, and economic burdens placed on the lower classes as the Meiji leaders launched Japan on the path of modernization in order to build a "rich and powerful nation," the arrival of Western liberalism with its emphasis on freedom, equality, justice, and individual rights, and the ensuing advent of socialism, communism, and anarchism touched off numerous reform movements in the Meiji period. The more radical by-products of these movements forcefully challenged the established order of things in the Taishō era. Among the activists were a number of women. Their number was small, to be sure, but their commitment was firm, and many gave their lives to the cause.

From the outset of the Meiji era a handful of courageous women took part in movements to extend the rights of the people. In the so-called popular-rights (*minken*) movement, we find women activists like Kusunose Kita (1836–1920), Kishida Toshiko (1863–1901), and Fukuda Hideko (1867–1927) fighting for equal political rights for women.

In 1878 Kusunose challenged the authorities in her home prefecture in Tosa in Shikoku Island for denying her the right to vote in the local assembly election despite the fact that she, as head of the household, was required to pay taxes. At this time the Meiji government had allowed women to be household heads. In April 1878 at the governors' conference a proposal was submitted to grant women household heads, who were property holders and taxpayers, the right to vote in prefectural assembly elections, but the proposal was quickly defeated. In September of that year Kusunose protested this inequity. The governor rejected her complaint, saying the duty to pay taxes had nothing to do with political rights.[43]

Tosa was one of the places where the popular-rights movement got started and had popular support, so it is not surprising that Kusunose took the stand that she did. In 1880 one of the towns in Tosa defied the prefectural governor and granted the suffrage to both male and female household heads. It also permitted men and women over twenty, whether they were household heads or not, to stand for local elections. The example was followed by a neighboring village. But in 1884 the central government revised the regulations on local government and deprived the local governments of the authority to decide on voting rights, and women's suffrage in those communities was eliminated.[44]

Kishida Toshiko, who later married Nakajima Nobuyuki, one of the founders of the Liberal party, joined the popular-rights movement early in her life. When she was barely twenty she asserted:

We have had in our country from antiquity the inimical custom of "respecting men and denigrating women." But society is preserved by the cooperation between men and women. In order to improve the society and plan for the progress of humanity, it is imperative that equality between men and women be achieved. In the West, in order to win political rights women are actively engaged in various movements such as submitting petitions to their parliament. Undoubtedly they will soon win the right to participate in politics and make equal rights between men and women a reality.[45]

In response to the argument that if men and women were made equal, and the wife did not submit to the husband, there would be endless family squabbles and the divorce rate would soar, Kishida responded:

By whom and when was it decided that it was the women's way to remain quiet and not respond even when men say unreasonable things? . . . Women alone should not be blamed for quarrels between husbands and wives. . . . Reflect for a moment. There are only a few instances when trouble results because the wife abuses her authority. Today, because men's rights are in ascendancy the whole society is being harmed. . . . If the rights of men and women are made equal, relations between the sexes will be harmonious, the true sentiment of love will deepen between husband and wife, and true love will prevail. Let me ask you men who love freedom and value people's rights, you say you want to reform the society and advance the rights of the people. Why do you, in this matter of equal rights between men and women, unite with those who are conservative and obstinate? [46]

After she married Nakajima Nobuyuki in 1886, Kishida ceased making "radical" pronouncements publicly and became a faithful supporter of her husband. Fukuda Hideko, who was inspired to become a political activist after listening to one of Kishida's public lectures, claimed that she stopped seeing Kishida because her way of thinking changed after her marriage. [47]

Fukuda, whose recollections are translated in chapter 2, was involved in various reform movements over a longer period of time than any other Meiji woman. Starting her activist life as a supporter of the popular-rights movement, she joined the radical wing of the Liberal party and then advocated socialistic reforms later in her life. Her life serves as a bridge between the *minken* movement, which focused on the extension of political rights, and the socialist-communist movements of the twentieth century and the Taishō era when social and economic reforms became the primary objective of the activists.

The pace of industrialization in Japan quickened toward the later years of the Meiji era, and a considerable body of factory workers came to constitute the country's work force. The plight of the young girls and women in the silk filatures and textile plants became a matter of urgent concern for reform-minded social and political leaders, especially Christian humanitarians. Many socialists and communists got their start as social critics and many reformers as Christians.

The Russo-Japanese War constitutes one watershed in the reform movement. A number of idealists opposed the war. Yosano Akiko (1878–1948), a romantic poet, called upon her younger brother not to be killed or kill in the war.

> Oh, my young brother. I weep for you.
> Please do not die.
> You, the youngest of their children,
> Our parents loved you the most.

> Did they hand you a sword,
>   and tell you to kill?
>
> Did they raise you for twenty-four years,
>   telling you to kill and be killed?
>
> Whether the fortress of Port Arthur falls,
>   or does not fall, does it matter?
>
> Is it any concern of yours? [48]

The government resorted to harsh measures to quell the pacifists and reformers. This had the opposite effect because repressive measures turned a number of reformers to more radical movements like anarchism, syndicalism, and eventually Bolshevism. In order to elicit public support for their cause Sakai Toshihiko (1870–1933), a socialist, Kōtoku Shūsui (1871–1911), an anarchist, and Uchimura Kanzō (1861–1930), a Christian reformer, formed the Heiminsha (Commoners' Society) in 1903 and began publishing the *Heimin Shimbun* (Commoners' News) in late 1903. Despite government interference, they managed to keep their publication in print until 1905. A number of women activists joined the Heiminsha circle, including Kanno Sugako (1881–1911), Fukuda Hideko, and Itō Noe (1895–1923).

The reform movement soon split between those who favored a more moderate approach to achieve their goals and those who favored a more radical approach. The latter inclined toward anarcho-syndicalism; their leader was Kōtoku Shūsui. In 1905 Kōtoku arrived in the United States and remained in San Francisco until the earthquake of 1906. He became acquainted with a number of anarchists and embraced their radical philosophy. Among Kōtoku's followers was Kanno Sugako, who went to live with him even though he was married. Earlier she had lived with Arahata Kanson (1887–1981), seven years her junior, an early convert to socialism and communism. Kanno was more radical in temperament than Kōtoku, and she became the key figure among a group of young anarchists who plotted to assassinate the emperor. Even though Kōtoku was not directly involved in the plot, known as the Great Treason incident, he was charged as the ringleader, and the affair came to be identified with him, although in fact Kanno was the person who held the plotters together. Her reflections, written while she waited for her execution, reveal a remarkably sensitive personality. These constitute chapter 3, together with a biographical sketch.

The execution of Kanno, Kōtoku, and their comrades put a damper on the radical political movement for a few years. Public opinion was inclined to condemn Kanno, and looked instead to another person as a model for women to emulate. This was Nogi Shizuko, who committed suicide with her husband, Nogi Maresuke, the general who led the Japanese forces against Port Arthur in the Russo-Japanese War, upon the death of Emperor Meiji in 1912. In fact, those who were about to emerge as champions of feminism hardly seemed to be affected by Kanno's fate. Hiratsuka Raichō, the founder of the Seitōsha (Bluestocking Society), recalled that she hardly paid heed to the Great Treason incident.[49] But Mrs. Nogi's suicide was another matter. The champion of the movement to purify the morals of Japan and an opponent of brothels, Yajima Kajiko, praised her action as a "beautiful deed, the true flowering of loyalty to the lord and love of country."[50]

The sociopolitical reform movement was given fresh impetus with the outbreak and success of the Bolshevik Revolution in Russia in 1917. But prior to this a feminist movement led by women who were initially more interested in literary activities emerged under the leadership of Hiratsuka Raichō. She and her friends organized the Seitōsha in 1911 and began publishing the journal Seitō. Their object was to free women from traditional moral and social strictures and enable them to develop their individuality to the fullest by providing them with a forum to reveal their literary talents.

In the statement of purpose for the journal Hiratsuka wrote, "The time has passed when women can continue to slumber idly. We must wake up and make full use of the talents given us by heaven. The Seitōsha will be an instrument for women's thought, literature, and moral perfection."[51] This was a time when the country was poised for the revival of liberalism (which had enjoyed a brief period of popularity in the early Meiji years) and embarked on an era of "Taishō democracy." The Taishō years (1912–26) were also a time of cultural renaissance. Major literary figures appeared. Popular culture spread through the urban centers, if not throughout the nation. Magazines directed to mass readership began appearing in large numbers. Women's magazines such as Shufu no Tomo (Friend of the Housewife) and Fujin Kurabu (Women's Club) won large readerships. A magazine that dealt with serious social and political questions, Fujin

Kōron (Women's Public Discourses), appeared and was read by women concerned about current affairs. It had a far larger circulation than *Seitō*, whose readership tended to be limited to more literary as well as more radical groups.

The first issue of *Seitō* included the following poem by Yosano Akiko:

> The day when the mountain will move is coming.
> When I say this, no one believes me.
> The mountains have been asleep only temporarily.
> In antiquity, mountains, all aflame, moved about.
> No one need believe this.
> But, all of you, believe this.
> All the women who had been asleep
> Have now awakened and are on the move.[52]

Hiratsuka Raichō's essay about women's being the sun in the beginning appeared in the same issue. In January 1913 she wrote in another journal her declamation about being a "new woman":

> I am a New Woman.
> I yearn each day to become a truly New Woman.
> Each day I work to become a New Woman.
> The sun is truly and forever new.
> I am the sun.[53]

Hiratsuka explained later that she did not intend *Seitō* to become a vehicle for social or political protest, though she resented "the oppressive environment and old morality that surrounded women," and she strongly objected to the unjust circumstances that kept women from developing their natural talents. The magazine could not help but be controversial. Hiratsuka and her friends, for example, criticized the traditional family system, which hindered the free development of women's talents and stifled their social and emotional life. In defending freedom of love, Hiratsuka asked, "Why is it immoral to lose one's virginity? Why do people indiscriminately criticize unmarried women who lose their virginity?"[54]

Hiratsuka, however, was not a political extremist and felt uneasy about the radicalism that began to color the articles in the journal. As a result, in 1915 she turned over the editorship to Itō Noe (1895–1923), a young woman who was barely twenty.

Itō was one of the most remarkable young women of this era. She was independent-minded, individualistic, and iconoclastic. If one of the distinctive characteristics of the New Woman was to assert her individuality and develop her personality to the fullest, no better example can be found than Itō Noe. She was deeply impressed by Emma Goldman's views on male-female relationships and her ideas on the importance of self-fulfillment. Unfortunately, although she wrote a large number of essays, she did not leave her memoirs for posterity, because she was murdered by the gendarmes before she reached the age of thirty.

Itō began writing for the *Seitō* when she was only seventeen. In taking charge of the journal she stated that her policy would be "no rules, no fixed policies, no principles, no advocacy of any causes." In an essay she published in *Seitō* in 1913 she expressed her beliefs about the need to give free expression to one's inner feelings. She wrote:

> When I was in girls' school all our teachers taught us that to achieve happiness we must learn to be satisfied with our lot. They taught us to eliminate all the impulses that well up in our hearts. They told us to close our eyes. . . . They said peace and happiness founded on ignorance is a pitiful thing, like a blind snake playing with a rosary. What they taught us was full of contradictions. If they believed that happiness based on ignorance is a pitiful thing, why did they not teach us to destroy the environment and customs to free the impulses that well up within us? Why did they not teach us to open our eyes and look at reality directly and comprehend that reality?[55]

Itō was willing to challenge anyone who mouthed moralistic cant, platitudes, or sanctimonious blather, whether they were traditionalists or modernists. She scoffed at Shimoda Utako, who was highly regarded as an educator of upper-class girls:

> There is nobody as hateful as the narrow-minded, obstinate women educators of Japan. With their narrow outlook, opinionated views, ignorance, and superficiality, how could they expect to undertake true education? This is not the time to be talking about perfect morality, perfect common sense. Such empty, formal, vacuous words will soon be worthless. . . . Your writings are amorphous and pointless. If they are indications of the kind of person you are, you are not even worth spitting at.[56]

She criticized rich women who soothed their consciences by doing charitable work, and derided the Christian reformers who were seeking to abolish public brothels, because they were unwilling to get at the root cause of this institution, poverty. She lashed back at Yosano Akiko when the latter criticized her for her rashness. Itō taunted old-line socialists like Sakai Toshihiko for losing their zest for combat and simply indulging in avuncular paternalism.[57]

Itō lived the life-style she espoused. While she was attending high school she fell in love with her English teacher, Tsuji Jun, and began living with him. Then when she became acquainted with Ōsugi Sakae (1885–1923), a leading anarchist, she left Tsuji and went to live with Ōsugi. Ōsugi believed in free love, and though he was married, continued his relationship with Itō as well as with another social activist, Kamichika Ichiko (1888–1981). His wife suffered in silence, but Kamichika could not curb her jealousy and stabbed Ōsugi in the neck. Ōsugi survived, but Kamichika was sent to prison.

This incident shocked their socialist friends and they turned against Ōsugi and Itō. For the next seven years the two carried on their work almost in isolation from the other leading social activists. They went into the industrial district of Kameido in Tokyo and worked with union organizers, gaining a circle of new supporters among workers and students. On September 16, 1923, in the aftermath of the Great Earthquake, Itō, Ōsugi, and his six-year-old nephew (a boy, born in the United States, who was visiting Japan with his mother) were apprehended by the military police and murdered.

In the 1920s the feminist movement experienced a cleavage between those advocates (among whom was Hiratsuka) who called for government aid and subsidies to mothers and those who believed that a revolutionary transformation of the society had to take place before equality for women could be achieved. The former were influenced by the writings of the Swedish feminist Ellen K. S. Key (1849–1926), whereas the latter tended to embrace the views of communists and anarchist thinkers like Alexandra Kollontai (1872–1952) and Emma Goldman (1869–1940).

In addition to the Bolshevik Revolution, political radicalism got a boost from the socioeconomic problems that resulted from World War I and its aftermath. The wartime inflation caused rice riots led by hard-pressed housewives in July 1918. The riots and demonstrations lasted for six months and spread throughout the country with perhaps a million people participating in them.[58] These disturbances led to government crackdowns on the press and critics of the existing order of things. But government oppression caused the opponents to become more militant. At the same time the economic downturn that followed the end of World War I led to increasing labor unrest. In 1919 about five hundred strikes broke out with 63,000 workers participating.[59] These developments offered the socialists, communists, and anarchists opportunities to revitalize their movement.

The anarchists had been weakened considerably after their leader, Ōsugi Sakae, alienated his fellow leftists with his affairs with Itō and Kamichika Ichiko. The group that became the major rival of the anarchists and communists in the labor field was the moderate socialists who had come out of the earlier Christian reform movement. Among the early activists in this group were Kagawa Toyohiko (1888–1960), who devoted his life to helping the poor, especially the urban slum-dwellers, and Suzuki Bunji (1885–1946), another Christian social worker. They believed that the workers' problems must be solved through harmonious cooperation between the employers and workers. In 1912 they organized the Yūaikai (Fraternal Association). Seeing that the Yūaikai approach was not very effective, Suzuki concluded that workers must be organized in unions. In 1919 the Yūaikai's name was changed to the Dai-Nihon Rōdō Sōdōmei Yūaikai (Yūaikai All Japan Federation of Labor). The leadership of the Sōdōmei was taken over by moderate labor organizers like Nishio Suehiro (1891–1973), who rejected the more militant approach advocated by the anarchists and the communists. The radical labor leaders split with the Sōdōmei and formed a rival labor organization, the Nihon Rōdō Kumiai Hyōgikai (Japan Labor Union Council) in 1925.

The spirit of reform, and possibly the revolutionary transformation of the society, spread into other areas of the society during the Taishō years. Movements to improve the plight of tenant farmers and outcastes (then referred to as *eta* or *hinin,* at present as *hisabetsu-burakumin*), the fight for universal suffrage, the feminist movement, labor activities, and political radicalism all enlivened the sociopolitical scene.

One reform movement that received little support from the reformers was the struggle of the Koreans to gain their independence from Japan, which had annexed their country in 1910. A number of Koreans participated in the labor movement and in left-wing political circles, but there was little reciprocal support for their national cause. One person who did join hands with a group of Korean activists in Tokyo and gave her life to their cause was Kaneko Fumiko (1903–26), who became an associate of a Korean anarchist, Pak Yeol (1902–74). In the aftermath of the Great Earthquake when anti-Korean sentiments reached white-heat intensity, Kaneko and Pak were charged with conspiracy to assassinate the emperor and were condemned to death. Their sentences were then reduced to life imprisonment, but Kaneko rejected the reprieve, tore the document up, and hanged herself. Excerpts from the memoirs she penned in prison constitute chapter 4 here.

Kaneko was outside of the mainstream of women activists who congregated around the socialists, communists, and anarchists. In most instances these women were wives, sisters, daughters, or friends of activist men. They drew public attention to their cause when, during the second May Day parade in 1921, they marched with a banner inscribed with the words "Red Wave Society" and ended up scuffling with the police. Sakai Toshihiko's daughter, Magara (1903–83), was among the founders of the Sekirankai (Red Wave Society), which was organized as an off-shoot of the Nihon Shakaishugi Dōmei (Japanese Socialist Alliance) in 1921. Kutsumi Fusako (1890–1980) was another member of this group. She was drawn into the socialist circle through her contacts with Sakai Toshihiko and later married a communist leader, Mitamura Shirō. Hashiura Haruko (1898–1975) caught the public's attention when a photograph of her being arrested by the police during the May Day march appeared in the newspapers. Yamakawa Kikue (1890–1980), a mainstream socialist, acted as an adviser to the Sekirankai. Selections from their memoirs and interviews constitute chapter 5.

Although the Sekirankai did not remain a cohesive and effective organization, some of the members continued to work for the socialist-communist cause. The Marxist circle, however, was not a unified group but went through periods of gyrations, internecine conflicts, and eventual fragmentation. When the Communist party was organized covertly in 1922, the government moved swiftly to crush it and arrested the leaders in June 1923.

Faced with government harassment, the party leaders decided to dissolve the party in March 1924. At the same time the group began to fragment. Yamakawa Kikue's husband, Yamakawa Hitoshi, decided that instead of trying to resurrect the party, they should form a legal proletarian party to prepare for elections that were to follow the enactment of universal manhood suffrage in 1925. So he and those who agreed with him formed a proletarian party. The women members asked the party to include in its platform the abolition of the system of household headship, the elimination of all discriminatory laws against women, the banning of public brothels, and equal pay for equal work. Initially the men rejected the proposal to eliminate household headships and the call for equal pay, but the women fought for their demands and won.[60]

The proletarian party was immediately dissolved by the government. The socialists then formed the Rōnōtō (Labor Farmer party), but the leadership was soon taken over by the communists, so the moderates then formed the Shakai Minshutō (Social Democratic party) with links to the moderate labor union, the Sōdōmei.[61]

In 1926 the Comintern directed the Japanese communists to establish an underground party. But the communists split over the issue of Fukumotoism. Fukumoto Kazuo (1894–1983), who had emerged as a key Japanese communist ideologue, contended that intellectual purity in Marxist thought must be achieved before a strong Marxist movement could be established in Japan. He argued that "division before unity" was a necessary process. Pure Marxists must be separated from false Marxists. The Communist party must be purged of fellow travelers and social democrats; it must be a party of pure Marxist thinkers.[62]

Fukumoto's position was rejected by the Comintern because it would cut the party off from the masses. Yamakawa Hitoshi, who favored keeping the party dissolved while working through the labor movement, found his position being condemned by the Comintern also. In 1927 the Comintern issued a thesis which asserted that "without an independent, ideologically sound, disciplined, and centralized mass communist party there can be no victorious revolutionary movement."[63]

When Yamakawa Hitoshi departed from the Moscow line, Kikue followed her husband's political course and joined the social democratic forces. But a few women stayed the course with Bolshevism. Among them was Tanno Setsu (1902–1987), whose husband, Watanabe Masanosuke, continued to adhere to the official Comintern line.

Tanno Setsu became involved in the labor movement through her friends in the mining community in Hitachi in Ibaraki prefecture. After she moved to Tokyo she joined a socialist study group, the Gyōminkai (Enlightened People's Society), and worked in the communist-led labor movement. Her story is related in chapter 6, together with brief excerpts from recollections of women who were active in the fight for farm tenancy reforms.

The internecine dispute among the Marxists became an academic matter because the government set out to eliminate the socialists and communists in Japan. On March 15, 1928, the Tanaka Giichi government began making mass arrests of those suspected of being socialists or communists. Over twelve hundred persons were arrested and over five hundred were indicted in the end. Those who escaped arrest went underground and tried to keep the communist movement alive. Among them were Tanno Setsu's husband, Watanabe, and Kutsumi's mate, Mitamura Shirō.

On April 16, 1929, the government struck again and arrested over seven hundred persons. Mitamura escaped the dragnet but was arrested later that month. These arrests virtually eliminated the communist threat—if ever there was a threat—to the established authorities. The movement was dealt a near fatal blow when two communist leaders, Sano Manabu and Nabeyama Sadachika, defected from the cause in June 1933. Mitamura also broke with the Comintern and the Communist party but insisted that he had not abandoned his commitment to effect a social and political transformation of Japan (see Kutsumi's memoirs in chapter 5). Of the communists in jail, 35 percent followed Sano and Nabeyama and defected; 65 percent of those awaiting trial defected by the end of 1934.[64] So the communist movement in Japan virtually expired. But a handful continued to fight for the communist cause even in the thirties. Among them was Yamashiro Tomoe (1912–) and her husband, Yamashiro Yoshimune. Yamashiro's story is related in chapter 7.

The decade of the 1930s and the war years were bleak ones for those who favored socialism or communism. They were years in which the movement to improve the plight of women was set back in the face of the powerful tide of nationalism and militarism. All "progressive" ideas and movements were condemned and suppressed as being unpatriotic.

Many of the feminist reformers were in prison or remained silent or even joined patriotic women's organizations to support the war effort. All women's organizations were brought under the all-encompassing umbrella of the Dai-Nihon Fujin Kyōkai (Greater Japan Women's Organization) in 1941, and their activities were closely supervised from the center. Many prominent feminist reformers rallied to the nationalistic cause and lent their names to the efforts of the government leaders to marshal national support for their nationalistic, imperialistic efforts. Yamakawa Kikue found herself being blacklisted by some of her former liberal colleagues.[65]

In wartime, of course, everybody is expected to subordinate his or her individual interests and concerns to the war effort. Women manned the home front, working in factories, shops, and fields while their fathers, sons, husbands, and brothers went off to the battlefields. They endured the privations, the bombings, and the loss of family members in the war.

The aftermath of the war saw the country filled with mothers who had lost their sons, and wives who were widowed in their youth. For the young girls who survived the war, however, the future looked brighter than it did for their mothers. The reforms introduced under the auspices of the occupation authorities included the granting of the franchise to women and the revision of the legal system to provide equality for women. The wife was no longer treated as a minor but was given the right to own property, enter into legal agreements, and divorce her husband. Girls were given the right to marry at the age of sixteen without parental consent and were accorded the same right to inherit the family property as their brothers. Legally, then, the patriarchal family system was replaced by one in which equal rights were guaranteed for women even though in fact many of the old practices persisted. Nonetheless, women interested in politics could now run for office. In the first election under the new constitution, held in 1947, thirty-nine women were elected to the more powerful lower house of the Diet.[66] Educational opportunities improved significantly for girls, but job opportunities remained restricted, and social institutions and practices were slow to change.

The women activists who survived years of tribulation, and in some cases prison terms until the end of the war (like Yamashiro Tomoe and Kutsumi Fusako), saw many of their dreams being realized. Some resumed their political activities, and a few, like Kamichika Ichiko, succeeded in being elected to the Diet. Some, like Hiratsuka, were honored for their pioneer work while others remained silent in obscurity. Still others, who had lost their lives for the cause, were not around to see the dawn of the new age.

TWO

PEOPLE'S RIGHTS AND NATIONAL RIGHTS
Fukuda Hideko

Fukuda Hideko (1865–1927) was a product of the movement for "popular rights and freedom" which rose in the mid-1870s in opposition to the new oligarchy that was being established by the Meiji leaders. While the center of this movement was Tosa in Shikoku, where Itagaki Taisuke (1836–1919), a prominent liberal leader, emerged, the movement had adherents throughout the country. Fukuda's home, Okayama prefecture, was no exception. Fukuda was an early convert to the movement for popular rights for both sexes, not just rights for men, which the male supporters of the movement had in mind. She remained a strong advocate of freedom and justice throughout her life, undaunted by political persecution and hardships. In this respect, she remained more faithful to the cause than such other early supporters of the movement as Nakajima (Kishida) Toshiko. Nakajima had inspired Fukuda to join the fight for equal rights, but she became a respected member of the establishment after she married Nakajima Nobuyuki, a prominent member of the Liberal party and, eventually, a member of the House of Peers.

An account of Fukuda's life up to the turn of the century is given in her autobiography, *Warawa no Hanseigai* (Half of My Lifetime), which was published in 1904.[1] This was the first woman's autobiography to be written in Japan.[2]

Fukuda's father, Kageyama Katashi, was a low-ranking samurai of Bizen-han (in Okayama prefecture). To supplement his income he ran a small private school and also raised vegetables. Following the Meiji Restoration, he became a policeman. Fukuda's mother, Umeko, was an edu-

cated woman, and when the Okayama prefectural government established a girls' middle school in 1872, she became a teacher there. Soon
after, she left to establish her own private school.

Fukuda Hideko was the Kageyamas' third child and second daughter.
The family had two boys and two girls. As her memoirs indicate, Fukuda
was a bright girl, eager to learn. In this she was encouraged and supported
by her mother. When she finished elementary school in 1879, she became
an assistant tutor at her school. At about this time she received proposals of
marriage, but, as her memoirs reveal, she rebuffed them. She could not
abide the idea of arranged marriages, a characteristic shared by all of the
women in this volume. Incidentally, one of her suitors became a leading
politician and prime minister, Inukai Tsuyoshi; another became an admi-
ral in the navy.[3]

Fukuda was drawn into the radical political circle by a local friend,
Kobayashi Kusuo. He was born into a lower-ranking samurai family in
Bizen and had gone to Kyoto to study. While there, he studied French and
translated a biography of Joan of Arc, which he suggested Fukuda should
read. The book inspired Fukuda, and she dreamed of becoming a patriot
like Joan of Arc.[4] In early Meiji, the advocates of popular rights were also
proponents of national rights. They saw no conflict in espousing liberal
political ideals at home while favoring the extension of Japan's national
authority abroad.

In addition to her friendship with Kobayashi, to whom she was eventually engaged, Kishida Toshiko's inspiring speeches stirred Fukuda's political interests. As she relates in her memoirs, she left Okayama for Tokyo
and was attracted by the radical liberal activists' circle, led by Ōi Kentarō
(1843–1922).[5] In 1885 she joined the plot to sail to Korea and create a disturbance large enough to undo the Sino-Japanese accord concluded by Itō
Hirobumi and Li Hung-chang in 1885.[6] The plot known as the Osaka
incident was exposed, and Fukuda and her friends were sent to prison. In
1889 they were released, thanks to the general amnesty decreed on the
adoption of the constitution.

After they were released from prison, Ōi Kentarō proposed to Fukuda,
even though he was already married. His wife was mentally ill, and Ōi
promised Fukuda he would divorce her as soon as he could arrange a satisfactory financial settlement. Meanwhile, he suggested that they live together and Fukuda agreed. In reality Ōi's wife was dead, and Ōi was

having several affairs while he was living with Fukuda. Fukuda had a son by him and tried to convince him to marry her, but he refused either to marry her or to break off the other affairs. In this respect, Ōi was typical of many of the male advocates of human rights and justice. Often the women who followed the leadership of male reformers found themselves being betrayed repeatedly by their men. Many of these men advocated equality of the sexes and liberation of the girls and women locked in brothels, and yet they were unfaithful to their wives and lovers and spent time in the brothels. As her memoirs indicate, Fukuda grew increasingly disillusioned with her fellow conspirators in the Korean affair as she witnessed their shameless behavior in the brothels.

Finally awakening to Ōi's insincerity about their relationship, Fukuda left him and started a girls' vocational school in Tokyo in 1891. Her family came to Tokyo to assist her in teaching the students. But because of a series of misfortunes and deaths in the family, Fukuda was forced to close her school. It was then that she met and married Fukuda Yūsaku. Fukuda had gone to the United States in 1886 and attended the University of Michigan. After graduating, he returned to Japan in 1890. Fukuda Yūsaku's parents opposed the marriage because they had made plans for Yūsaku to marry his cousin. Yūsaku's trip to America was partly to avoid marrying his cousin. On his return, his parents expected him to return to Tochigi prefecture and fulfill his family responsibilities. All sorts of pressures were exerted to break up the relationship between Yūsaku and Hideko, but Yūsaku was firm and renounced his rights as the family heir. They were finally married in 1898. During this time the couple had two children, and endured hardship and privations in order to stay together. In the spring of 1900, Yūsaku suffered a mental breakdown and died. Hideko was left with the task of supporting three children, two by Fukuda and one by Ōi. She started another school, this time a technical school for women. She was assisted by a young man, Ishikawa Sanshirō, who had been a schoolboy in the Fukuda household. Though he was eleven years her junior, they began to live together.

During this period, Fukuda met Sakai Toshihiko, who was emerging as a leading socialist. Through his help, she found a job for Ishikawa with the *Yorozu Chōhō* (Comprehensive Morning News), a newspaper critical of the government. In 1904 when it appeared that a war between Russia and Japan was likely to break out, Sakai, his fellow socialist Kōtoku

Shūsui, and a Christian humanist, Uchimura Kanzō, left the *Yorozu Chōhō* in disagreement with the president of the paper, who favored going to war against Russia. They then started their own weekly paper, the *Heimin Shimbun* (Commoners' News). Fukuda joined the Heiminsha circle and supported their antiwar stand.

The Heiminsha's politics were not popular, but they did find some supporters. A month before the outbreak of the war, Heiminsha stated in an editorial: "We absolutely oppose war. From the moral standpoint, wars are terrible crimes. From the political standpoint, wars are destructive and evil. From the economic standpoint, wars cause severe losses. Social justice is undermined by wars, and the happiness of myriads of people are destroyed."[7]

Fukuda's shift from liberalism to socialism was, in part, the result of her disillusionment with the unprincipled behavior of her former liberal comrades. She remarked, "I regret the arrogance of the aristocracy and the rich businessmen, but I also abhor the depravity and insincerity of the leaders of the Liberal party with whom I shared the joys and pains of life in the past. Though I am a woman, my desire to serve my country will not cease till I die. This desire led me to appreciate the theories of socialism. It has finally led me to abhor the words and deeds of the imperialists who dedicate themselves to the pursuit of self-interest."[8] The true heirs of the early Meiji advocates of freedom and popular rights were, she decided, the opponents of the Russo-Japanese War and the advocates of socialism.

Once the Russo-Japanese War broke out, the government set out to curb the *Heimin Shimbun,* whose policy it was to actively oppose the war. Finally, in January 1905, the authorities closed the paper down and arrested Sakai, Kōtoku, and others. Ishikawa then joined others in publishing a Christian socialist magazine called *Shin Kigen* (New Era). Fukuda's school had failed because of financial problems and she now turned her energies toward the new magazine.

At about this time Fukuda also became acquainted with Tanaka Shōzō (1840–1913), a Diet member who led the protest movement against the Ashio Copper Mine for poisoning the waters of the Watarase River in the Kantō Plain. Yanaka village downstream was the most seriously affected, and Tanaka's appeal for assistance to the villagers became a rallying point for social reformers.[9] Fukuda became a staunch supporter of Tanaka's cause. In 1907 she started a magazine, *Sekai Fujin* (Women of the World), and published articles publicizing the affair and highlighting the plight of the villagers of Yanaka. She also published articles dealing with the wretched, dangerous working conditions in the Japanese textile factories, injustices in the family system, women's rights, and other reform issues that she felt should be brought to the public's attention. Many of the articles in the magazine were written by her socialist friends, and so, even though the circulation was very small, the journal became the target of government suppression. In August 1909 the authorities banned the magazine.[10]

In February 1913 Fukuda published an article in Hiratsuka Raichō's journal, *Seitō,* advocating socialism as the best solution to women's problems. She wrote: "Complete liberation entails not just liberation of women but the liberation of 'that which is human.' What is necessary is not the freedom of women but freedom of 'humanness.' Unless a thoroughgoing communist system is established, there will not be a satisfactory knowledge of that which is human in us. When a communist system is put into effect all scientific knowledge and mechanical power will be utilized for the equality and benefit of all."[11] The government immediately banned the issue.

Ishikawa left Japan for Belgium in 1913, partly to escape the government's increasing pressure on the socialists, but also to ease off on his relationship with Fukuda. Fukuda was forced to peddle yard goods to support her three children. When Kamichika Ichiko met Fukuda in the early 1920s she was still selling them and had then distanced herself somewhat from politics. When Kamichika saw her at one of the discussion sessions at Sakai Toshihiko's home, Fukuda seemed hardly interested, merely listening to the discussion from the next room.[12]

The last years of her life were cheerless ones. Her son by Ōi left her for Manchuria; her younger son by Ishikawa died in 1921. Ishikawa returned from France in 1920 but did not reestablish their relationship. In April 1927 Fukuda died after sixty-one years of turbulence and relative poverty. It is reported that she used to say, "Men are worthless. They are easily bought off by titles of nobility and medals. In this respect women are more reliable. Among women there are no fools who go about proudly dangling medals around their neck."[13] Not until 1966 did anyone think of honoring her memory by erecting a memorial to her.

Half of My Lifetime

FUKUDA HIDEKO

At eight or nine I was praised as a sharp child by my family, and my teachers at school liked me because I was a lively, unspoiled child. When I was eleven or twelve, I was asked to speak on the *Abstracts from the Eighteen Histories* and Rai Sanyō's *Unofficial History of Japan* before the prefectural governor and members of the educational committee.[14] It was a great honor, and I was elated. I felt there was no one as smart as I in the entire world, and I felt proud whenever I ran into the people of our community.

I was appointed an assistant teacher in our school when I was fifteen and was paid a monthly salary of three yen to help the school children with their studies. In addition to my teaching duties, I tutored thirty to forty children at home and helped them review their lessons. Through this extra work I succeeded in helping the students pass two grade-levels of examination in one year. Their parents had great confidence in me, and my private school at one time was almost better attended than the public school.

I will remember my seventeenth year forever. A large number of advocates of freedom and people's rights gathered in our community. Kobayashi Kusuo,[15] a close friend, was a supporter of the movement. He used to say that he wanted to unite the people, become their leader, and petition the government to establish a national assembly. He wanted our prefecture [of Okayama] to take the leadership in arousing the people from their illusions.

My mother composed a song about the movement, patterned after the Ōtsu ballad. It went:

Claiming that it is for the good of the emperor, heroic men from many provinces, led by the men of Okayama of Bizen, etch their flaming ideals in ink, and shoulder the heavy burdens of the nation. They go on the road, willing to sacrifice their lives, forsaking their wives and children. Patriots leave their homes and head for the capital. Their hearts ache as they labor to establish the national assembly. Soon the fog and clouds will vanish, and spring will greet freedom and people's rights.

This ballad was different from other topics intoned in the Ōtsu ballad because it dealt with current affairs. It was in tune with the mood of the people, who were in a state of frenzy about popular rights. I was asked often to strum the Chinese lute and sing the ballad.

Before this, when I was fifteen, I took lessons in tea ceremony, flower arrangement, sewing, and the general rules of etiquette because, I was told, girls had to be well-versed in these things. Moreover, hoping to make me behave like a girl rather than a boy, my parents decided to try to change my behavior by having me take music lessons. So I had to take daily lessons in how to play string instruments like the two-string koto and the Chinese lute. Those days were very busy, for I worked at these lessons well into the night, day after day.

When I was sixteen, a certain family proposed that a marriage be arranged between their son and me. I was opposed to it because the young man lacked the qualities that I wanted in a husband. My feelings placed my parents in an awkward position. They told me that our family was beset with financial difficulties and was on the verge of bankruptcy. I would not be able to stay at home with them forever. The marriage proposal, in their opinion, was a good one. They urged me to accept the proposal. I told my mother that I was grateful for their having raised me thus far. Thanks to them I was now capable of making my own living. Even if I had to leave home I would not starve. But I asked her to let me stay with them indefinitely. In return I would hand over to them my earnings from school. In this way, I would be able to help ease their financial difficulties somewhat. I pleaded with my parents with all my heart. They must have concluded that I could not be easily dissuaded, and they turned down the proposal.

There are many women who, coerced by their parents, mechanically and ritualistically marry men whom they do not love. After my experience, I vowed to help these unfortunate women so that they might follow the path of independence and self-reliance.

Once discussion about my getting married was dropped, I devoted all my energy to school work. I resigned my job as assistant teacher and established my own private school. I taught the pupils conscientiously, and the reputation of my family, which had been known for its educational work for generations, spread widely in our region. The number of students who wanted to enroll in the school grew daily. I rented a room in the local Buddhist temple for use as a classroom, and at night I held classes for people who could not attend classes during the day, such as women and children of poor families. My mother and my older brother helped me, and we abandoned the old-fashioned way of teaching and adhered strictly to progressive pedagogical methods.

During this period (1881) the renowned Madame Kishida (the wife of the late Nakajima Nobuyuki) came on a lecture tour. She stayed at our house for three days and delivered public lectures. People crowded into the lecture hall, which was always packed to capacity. I was beside myself with excitement when I heard her speak so eloquently on the principle of women's rights. While she was with us I got together with the wives and daughters of community leaders and organized a women's social club to work for the unity of women. We were the first in Japan to organize such a club. We invited speakers and champions of natural rights, freedom, and equality to come and speak to us. Our aim was to work for the abolition of backward customs from the past, which had kept women in a state of oppression. The times were propitious, and applications for membership kept pouring in, and our organization continued to flourish.

[Fukuda got into trouble with the authorities when an outing by the Liberal party members led to a minor clash with the police. They ordered her school to be closed, so she took the opportunity to go out to Tokyo and work for the Liberal party. This was in 1884. In Tokyo she enrolled in a girls' school to study English. She also commenced working for the feminist cause.]

I founded the Benevolent Publishing Firm in order to enlighten my fellow women. My object was to teach women to become independent and self-sufficient so that they would cease being slaves to men, and to make it possible for us to fulfill our natural functions as women without hindrance. I also hoped to influence men so that they would cease behaving in a tyrannical and vulgar fashion. My friend Tomii Oto and I made plans to gain the support of prominent people from many places, raise funds, and form a major organization. But our plans did not work out as we had hoped. Unfortunately, Madame Tomii had to return to her hometown. [Tomii was prevented by her family from returning to Tokyo. As was noted above, in 1885 Fukuda got involved in the Osaka incident. Her recollections follow.]

The tranquillity of my studies was disrupted by reports of disturbances in Korea and the beginning of Sino-Japanese negotiations over that country. My sense of outrage and indignation was aroused by the pusillanimous behavior of our government officials. They were bent on oppressing the people at home but were cowardly in dealing with foreign affairs. They were willing to sully our national honor while pursuing their own ephemeral honor. They concentrated on enhancing their personal ease and comfort while they ignored developments destined to plague the nation for a century. . . .

In Osaka, I stayed at Mr. Andō's home for several days and then moved to an inn near the dock to wait for our journey to Korea. One day Isoyama sent a message saying that Kobayashi had arrived and I was to hurry over to his inn. When I got there, I found my comrades in the midst of a drinking party with beautiful geishas. I could not understand how these men could party so, and I castigated them for their behavior. I told Kobayashi that I had rushed over here expecting to hear about some urgent business. Instead I was exposed to idiotic, repulsive behavior. If people whom I respected and relied upon behaved this way, it was not surprising that other young activists spent all their time in brothels. I was ashamed even to talk to them, and after telling them off as caustically as possible, I left.

It turned out that Isoyama had invited me there as a prank to see how I would react. When I certainly got angrier than they had expected, they all were embarrassed. The atmosphere was thoroughly dampened and they cut short their party.

Several days later, the explosives were ready and we were set to depart. But the day before the scheduled departure, no one could find Isoyama. His nephew Tazaki discovered that he was hiding in a brothel. When I went there to find him, the mistress of the house came out and told me that he was not there. I told her that Isoyama may have told her to say that, but that I was a close confidant of his and I knew that he was there. I told her that I was on urgent business, and that if Isoyama knew that it was me, he would see me. The mistress then said, "I am sorry. He told me to say that he was not here, no matter who came. That's why I lied to you. Please forgive me. You are a woman, so I am sure he will not get mad." She then led me to the back of the house. There was Isoyama seated before his favorite geisha, Yae. He had not expected the mistress to break her promise so easily, and so when I appeared he became completely flustered. This time I decided to watch my tongue. I pretended to sympathize with Isoyama and tried to persuade him to come and talk with Arai and Kobayashi. I finally persuaded him to leave and come with me in the rickshaw, and we set out on our way to Kobayashi's inn. On the way, Iosyama said that he wanted to pick up another comrade to come with him, and left the carriage. I did not for a minute dream that he was lying, so I let him go to fetch his friend. There are certainly devious people in this world. Isoyama took advantage of the situation to flee and vanish.

Unfortunately, we did not lose only Isoyama. He took with him a good deal of money, including that which an activist from Kanagawa prefecture had raised by forcing his way into the home of a rich man and appealing to the man's conscience. He had practically forced the man to give him the money. Now, Isoyama will use the money for his own sensual pleasures. He sacrifices the public good and justice in order to cater to a prostitute. What a contemptible idiot! That he is now imprisoned in disgrace is only right and proper. His comrades ostracize him as a turncoat, and the prison officials hold him in contempt. During the public trial he was even attacked and injured by an activist. He surely must now be aware of the perils of karmic retribution.

It is commonly said that when the wound heals the pain is soon forgotten. This applies most aptly to hot-blooded and righteous revolutionaries. As they got together some money, the men—even Ōi, Kobayashi, Arai, and Inagaki—forgot the difficulties facing us and went off to the bordellos. Left alone in the inn, I would reflect on the past, worry about the future, and fall into deep depression. I lamented the frail plight of women and felt bitter toward my comrades. I thought of the many complaints that I could lodge against them. Then I would remind myself that I was serving, not them, but our country and my fellow Japanese. I could not abandon the cause in mid-course.

Once when I was alone in the second-floor room of the inn and feeling depressed, I opened the sliding door and gazed down at a boat loaded with trash. On it was a beggar woman, with a child, two or three years old, strapped to her back. She was rummaging through the trash, picking out waste paper and putting it in her basket. The child must have been in pain as the mother bobbed and weaved, for it was wailing as if it were about to suffocate. The mother ignored the screeching child (almost as if she did not hear it) and continued to pick through the trash. Finally, she dug up what appeared to be fish guts and chicken entrails. She began to wash these and prepare them for cooking. I was overwhelmed at this pitiful sight and thought, "Alas, I never realized how miserable life could be. I am poor, but I am certainly better off than this beggar."

I was overcome with pity for the mother and child and called out to them from the second floor. Taking out a fifty-sen note, a small fortune for me then, I attached a weight to it and threw it down to the mother. She reacted as if it were a gift from heaven. She picked it up timidly, as though she were afraid to take it, and I called out to her and told her to use the money to buy food for the child. She seemed reassured by this and bowed over and over to thank me. I could not bear to see her thank me so profusely and closed the sliding door.

A little later, I decided to step outside. The landlady stopped me and said, "Was it you who gave some money to a beggar woman?" When I nodded, she said, "A moment ago the woman with a child on her back came here with tears in her eyes, saying that a woman guest had thrown some money to her and she had come to thank her. She asked me for your name. I didn't think it was wise to let a beggar have your name, so I told her I would convey her message to you, and sent her off. How much did you give her?"

Charity rewards the giver, not the receiver. I felt better than I had for days. Then I forgot about the incident like a haze that passes before one's eyes. Only later—like a scene from a novel—would I again meet this beggar woman where I least expected to.

In December of that year [1885], our momentous plot was uncovered and we were arrested at an inn in Nagasaki. We were then transported to a prison in Osaka, in Nakanoshima. Accused of crimes against the state, we were treated better than ordinary criminals.[16] While awaiting sentence, I was made a trustee and supervisor of a prison ward that housed first offenders and minors. I tried to help them reform and rehabilitate, and I taught the minors reading and writing. I won the respect of the inmates, who called me "teacher." During the three years I spent awaiting sentencing, I met a host of prisoners, and there were good people among them, people no one would have suspected of being criminals. There are many in society who have committed more serious crimes and perpetrated greater wrongs than these inmates, and yet they are free to strut about in the open road in broad daylight. Only those who have spent time in prison can realize the injustice of a situation in which the big criminals get away while the petty offenders are punished. Mention this to most people, and they cover their ears and refuse to listen.

I spent my time in prison sleeping and eating with the unfortunate women that society labels as major criminals and incorrigible villains.

Sometimes I acted as their mother, and at times as their friend. Their feelings of respect and love for me were much stronger than the sentiments that bind teachers and students in the outside world. Even among one's own family, the sense of unity forged by the common sentiments and emotions that prevailed in the little world that we inhabited is seldom found.

Even in prison spring comes. By April or May of my second year the weather had turned warm and misty. One day the guard came with a new prisoner. He ushered in a careworn woman of twenty-five or twenty-six. Just as the prison door was being opened the woman caught sight of me and began to wail. I had no idea why she was crying and assumed that she was frightened by the formidable prison atmosphere. Perhaps she was thinking of the hardships that awaited her. I felt sorry for her, and tears came to my eyes. After a moment she addressed me. "You may not remember me, but I have not forgotten you for one single day. I remember your face very well. Didn't you give some money to a beggar woman last year at the Hakkenya Inn? That beggar woman was me. Some quirk of fate has brought us together again. It must have been my husband and child who made this possible. They must want me to repent and also thank you for your kindness of last year. The child to whom you generously gave fifty sen caught smallpox and died a week ago. I too had caught the pox. My face is still marked. But I wanted at least to buy some incense and perform the seventh-day mourning ritual for my child, so I went out to pick through the trash for some waste paper. But I was sick and could not walk very far, so my basket remained nearly empty. I realized that I would not be able to earn enough money to buy a meal let alone incense. I was in pain and agony. Then I saw that some clothes were set out to dry in a house that seemed empty. I had no choice; I had to eat. But retribution was swift. I am ashamed to be seen by you in this miserable situation."

Then she began to wail as if she had lost her head. Through it all, she continued her story: "After you gave me that money, I went home and explained what happened, to my husband who was sick in bed. I regarded your kindness as a protection extended us by Heaven, and I bought some medicine and some candy for my child. The three of us were able to smile. For the first time in days we were all happy. But my husband's health grew worse and he eventually died. I kept up my courage, and with my child I continued to scrounge around for waste paper day after day. But Heaven did not listen to my prayers. I had never committed a single wrong no matter how poor I was, but Heaven afflicted us with disease and snatched away the child that I loved so dearly. Now I have been driven to this. Heaven is truly merciless."

I too was amazed by our second encounter, and I wept over the fate of this poor woman. There was nothing I could do but console her, together with other inmates, and encourage her to hope for an early release so that she could care for the souls of her dead husband and child. Indeed, she was released a week later. However, she was distressed at leaving and said she did not want to go out into the world and starve to death. She even said she wished she had committed a more serious crime so that she could stay in prison and continue to receive my help. She wept in anguish when she left.

The hardships of life led this weak woman to prefer the pains of prison to freedom and life. Who can deny that this is a miserable state of affairs? The government knows how to punish people well. But I ask them, "Have you devised ways to help those who have paid for their crimes? Can you guarantee that, once free, they will not be exposed to the hazards of starvation, and long for the security of prison life?"

[Fukuda resumes her account of the Korean venture after their arrival in Nagasaki, where they expected to board a ship to Korea.]

Arai got up and left the inn for Saga in the middle of the night. Only Inagaki and I from our party remained in the inn. Inagaki seemed to be exhausted from his recreational activities and fell asleep as soon as he lay down. I stayed awake, mulling over the fact that my comrades behaved as if we had enough money for them to spend their time in bordellos. If we really did have that much, I should be able to visit my parents and brothers and sister and say goodbye, for it was not likely that I would ever return to Japanese soil. I was half asleep with these thoughts still in my head when I heard noises. I opened my eyes and saw more than ten policemen holding lanterns in the very room we thought was as safe as a fortress. I got up, saying "What's the matter?" The innkeeper said the police were there to question the guests. "This is the end," I thought, and was ready to accept my fate. But because others were involved, I decided to try to talk my way out of the situation. When the police asked me about our plot, I feigned ignorance. I told them that I was only Inagaki's companion and knew nothing. The police nodded and put a rope around Inagaki but did not accuse me of anything. Then, to my chagrin, they found in my bedding the letter that I had written to Kobayashi [condemning him for indulging himself in brothels]. The man in charge became very stern and ordered his subordinate to arrest me too. They then told me that I would have to accompany them to the police station and advised me to dress warmly. I could no longer protest my innocence. I did what I was told and wrapped myself with so many clothes I looked like a potato bug. Then, surrounded by the police, I made my way to the police station. As soon as I arrived, a detective from the central government interrogated me with a barrage of questions. From what he said, it was clear that they had known about my visit to the park and my stopover at the emporium to buy the brush and paper. They knew everything. They were already aware of our plot two days before, when we thought our secret was safe.

After I was interrogated, I was put in a detention room. The prison was just like those I had seen in plays. It was about 3:00 A.M. when I was imprisoned. The sound of the prison doors being opened in the still of the night is eerily menacing. Although I was prepared to face a situation like this, the experience was so frightening my hair stood on end. My heart, which was weak to begin with, began to beat fast in an irregular rhythm. I felt as if I were about to suffocate. The police were oblivious of this and treated me like a common thief. They practically shoved me into a dark room and then barred the door. I told myself, "I don't care if I die right now. I am not going to submit meekly to an unjust punishment like this." I couldn't even cry. Even though I was a woman, I had decided to risk my life challenging the brutal government, and now I was learning the truth of the adage "If you win, you are a loyalist; if you lose, you are a traitor."

I told myself it was shameful of me to whine about brutality and ruthlessness. So I calmed myself and decided to cope with the situation by convincing myself that although physically I was alive, I was, in effect, already dead. Now, I would have to suppress all my feelings. As a result, I slept better in prison than I had in the inn. When I awoke the next morning breakfast was just about over in the prison mess hall.

When I had entered the prison that night, I felt as though I were being stuffed into a hole. When I looked around in the light of day, however, I saw that the ceiling was high and there was no way in which I could hang myself. The window was only large enough to let in a little light. The cell was made of iron bars. Even the strongest of men would not be able to break out. I asked for some water to wash my face, and then they passed me my breakfast through a tiny opening. I thought I wouldn't be able to eat, but the food tasted better than I had expected and I finished quickly. My equanimity surprised me.

After breakfast I walked about the cell and noticed that there was a small opening in the wall from which I could see the floor of the next cell. Looking in, I could see one of my comrades pacing back and forth in his cell, wrapped in his red blanket. It was Naitō Rokushirō. I wondered where Arai's and Inagaki's cells were. As I got accustomed to the idea of being in prison, I began to think about my parents at home and our supporters in Tokyo and Osaka. When I thought about them I felt like crying.

The next morning, after breakfast, I was taken to the interrogation room and was asked by the police about my place of residence, occupation, age, place of birth, and so on. They then asked me why I had come to Nagasaki. I told them that I came to see the sights. The interrogator then told me that we had been arrested because they had concrete evidence about our plans. Would it not be more consistent with our professed principles if we just told them everything in a candid manner? He had a valid point, and so I told him my reasons for participating in the project.

[Fukuda and her comrades were transported to Osaka and held in prison while they awaited their trial.]

While in prison I read every day. If I were free, I could have obtained newly published books and pursued academic learning, but we were permitted to read only a few Chinese classics, like the Confucian *Analects* and the *Great Learning,* as well as other books, like the Bible, or books on primitive men, and so on. At one point, I decided to study English on my own by building on what I had once learned from a Westerner. I worked at it for days, but I could not make any progress, so I am ashamed to say I gave it up. I also kept thinking of the things that I could do after my release. I made all sorts of plans and indulged in my fantasies, but after I gained my freedom all these dreams failed to materialize. After suffering numerous disappointments, I allowed myself to degenerate and waste half my lifetime as if I were living in a dream. I am now determined to spend the remainder of my life as a worthwhile person.

The malelike side of me developed early, but I developed late as a woman. But I was aware that as a woman I would eventually have to marry. I had decided earlier that when the time came to choose a husband I would pick as the ideal person a man of heroic stature, a famous man. But I lived in a narrowly circumscribed world. I was incapable of distinguishing between a bat and a bird. The man whom I believed to be a heroic figure was Kobayashi, and he became my teacher. He taught me about freedom and popular rights, and I admired and respected him, eventually agreeing to marry him. But we were not in a position to start our own family at that time, so I only informed my parents and brothers and sister about my plan so that they would know what to expect. Kobayashi and I agreed that we would first devote our energies to serving our nation. But, as was noted earlier, my school was suddenly shut down. This led to my departure for Tokyo. There, I became involved in numerous projects, which demanded that I sacrifice my own interests. Finally, I was practically homeless. The other activists received the assistance of Ōi, Kobayashi, and others while I barely managed to keep going by working as a hairdresser and a washerwoman. Then the Korean project was launched.

En route to Nagasaki, not only Kobayashi, who was pledged to become my husband, but others, who had left their wives and children, their entire families, back in their hometowns, made all sorts of excuses to indulge themselves with prostitutes. And they felt no shame over this. Then there was Isoyama, who shamefully betrayed the group. I began to wonder if self-centered people like these were capable of carrying out our momentous plan. That was why I had written a farewell letter to Kobayashi in Nagasaki.

When I received word that the public trial was to start, I worried that the letter, written in a very emotional moment, would be made public. I was ashamed of what I had done, and I also felt sorry for Kobayashi. I was certain he would be conscience-stricken when he saw the letter, but he was also sure to be angry at me for being so rash. I was too inflexible then. I could not keep silent about the fact that he had sullied our love and crushed our sacred relationship underfoot. Only because I had expected to die within the week had I decided to fully reveal my feelings.

When the time came to appear in court, I was delighted at the thought of breathing the air of freedom for the first time in three years. I was also eager to see my relatives and friends, who had come from my hometown, and to inquire about my parents. Escorted by the guards, I got on a rickshaw and left the prison gates. The streets from the prison to the Edobori courthouse were a wall of people. The congestion was incredible. I was told later that the citizens of Osaka are basically ill-informed about politics, but that our impending trial had finally aroused the public's interest.

By December 1885 the number of suspects rounded up by the authorities had grown to about two hundred. But many had been cleared during preliminary hearings, and by the time of the public trial only sixty-three people remained. This number, however, was too large to be tried all at one time in a single courtroom. So we were divided into nine groups, and three defense lawyers were assigned to each group.

On the opening day, the prosecutor read the charges. When he came to the part that stated "Isoyama Seibei . . . was disappointed by the cold treatment accorded him by Ōi and Kobayashi and decided that they did not deserve his support," one of the defendants, Ujiiye Naokuni, who was seated in the third row, clearly became angry and agitated. The prosecutor read for a bit more, and then Ujiiye suddenly leaped up and attacked Isoyama Seibei, who was seated in the first row, grabbing him by the throat. Pandemonium broke out in the court. The police standing by the front door had to draw sabers to restore order. Finally the guards and jailers managed to pull Ujiiye away from Isoyama. Ujiiye indicated that he wanted to say something, but the presiding judge ordered the guards to remove him. The judge then recessed the court, saying that he wanted to confer with the other judges in his chambers.

The trial was reopened in the afternoon and continued without incident. Unlike the first day, when all sixty-three defendants were brought in to hear the charges, for the remainder of the trial the nine groups were brought separately into the courtroom under guard and tried one group at a time. Those wishing to observe the trial began lining up in front of the courthouse gate every day at about 3:00 A.M. Some only managed to get in after three or four tries. Each day we entered the courtroom by weaving our way through the large crowd.

During the trial Kobayashi wrote notes to me on his slate, unnoticed by the guards. (The defendants were given a slate so that they could jot down notes for their defense.) He complained about my cold behavior toward him. However, I had decided by now not to trust him, and I told him that he was a hypocrite who spread his love in all directions. I was not going to let him toy with my love.

To my surprise I got a letter from Ōi expressing his deep love for me. When I was living in Tokyo I used to visit him often to ask him to help Madame Tomii escape from her home. I also used to consult him about raising travel money for our project. At the time, he seemed to have low regard for women who took an active role in politics. He seemed to be particularly hostile toward my involvement in national affairs. So I was completely surprised by his letter. I couldn't understand his feelings and thought that he was interested in me because I was different from most other women. So I ignored his first letter and those that followed. Then he began to show his interest overtly. I thought it was strange, but on the other hand, I felt that I could no longer ignore him. So I wrote him a note expressing my appreciation, and then we began to exchange notes often. Eventually I forgot my disillusionment with men. In retrospect, I regret this very much, for this led me to the depths of unhappiness and misfortune.

Now I am chagrined and horror-struck at what resulted from my relationship with Ōi, but at that time I had no way of foreseeing what would follow. I felt that I had found a future husband in this famous and heroic figure. From then on, I looked forward to my court appearance and anxiously waited for Ōi to appear. I was intoxicated with excitement. My spirits, which had tended to flag till then, were uplifted as a feeling of mutual respect blossomed. Suddenly I began to feel as if my own character had been purified.

The trial came to a close in the midst of this pleasant, dreamy atmosphere. I was sentenced to a prison term of a little over a year, with minimal restrictions. The leaders of our group, such as Ōi and Kobayashi, were sentenced to longer prison terms, and they all appealed their sentences. I alone among the leaders started to serve my sentence immediately. I expected to be kept in prison in Osaka where my comrades were detained, and I hoped to have easy access to information about them. However, I was told that I was to be sent to Tsu city in Mie prefecture. I was greatly disappointed at this news and felt like a person stranded on a desert island.

Only the fifteen or so of us who were sentenced to prison terms were sent to the prison on Ise Peninsula. The scenery along the way could elicit poems from travelers comparable to the poems written about the fifty-three scenic stops along the Tōkaidō. But since I was in persimmon-colored, tight-sleeved garb and was bound by a rope around my waist and guarded by the police, I found little pleasure in the scenic sights and could hardly wax poetic. The police who had escorted us from Osaka were replaced at Kusatsu, so we were deprived even of the company of the police that we had gotten to know. We were all depressed by the time we arrived at the prison in Ōtsu city. It was already twilight, but because we were expected, the warden was still there. He delivered a speech in a loud voice. I can still remember it. "I am Hiramatsu Gitō, the warden of this prison. You are convicts who have been transferred here from the Osaka prison. Now that you are under my jurisdiction I expect you to obey the prison rules carefully, and I hope you will try to get pardoned as soon as possible and gain your freedom. Now state your name, occupation, and status." We all did so.

When it came to my turn the warden said, "You don't have to tell me your name. You must be Kageyama Hide. Your parents are no doubt unaware that at such a tender age you have participated in the nefarious plot, and that you are right now standing before me this way. Ah, they must be constantly worrying about you whether it be winter or summer. They wonder about where you are and what you are doing. No doubt you think about your parents, too. You made the mistake of thinking that your actions would serve the national interest. You must long to be with your parents. Those who are loyal to the nation must also be filial to their parents."

He spoke to me in a genuinely sympathetic fashion, almost in tears. His words left me sad. I had kept my feelings under control in front of my comrades until then, but after he finished I was so homesick that the tears began to pour out of my eyes as if a dam had burst. I was unable to look up for some time. The warden became pensive and said, "I understand, I understand. From now on just obey the prison rules strictly and help the other misguided women convicts reform and become virtuous. Work toward the enlightenment of our fellow countrymen and live up to the ideals of loyalty and patriotism. Even though your sentence is only a year and a half, there is a chance for an early pardon. So work toward being released sooner, even if it means just one day. Then you can return to your parents and serve them as a filial daughter."

After that, whenever he made the rounds of the prison, the warden spoke to me sympathetically. Because of his attitude, I ignored the fact that I was under light sentence and was not required to do any prison work, and I spent my time helping the other women inmates with their studies.

We had to get up at five in the morning. When the women guards came to open the cell doors, I, like the others, had to sit properly on the floor and bow my head. Then we were all taken to the well, where we lined up to wash our faces. Next, we went to the dining room for breakfast, and after that we started the day's work. Some inmates busied themselves sewing garments, other worked at the loom, still others spun threads. The amount of work the seamstresses were expected to produce each day depended on what they were sewing. For red tight-sleeved kimono without linings the quota was three; with linings, two; cotton quilt garments, one and a half; and trousers, four. For mending garments a quota was fixed depending on the amount of mending each garment required. The guards handed each inmate her day's quota of work.

My sentence was light, so I was not required to work. I could have spent the whole day reading if I had wanted to. But I decided that I too would work like the other women convicts in order to modify the public's perception of me. So each day I did my quota of work. However, I quit two hours before the others to return to my cell to read. Consequently, when I left the prison I was paid a considerable sum of money. Those under maximum labor sentence had to turn over 70 percent of their earnings to the government and were permitted to retain only 30 percent. In my case, only 30 percent of my earnings went to the government.

After one year in prison, I was given four merit points. If I had earned one more point, I would have been paroled. One day, Mr. Kozuka Yoshitarō came from Osaka to see me. Hearing that he was from Osaka, I was elated, but I also felt nervous. Escorted by a guard, I entered the visitors' room. Mr. Kozuka greeted me with a smile and apologized for not having kept in touch with me. He said he had been asked by some prominent figures to go about visiting prisoners. He then explained, "On the anniversary of the founding of our nation, a constitution is scheduled to be promulgated. On that occasion His Majesty will graciously"—at that point a guard interrupted Mr. Kozuka, saying that the prison authorities had not received formal word on anything and so Mr. Kozuka must not speak carelessly. But Mr. Kozuka continued: "You do not seem to be aware of anything, but you should be notified soon. I will come back to see you again tomorrow. Are your clothing and possessions in order? Are you prepared to gather them at a moment's notice?" He advised me on some other matters in a kindly way and then left.

The entire visit left me completely surprised. I decided that I would receive further news in a day or two and began to prepare myself. Sure enough, that evening the guard told me to collect my books and other possessions and go see the warden. "This is it!" I thought to myself. I felt as if I were going to Heaven. The warden and other prison officials were seated in the waiting room when I entered. The warden then read out the imperial decree on general amnesty. He formally told me, "Your criminal record has been cleared by the general amnesty. As of today you are a free person. I hope you will dedicate yourself ever more to the service of the country."

On hearing this I suddenly experienced a strange sensation. Until yesterday, nay till today, I had been treated as a traitor, but in an hour's time I had been converted into a loyal, patriotic citizen and a beneficiary of the general amnesty. Truly an enigma. Whoever said "Life is like a dream" was indeed right. For a moment I was in a daze. Because Mr. Kozuka had warned me in advance, I was ready with fresh clothing and left the Mie penitentiary with six of my comrades.

When we arrived at the Umeda Station in Osaka we were given a rousing welcome by an enthusiastic crowd. Shouts of "Banzai" thundered across the station as the crowd rejoiced in our safe return from prison. As soon as we arrived at the station prominent figures rushed over to shower us with bouquets of flowers. And my father, whom I had longed to see after seven years of separation, was there. He was being helped by relatives because he was still weak from his recent illness. I had not expected to see him at the station because of his poor health, but there he was. I cried out tearfully to him. Other people were weeping as well. Such was only to be expected.

Accompanied by my father, my comrades and I were taken all over Osaka in rickshaws. Everywhere we went people were waiting to greet us. And we saw big red-and-white banners with slogans welcoming and congratulating us on our freedom. My father, seeing my safe return from prison and the enthusiastic welcome given us by the people of Osaka, was deeply moved. He said it let him forget all the worries he had experienced and that he would have no regrets if he died right then and there. He had not expected such an enthusiastic welcome from such people as Nakae Chōmin, now deceased, and Kurihara Ryōichi.[17]

We arrived at our inn expecting to have time for a little rest, but visitors continued to crowd in. We felt obliged to greet and thank everyone, so we were kept breathlessly busy.

The following day, we went to the station to greet Ōi, Kobayashi, Arai, and others who were scheduled to arrive from Nagoya. When they arrived, we presented them with bouquets of flowers. They then set out on foot to *Shinonome* newspaper. But thousands of welcomers and spectators had jammed the Umeda Station, and we were all hemmed in by the crowd. We barely managed to get to the newspaper. There were so many people that our feet hardly touched the ground as we moved forward. A huge crowd had gathered at the newspaper as well. The doors were closed, and only those with urgent business were allowed to enter. The crowd kept shouting, "Ōi, banzai, freed prisoners, banzai!" There were fireworks, and sword dancers whirled about.

Master Nakae told me that today is the day when we revere women above men. I was, he said, the single bright red flower in a field of green. My work as the only woman among men was exceptional and was one of the most notable aspects of the Osaka incident. He made me sit on top of the table and showered me with drinks and food. We did not get back to our inn until nightfall.

THREE

REFLECTIONS ON THE WAY TO THE GALLOWS
Kanno Sugako

By the turn of the century, many of the early Meiji advocates of people's rights had joined the establishment, no longer offering a radical opposition to the vested interests. The socialists, who were by now beginning to raise their voices on behalf of social justice and political freedom, were, as Fukuda Hideko observed, the true heirs of the early Meiji popular-rights movement.

The first woman to stake her life in this cause was Kanno Sugako (1881–1911). Born in Osaka, Kanno's early life was marked by difficulty and struggle. Her father's fairly successful small mining business had begun to falter by the time she was eight or nine. Furthermore, Kanno's mother died when she was ten. Her father remarried, but unfortunately, her stepmother turned out to be the proverbial sadistic stepmother, who was convinced that Kanno was cunning and evil because she was born in the year of the serpent (*kanoto-no-mi*).

At fifteen Kanno was raped by a miner, and this traumatic experience left her with a lasting sense of shame and guilt. (Years later she claimed to have discovered that the miner was encouraged by her stepmother to rape her.)[1] Kanno's interest in socialism was aroused when she read an essay by Sakai Toshihiko in which he counseled rape victims not to be burdened with guilt. After reading this essay, Kanno began to read Sakai's other writings and eventually gravitated to the circle of socialists.

When Kanno was seventeen, she married into a merchant family in Tokyo. Although she felt no attraction to the man she married, the union enabled her to escape the harassment of her stepmother. However, after her stepmother abandoned the family when Kanno's father suffered a stroke in 1902, Kanno returned home to nurse him and take care of her young brother and sister.

This was the period when Yosano Akiko was winning renown as a writer and poet, and, influenced by her, Kanno decided that she too would become a writer. At that time aspiring writers would apprentice with established writers and learn the craft under them. The most renowned writer in the Osaka region during this period was Udagawa Bunkai (1848–1930). Even though Kanno had only an elementary education, she so impressed Bunkai that he agreed to help her. He got her a job with a newspaper in Osaka and worked with her on her short stories and articles. Despite the differences in their ages (Bunkai was in his mid-fifties and she was twenty), Kanno became emotionally involved with him and they became lovers.[2]

By 1903 Kanno had become interested in the reform movement being undertaken by Japanese Christian leaders. She became affiliated with Yajima Kajiko's Fujin Kyōfūkai (Women's Moral Reform Society), which was working to end the system of legalized brothels in Japan, and wrote a series of articles attacking this institution. When the Russo-Japanese War broke out in 1904, she joined Christian and socialist opponents of the war and became part of the Heiminsha group led by Sakai and Kōtoku.

In 1906 when the publisher of a local newspaper in Wakayama prefecture, the *Murō Shimpō* (Murō News), was jailed for writing articles critical of the government, Sakai Toshihiko arranged to have Kanno Sugako keep the paper functioning in the absence of the publisher. A young socialist, Arahata Kanson (1887–1981), also joined the newspaper's staff. Although six years her junior, he and Kanno entered into a common-law marriage in 1906. When the publisher was released from prison, Kanno left the paper and moved to Tokyo, where she got a job with the *Tōkyō Dempō* (Tokyo Telegraph). Arahata became a reporter for the *Heimin Shimbun*. By this time (1907) Kanno had contracted tuberculosis. She continued working, and these difficulties made her more irritable than usual. Soon Kanno and Arahata's relationship became so strained that they separated, though their friends still saw them as husband and wife.[3]

While Kanno was editing the *Murō Shimpō* she published a short essay in which she expressed her views on the status of women.

In these postwar years there are many tasks facing the nation in politics, economy, industry, education, and so on. But for us women the most urgent task is to develop our own self-awareness. In accordance with long-standing customs, we have been seen as a form of material property. Women in Japan are in a state of slavery. Japan has become an advanced, civilized nation, but we women are still denied our freedom by an invisible iron fence. There are women who take pride in their apparel, who are content to eat good food, and who regard going to the theater as the highest form of pleasure. We could ignore for the time being these pitiful women with slavish sentiments and hapless plights, women who give no thought to anything but their own self-interest. But women with some education and some degree of social knowledge must surely be discontented and angry about their status. . . . Our ideal is socialism, which aims at the equality of all classes. But just as a great building cannot be destroyed in a moment, the existing hierarchical class system, which has been consolidated over many years, cannot be overthrown in a day and a night. If we act too hastily we are likely to produce a history of repeated mistakes. But we must cling to the ideal of a new society as our hope and entry into a new, sun-lit world. So we must first of all achieve the fundamental principle of "self-awareness," and develop our potential, uplift our character, and then gradually work toward the realization of our ideal.[4]

In June 1908 Kanno attended a socialist-anarchist rally where red flags were hoisted and anarchist songs were sung. The authorities arrested the leaders of the gathering, among whom were Ōsugi Sakae, Arahata, Sakai, and Yamakawa Hitoshi (1880–1958). These were all prominent leaders in the socialist-communist-anarchist circles of the late Meiji and Taishō eras. Kanno went to the police station to inquire about her comrades and was shocked to see the brutal manner in which the men were being beaten. Furthermore, she too was thrown in jail for visiting her friends. This experience convinced Kanno that peaceful change was not possible under the existing system. "It is necessary," she decided, "to arouse the people of the society by instigating riots, undertaking revolutionary action, and engaging in assassinations." When she appeared in court after her arrest following the Red Flag incident and was asked by the judge about her political convictions, Kanno responded forthrightly. "My beliefs are closest to anarchism," she replied.[5]

She was not held responsible for the Red Flag incident and was not

sentenced to prison, but she had spent over two months in jail while awaiting trial. Her comrades were sentenced to prison terms of one to two and a
half years. Kanno had contracted tuberculosis before her arrest, and her
physical condition deteriorated during her incarceration. To make matters worse, she had also been fired from the *Murō Shimpō*.

Following her release from prison, Kanno met the activist Kōtoku
Shūsui, for whom she had developed a strong respect and admiration.
Kōtoku was not in Tokyo for the Red Flag incident and so had not been
incarcerated. Earlier in 1905, though, he had spent five months in prison
for his writings in the *Heimin Shimbun*. Upon his release, he left for the
United States and there became acquainted with a number of anarchists.
By the time he returned to Japan six months later, he had become a firm
convert to anarchism.[6] By early 1909 he had divorced his second wife
and was living with Kanno. Despite his ideological belief in equality for
women, Kōtoku often treated women as mere sexual objects and was a
frequenter of the brothels. Like many male reformers of this era, he saw
no contradiction in his professed humanitarian ideals and his visits to, and
hence support of, publicly sanctioned brothels, prewar Japan's most in-
humane exploitation of impoverished young girls. In her personal life,
Kanno too had affairs with a number of men, including her stepbrother.[7]
Such behavior provided the foes of women activists a convenient weapon
to discredit their work as the ravings of loose, immoral women.

Kanno and Kōtoku's affair outraged their comrades, who saw this as
a betrayal of Arahata, who was then still in prison. Ōsugi charged that
"Shūsui stole the woman of a comrade in prison, and Kanno abandoned a
foot soldier in favor of an officer."[8]

In 1909 Kanno and Kōtoku started the journal *Jiyū Shisō* (Free
Thought). From the beginning, the authorities moved to prevent its publication and constantly harassed Kanno and Kōtoku. Kanno was soon arrested for publishing the journal and sentenced to a fine of four hundred
yen or three months in prison. Unable to raise the money, she returned to
prison. Prior to this, however, she had become involved in a plot to produce a bomb to assassinate the emperor. The plan was hatched by Miyashita Takichi (1875–1911), a factory worker who had become a student of
socialism and anarchism.[9]

Miyashita's scheme had interesting roots. A member of the Heiminsha
circle, Morichika Umpei (1881–1911), had introduced him to the theory
that the emperor system was based on a myth created by establishment

historians. He had also read a pamphlet published by a Zen monk and an anarchist, Uchiyama Gudō (1874–1911). Explaining the reason for the poverty of tenant farmers, Uchiyama wrote:

> There are these leeches: The emperor, the rich, the big landowners. They suck the people's blood. . . . The big boss of the current government, the emperor, is not the son of the gods, as the teachers have misled you to believe. The ancestor of the present emperor came out of the corner of Kyushu and killed and robbed people. He then destroyed his fellow thief, Nagasune-hiko. . . . That the emperor is not a god becomes obvious if one thinks about it even for a moment. When it is said the dynasty lasted for 2,500 years, it may sound as if he is divine, but historically the emperors have been tormented by foreign foes and domestically they have been treated as puppets by their vassals.[10]

Kanno was enthusiastic about carrying out the plan, hoping to emulate Sophia Perovskaya, who had participated in the assassination of Alexander II of Russia. But Kōtoku, informed of the plan, began to lose enthusiasm and started to distance himself from the plotters. The four who were directly involved in the plot were Kanno, Miyashita, Niimura Tadao (1887–1911), an admirer of Kōtoku, and Furukawa Rikisaku (1884–1911), who was recruited into the group by Kanno.[11] Miyashita made the bomb and turned it over to his friend Shimizu Taichirō for safekeeping. Shimizu betrayed him to the police.

Kanno, some observers believe, was the central figure and the moving force of the conspirators, not Kōtoku Shūsui, though the government and most historians have made him the focus of attention. One of the defense lawyers, Imamura Rikisaburō, later asserted, "She was not a likable woman. If Kōtoku had not been ensnared by a woman like that he would not have ended his life in that manner. The Great Treason incident was all Kanno Suga's doing."[12] Arahata Kanson (who seems not to have forgiven her for her leaving him for Kōtoku) years later questioned her philosophical understanding of the issues and ascribed her actions to her pessimistic outlook, misanthropy, and world weariness caused by her long struggle with tuberculosis.[13] But this assessment ignores Kanno's strong commitment to her convictions, her passionate desire to redress social injustices, her formidable sense of responsibility, and her courage.

When the plot was uncovered in May 1910, Kanno was serving her prison term. The authorities (under Prime Minister Katsura Tarō, who had been directed by the *genrō* [elder statesman] Yamagata Aritomo to come down hard on the leftists) rounded up everybody who had the slightest connection with Kōtoku and charged them with complicity in the plot. Twenty-six people were put on trial, and Kanno was the only woman. The trial opened on December 10, 1910, and was closed to the public. Of the twenty-six, twenty-four were sentenced to death and two were given prison terms. Later the death sentences of twelve men were commuted to prison terms. In all, twelve were executed, including Kanno, Kōtoku, Miyashita, Niimura, and Furukawa. Also among the executed were Morichika Umpei and Uchiyama Gudō.

Kanno faced her accusers with courage, making no attempt to evade responsibility or bend her principles. During her preliminary interrogation she remarked:

> Basically even among anarchists I was among the more radical thinkers. When I was imprisoned in June 1908 in connection with the Red Flag incident I was outraged at the brutal behavior of the police. I concluded that a peaceful propagation of our principles could not be conducted under these circumstances. It was necessary to arouse the people's awareness by staging riots or a revolution or by undertaking assassinations. . . . I hoped to destroy not only the emperor but other elements too. . . . Emperor Mutsuhito, compared with other emperors in history, seems to be popular with the people and is a good individual. Although I feel sorry for him personally, he is, as emperor, the chief person responsible for the exploitation of the people economically. Politically he is at the root of all the crimes being committed, and intellectually he is the fundamental cause of superstitious beliefs. A person in such a position, I concluded, must be killed.[14]

When she was asked by the presiding judge if she wanted to make a final statement in court, she responded:

> I have no regrets. I am only chagrined that our plan ended in failure. It is my fault. I am a woman . . . and lack will power. . . . This is my shame. There are many pioneers who sacrificed their lives by courageously putting their plans into effect. They set examples for us to emulate. I feel that I have failed these pioneers. I shall die without

whimpering. This is my destiny. Those who sacrifice their lives for a cause are accorded the highest honor and respect by later generations. I shall die as one of the sacrificial victims. I have no regrets. But I do have one request. I am prepared to die. I was prepared for this from the very moment we hatched this plan. I have no complaints no matter how severely I am punished. But my plea is for the many people other than myself. These people have no connection with us. From the outset I knew that our plan would not succeed if we let a lot of people in on it. Only four of us were involved in the plan. It is a crime that involves only four of us. But this court, as well as the preliminary interrogators, treated it as a plan that involved a large number of people. That is a complete misunderstanding of the case. Because of this misunderstanding a large number of people have been made to suffer. You are aware of this. These people have aged parents, young children, and young wives. If these people are killed for something that they knew nothing about, not only will it be a grave tragedy for the persons concerned, but their relatives and friends will feel bitterness toward the government. Because we hatched this plan a large number of innocent people may be executed. If such an injustice should be the end result . . . I may die, but my sorrow will linger on.[15]

Her outrage at the wholesale conviction of innocent people is expressed in the memoirs she wrote a few days before her execution. Regarding her own situation, she remained steadfast, her only disappointment possibly being the information the prosecution passed on to her about Kōtoku's efforts to reconcile himself with this former wife.[16]

On January 24, 1911, eleven of Kanno's comrades were executed. On the following morning she herself was hanged.

The newspaper *Miyako Shimbun* reported: "She mounted the scaffold escorted by guards on both sides. Her face was covered quickly by a white cloth. . . . She was then ordered to sit upright on the floor. Two thin cords were placed around her neck. The floor-board was removed. In twelve minutes she was dead."[17]

Public reaction to her execution was cool. The *Tokyo Asahi News* commented, under the headline "Personification of Vanity," "She lived her life without believing in the gods or spirits. She indulged herself by reading biographies of Russian anarchists and nihilists who had given their lives to their so-called principles. It is said that she prided herself as a pioneer among Japanese women."[18] Hiratsuka Raichō, who was to organize her Seitōsha several months later, recalled, "I hardly took any interest in the Great Treason incident, which caused such a commotion in the society."[19]

Reflections on the Way to the Gallows

KANNO SUGAKO

This is written as a record of the period from the time the death sentence was pronounced to the time I mount the scaffold.[20] I shall write things down candidly and honestly in a straightforward fashion without any effort at self-justification.

In the women's prison in Tokyo. January 18, 1911. Cloudy. Needless to say, I was prepared for the death sentence. My only concern day and night was to see as many of my twenty-five fellow defendants saved as possible.

I boarded the prison carriage just before noon. From the window of the carriage I could see in the dim sunlight saber-bearing figures solemnly standing guard en route. They seemed to presage the verdicts of the trial, and I waited impatiently for the court proceedings to start at 1:00 P.M.

The time came. We climbed up to the second floor, then to the third floor, and then down again to the second floor to the courtroom of the Supreme Court. The security measures along the corridors and in the courtroom during the proceedings were extremely tight. The court was packed with people—lawyers, newspaper reporters, and spectators. I tend to get dizzy easily, so I felt a bit faint, having climbed many stairs and because of the stifling presence of the crowd in the courtroom. After I calmed down, I looked around at my fellow defendants. They were all sitting circumspectly, looking worried. They looked as if they were afraid to smile at each other. A pride of hungry lions. Their nails and teeth had been filed and smoothed down. There they sat before me. Twenty-five sacrificial lambs.

Soon the judges entered through the left door at the front of the courthouse. Will it be life or death? Many of the defendants' hearts must have beat faster. The clerk read the names of the defendants. Chief Justice Tsuru Jōichirō said a few words of instruction. Then, contrary to the usual procedure, he left the verdicts to the end and proceeded to read the lengthy arguments, sipping occasionally from a glass of water. As he continued to read, it became clear that he was arbitrarily linking even those who were clearly innocent to Article 73 of the criminal code.[21] His sophism became increasingly blatant. My concern [for my fellow defendants] increased and finally overwhelmed me like a tidal wave. But until he read the verdict for each defendant, I kept hoping against hope that some, even one person, would receive a minimal sentence. But, aah, it was all in vain. . . . It was all over. Except for Nitta Tōru, who was sentenced to eleven years in prison, and Niimura Zenbei, who was given eight years, the remaining twenty-four of us were sentenced to death.

From the beginning, I feared that this would be the case, but the trial was conducted in such an unexpectedly meticulous fashion that I began to hope that it would be relatively fair. The verdicts came as a shock. I was so angry and upset that I felt as if my entire body were on fire, and I began to tremble.

My poor friends, my poor comrades! More than half of them were innocent bystanders who had been implicated by the actions of five or six of us. [Kōtoku Shūsui, Miyashita Takichi, Niimura Tadao, Furukawa Rikisaku, and herself, as she wrote in the diary entry for January 21. See below.] Just because they were associated with us, they are now to be sacrificed in this monstrous fashion. Simply because they are anarchists, they are to be thrown over the cliff to their deaths.

I was not the only person shocked by this unexpected turn of events. All the lawyers, prison officials, and police who had been present during the trial on the sixteenth and were privy to the truth about this affair certainly must have been shocked at these outrageous verdicts. You could read it on the faces of everyone in the court. The defendants remained voiceless and silent; for the moment they were frozen in irrepressible anger. Then cold smirks appeared on their lips.

I wanted to comfort my fellow defendants, but I was so upset and angry I could not think of the right words. I could only mutter to myself, "What a shocking, lawless trial."

Then the straw hat [that covers the face of the prisoner] was placed on my head. Because we were marched out in reverse order of our arrival, I was the first to leave. As I stood up I thought of my comrades. Though they will mount the same scaffold as I, we shall never meet again. Some of them must certainly feel bitter toward us. But they are all my comrades.

We stood side by side as fellow defendants. Farewell, my twenty-five friends. Farewell, twenty-five victims. Goodbye!

"Goodbye, goodbye!" That was all I managed to say.

"Goodbye, goodbye," they shouted after me. As I left the courtroom I heard someone shout "Banzai!" No doubt one of the zealous anarchists was shouting for the anarchist cause. As I stepped on the first step of the stone stairway someone shouted, "Kanno-san!"

When I returned to the detention room of the courthouse, I began to cool off and regain my composure. I felt somewhat ashamed of myself for getting so angry. But what an outrageous trial!

However, it should not have surprised me. My past experiences should have prepared me to expect this as a matter of course. We initiated our plot precisely because this kind of outrageous legal system and despotic political authority exist. It was absurdly foolish to hope, even for a moment, that the wielders of power—whose authority I do not acknowledge—might save my comrades simply because the court hearings were meticulously carried out.

Soon the prison carriage arrived. I left the dimly lit detention room. The blood-red face of Takeda Kyūhei, one of the defendants, showed in a small detention-room window. He shouted, "Goodbye!" I replied, "Goodbye!" Someone else shouted "Goodbye!" One word filled with so much emotion. The late afternoon sun hits the prison carriage from the side. The carriage carries me to Ichigaya, on a route that I shall never see again.

January 19. Cloudy. Though I was furious, I must have been exhausted from the strain of the past several days. I slept soundly from early evening, and today I feel refreshed. I have received permission from the prison authorities to leave some of my possessions to my friends as mementos. I will leave my formal silk kimono to Sakai Mā-bo, the single-layer kimono to Hori Yasuko, the black cloak and the lined garment of striped muslin to Yoshikawa Morikuni.[22]

I wrote postcards to the three lawyers, Isobe Shirō, Hanai Takuzō, and Imamura Rikisaburō, expressing my shock at the verdicts. I also wrote cards to Sakai, Hori, and Yoshikawa, telling them about the mementos.

In the evening, the chaplain, Numanami Masanori, appeared. He told me that one of the fellow defendants, Mineo Setsudō, came to appreciate the value of faith in an external power after he was sentenced to death.

The chaplain said he was impressed that Mineo showed no signs of fear or worry. He then urged me to seek solace in religion. I told him I could not be more at peace with myself than I now was. It is ludicrous for an anarchist who is against all authority to turn to Amida Buddha for peace and security simply because he faces death. But I can appreciate Numanami's position as a religious leader and as a chaplain. I have, however, my own beliefs and peace of mind.

We had sailed into the vast ocean ahead of the world's current of thought and the general tide of events. Unfortunately, we were shipwrecked. But this sacrifice had to be made to get things started. New routes are opened up only after many shipwrecks and dangerous voyages. This is how the other shore of one's ideals is reached. After the sage of Nazareth was born, many sacrifices had to be made before Christianity became a world religion. In light of this, I feel that our sacrifice is miniscule.

I told the court these thoughts on the last day of the trial. They are with me constantly. I am convinced our sacrifice is not in vain. It will bear fruit in the future. I am confident that because I firmly believe my death will serve a valuable purpose I will be able to maintain my self-respect until the last moment on the scaffold. I will be enveloped in the marvelously comforting thought that I am sacrificing myself for the cause. I believe I will be able to die a noble death without fear or anguish.

At night Tanaka, director of prison instruction, came to see me. He told me that my fellow defendants were fairly calm and serene. I was pleased to hear this. He also talked about instances in which people condemned to death faced their end admirably. I described the kind of coffin I wanted made for me and how I wanted to be dressed after death. I was afraid that the supporters of the emperor and champions of patriotism might dig up my corpse and hack it to bits. I did not want to look too shabby when this happened. After Tanaka gave me his blessings, Numanami brought me two pamphlets: the *Tan'ishō*[23] and *Outline of the Blessings of Faith*.

January 20. Snow. Snow has settled on top of the pine trees and the dead branches of the cypress trees. The world has been covered in silver during the night. Since the beginning of the year there have been several short flurries, but this storm doesn't look as though it will stop soon. Let it snow, let it snow! A foot, two feet. Pile it up high. Envelop this sinful city of Tokyo in snow, like a city buried in ashes. Level the entire landscape.

I wonder what the defendants in the men's prison are thinking of now as they look out at the cold snow from the three-foot iron windows?

Snow. Full of memories. As I stare out the iron window and observe the gently swirling snow, memories of many years float past my eyes, the many times that I looked up at the same sky with all sorts of thoughts and feelings. A combination of happiness and sorrow quietly presses against my chest. I long for those days, but I realize that all things are ephemeral. Everything now belongs to the past. I don't know what will happen to me tomorrow. Now I do not have time to enjoy reminiscing about the past. Oh, yes, I have the time, but my time is too precious. I must use the time to read, to write. And there are things that I must think about immediately. My mind is preoccupied with thoughts of things that I must take care of. Why do I feel so restless and harried? I don't understand it. Is it because a stack of books is facing me? Is it because I can't see the people I must see to have certain things taken care of? Is it because I haven't written my last words to my younger brother?[24] People tell me that I haven't changed at all, that I am still full of energy. But even though I am busy with all sorts of things, nothing gets done. Still, it doesn't matter. I'll do what I can and whatever's unfinished, I'll leave as it is.

Two or three days ago I got a letter from Sakai. He wrote:

> I saw your letter of the fourth. I hope you will write your prison diary as forthrightly and courageously as possible. I admire you for not giving up your English studies. There is a saying that goes something like this: "For each day that a person lives, there is one day's worth of work." We all could die tomorrow, but I am studying German and French bit by bit as if I were definitely going to live till I am sixty. I don't know how many days or months you have left. If we look at our lives from the standpoint of the eternal universe's time and space, they last only a split second. Isn't it wonderful that we can spend part of that moment exchanging lighthearted letters like this?

[Kanno had written Sakai on the fourth: "Now that the trial is over I have nothing at all to do. Since the first of the year I have been keeping a prison diary as a sort of record of my thoughts and feelings. I plan to write candidly about whatever comes to mind. Memories, impressions, confessions, hopes. I expect you will be able to see it sometime in the future. . . ."]

I certainly am calm. Since September of last year I've been playing tug of war with the dictionary, trying to learn English. I go at it with a nervous sense of urgency but am making very little progress. I am only one-third into Reader V.

I had gotten so that I could at least read a [Japanese] magazine without much schooling. It is only natural that I cannot come up to the hem of those who have a formal education. However, what bothered me most of all was that I did not know a foreign language, and I wanted at least to be able to read one. Though I started to study on my own several times, poor health or something else always interfered. So I had not been able to do anything about this till recently. It was due in part to my lack of will power and patience but also to the circumstances I found myself in that only in mid-September did I decide that the time had come for me learn to read at least some simple English selections. I had to do so before I died. So I started with a Third-level Reader. Now, I don't know when I will be executed. I probably don't have much time left, so I guess I won't be able to master the language. I regret this very much.

This diary will be written without any falsehood or pretense. Sakai need not worry about this. It will reveal the naked Kanno Sugako, just as I am. [Kanno then jotted down some random thoughts, which she inked out.]

—I must copy down two or three poems from my other diary [which evidently is lost].
—What are we puny things fighting about—in the midst of eternal time and boundless sky?
—Born in a tiny country, I am sacrificing my little body for a glimmer of hope.
—What a nation! It takes pride in spilling the life-blood of a hundred thousand people over one inch of the map.
—Another day spent guarding the shadows created by the sunlight that comes through the barred window.
—I know that the cliff drops one thousand fathoms, yet I rush down the path without turning back.
—I lie motionless in the cold night bed and listen time and time again to the stealthy sounds of sabers.
—I lie on my back for half a day, looking through the three-foot window and watch the leaves of the cypress tree sway in the wind.
—The gingko tree in the winter exudes a sense of reverence. It looks like a holy man coming from the snowy mountains.

—This wretched love. It continues to smolder like the smoke that keeps rising from glowing ashes.

—My last day will soon come. I smile as I think about my life. I can think about it forever. Is the strong, courageous child of revolution the same person as the weak, frail, weeping child? Is this me?

—Don't ask where the seed that dropped in the field is. Wait for the east wind that blows in the spring.

—We lined up by the railing listening to the song of the seashore where Hatsushima Island [near the Izu Peninsula] floated three *ri* off in the waves.

—Deep in the night the wounded person cries. Both the old and new wounds are painful.

—In coming and going, did I see through the straw hat, the pale face in the third window?

—His eyes said "forgive me," but my eyes were as cold as the ice in the northern sea.

—I cursed at the light and darkness that came and went through the iron window for two hundred days.

—The evening crow. It keeps solitary watch over the rain clouds floating slowly across the big sky.

—Autumn afternoon. In the hollow of the cherry tree two tiny frogs are having fun.

—The pillars of words in my heart. They collapse one after the other in the autumn wind.

—I remember when I said "I'm going to end my life at twenty-two" and cut the strings of the violin and wept.

—You and I. We go to our graves feeling as if our hearts are separated east and west by the sea.

—The cherry petals fall on the stone-covered path of the Daihikaku Temple. And the temple bell peals.

In the evening I received cards from Sakai and Tameko [Sakai's wife], Yoshikawa, and Kōtoku Komatarō.[25] I wanted to jot down my thoughts after reading the cards, but it was more than I could do. As I reread what I've written so far, this diary strikes me as totally disorganized and fragmentary. It's almost as if I'm writing down the mutterings of my dreams. It's distressing. Should I stop altogether?

January 21. Clear. The sun is shining on the snow on the pine tree branches. It looks like a painting by Maruyama Ōkyo [1733–95]. An exquisite scene.

When Sakai started his Baibunsha,[26] the first person to ask for help was a student in a women's college. She wanted the Baibunsha to write her senior thesis. What a comment on our society—comical and disgraceful at the same time.

I hear that Sakai Tameko is attending midwives' school. I admire her courage and initiative to begin studies at the age of forty. And I admire Sakai for helping his wife become independent and self-sufficient. I am sure this entails some inconvenience for him. Not every man would be so willing.

Kōtoku's mother died on December 28. She caught malaria and then pneumonia and died ten days after she got sick. I was told that when she came to Tokyo in November to see Kōtoku, she had planned to visit me too, but because Ochiyo [Kōtoku's former wife] was with her she held back and left without seeing me. Even though Kōtoku and I had broken off relations by then, she and I still saw each other as mother and daughter. When I heard that she had come all the way to Tokyo and did not visit me, I was hurt and felt she was being heartless. Now having heard what happened, I feel guilty to have thought ill of her even for a moment. I think of her with fondness. We were mother and daughter, and then we were no longer members of the same family. Now we have parted, never to see each other again. She had comforted me constantly with her letters and packages. The past is like a dream. Ah, life is like a dream. Time is the graveyard, and everyone is going to be buried eventually. It is only a matter of time. Here I am, weeping over the death of others. But I too will be buried soon.

I seem to have caught a cold. I have a bad headache, but I took a bath anyway. Bathing is one of the few pleasures of prison life. Visits, letters, and bathing. I have no family, am virtually alone, so I seldom have visitors or get letters. The bath we are allowed every five days is my greatest pleasure.

From the clear, blue sky the warm sunlight streams in through the barred window. Sitting before the desk, feeling relaxed after my bath, how happy I would be to simply melt away and fall asleep forever.

Yoshikawa wrote in his letter:

This day a year ago I was released from prison.[27] Of the three of us who left prison that day, Higuchi Den [a writer] is doing extremely well. In contrast, I am merely staying alive. Oka Chiyohiko [a printer] went back to his old nest in Chiba and is struggling with cold weather and hunger.

I wonder why Oka was imprisoned. Are those who are successful right and those in the depths of despair wrong? What about Morioka Eiji,[28] who lost his mind and jumped into an old well in Dairen? What about those people who abandon their principles like worn-out sandals because they fear government oppression and hope to save their skins? Isn't fate fickle? The human heart is so frail. Let those who want to leave, leave. Let those who must die, die. New shoots sprout only after the mammoth tree falls. In the springtime of the intellectual world, those of us who deem ourselves to be pioneers need not look back to fall and winter. We must look forward. We must rush forward. We must rush toward the light that offers us hope.

It seems that the authorities are watching our comrades in the outside world with even greater vigilance. The trial's shocking and outrageous results show that the government is planning to take advantage of this incident to adopt extreme, repressive measures. Persecute us! That's right, persecute us! Don't you know that for every force there is a counterforce? Persecute us! Persecute us as much as you wish. The old way is fighting the new—imperialism versus anarchism. Go ahead: Take your piece of stick and try with all your might to stop the onrush of the Sumida River.

Chaplain Numanami comes and asks me, "How are you?" I reply, "Same as usual." He says, "You have peace of mind because your life is founded on faith in your ism, your cause. Some people may be chagrined about the whole affair, depending on how deeply they were involved in it. You were involved in the affair from the beginning to the end, so you must have been prepared to face anything." What he said pleased me. It was much better than his trying to convert me.

I am sure many fellow defendants are deeply distressed about what has happened. This incident is unprecedented in history, but the punishment is unprecedented too. This affair should not be labeled a conspiracy by the anarchists. Rather it should be called a conspiracy concocted by the public prosecutors. The invocation of Article 73 in the trial was truly idiotic. The public charges and the truth of the matter were totally unrelated, like a novel written by a third-rate writer. Only the five of us—Kōtoku, Miyashita, Niimura, Furukawa, and I—were involved in the conspiracy, the group that the prosecutor called the "reserves under Kōtoku's direct command." The prosecutors linked the others to the conspiracy simply because of the idle talks we had with them in the past, talks that were as ephemeral as smoke drifting in air.

The prosecution argued that the affair was a conspiracy of the anarchists—so-and-so is an anarchist, or so-and-so is a friend of an anarchist; therefore, they were participants in the conspiracy. Using this kind of outrageous reasoning, they went about arresting people. Rushing to fight for honor and fame, the authorities strove to bring as many as possible to the dock. They resorted to deceit, double-dealing, threats, and, in extreme cases, methods similar to the tortures used in the past. Some were questioned continuously day and night without rest or sleep. The prosecutors latched onto the common complaints that ordinary people, not necessarily anarchists, mouth about the government. They presented these casual discussions as if they were linked in a profound way to the conspiracy.

Even though one were to let them interpret these discussions as broadly as possible and define them as being conspiratorial, they can in no way be linked to Article 73. At most, the prosecutors might prove a plot to stage a civil uprising. But the prosecutors and judges who conducted the preliminary investigation questioned the accused in detail about anarchism. When the ideals of anarchism—and these were merely ideals—were expressed, the prosecutors concluded that because anarchism believes in absolute freedom and equality it perforce also naturally rejects the imperial family. Through such reasoning they managed to get their inferences into the records of the examination. They then used these theories and ideals, which have no relationship with the current affair, to entrap completely innocent people.

The more I think about this the madder I get.

You poor pitiful judges. All you wanted to do was protect your positions. To safeguard them, you handed down these verdicts even though you knew they were unlawful and arbitrary. You went against your consciences. You poor judges, poor slaves of the government. I should be angry at you, but I pity you instead. Here I am bound by this barred window, but my thoughts still spread their wings in the free world of ideas. Nothing can bind my thoughts or interfere with them. You may live for a hundred years, but what is a life without freedom, a life of slavery, worth? You poor slaves.

At 4:00 P.M. I was taken to the visiting room. Four people were there: Sakai, Mr. and Mrs. Ōsugi [that is, Hori Yasuko], and Yoshikawa. Before the visit, I was told by the warden that I was not to speak about the trial. This must have been a governmental directive, based on the fear that if the truth about the outrageous trial got out, our comrades might vent their anger against the government.

I remember how Sakai and Ōsugi looked when we were together during the trial of the Red Flag incident in room 3 of the court of appeals. Today they looked no different. Both are healthy and vigorous. We spoke a word here, a phrase there. I tried to avoid meeting their eyes, which were filled with tears. I tried to laugh and chat casually, but finally when the time came to say farewell, especially when it came time to shake Yasuko's hand, the tears that I had been holding back poured out as if from a broken dam. We both cried and held hands for a long time.[29] Oh, my dear friends, my comrades! When I blurted out "The verdicts were a surprise," Sakai said in anguish, "I expected you and Kōtoku to die for the cause but. . . ." That's all he said—his heart was overflowing with emotion.

Today I wrote a letter to Mr. and Mrs. Ōsugi and cards to Messrs. Sakai and Yoshikawa.

[To the Ōsugis she wrote, "Ōsugi, Yasuko, thank you for visiting me. I was pleased to see Ōsugi, looking so well. I hope both of you will take good care of yourselves and live for many years." To Sakai Tameko she wrote, "Please come and pay me a farewell visit when it is convenient for you. I am grateful for the sash you sent me. Thank you so much." To Yoshikawa she wrote, "I am prohibited from making even the slightest comment in my letters, so I am jotting things down in my diary. Please read it after I am gone."]

January 22. Clear. Last night, for the first time since I was jailed, I felt depressed. The final visit from my friends was nerve-racking. Since June 2, when I heard that our plot was uncovered, I have been convinced that I have to learn to discipline myself.[30] Right now I feel like a worthless person—to be overwhelmed, even for one night, by such irrational feelings. I despair for myself. How could I be such a weakling?

Maybe it is only a natural reaction. Asian heroes say that one's face should not reveal feelings of joy or anger, happiness or sorrow. In a way, this is a highly admirable ideal, but at the same time it is hypocritical. Maybe an idiot or a sage can really transcend joy and anger or happiness and sorrow, but ordinary people are filled with such feelings. Only by lying or pretending can they live without showing feelings. I am a weak person, emotional to the extreme. I hate lies, I dislike pretense. I detest all things unnatural. I cry. I laugh. I rejoice. I get angry. I let my emotions have free play. I don't care how others measure my worth as a human being. I will be satisfied if I can end my life without lying to myself.

Today, however, I feel very good. The sadness of last night has vanished. I wonder why I felt so bad? I was overjoyed to hear that my fellow defendants in the male prison wing are ready to face death, displaying a fortitude worthy of anarchists. When I heard this, I felt as if I were floating on air. Since we are responsible for their plight, I was very worried about how they might react. We are all human. It's only natural that they might find it intolerable to be punished so harshly for the truly tenuous connection they had with the affair. I am really impressed that they have decided to sacrifice all for the sake of their principles. They are worthy anarchists, worthy comrades. I am truly happy. I am proud to be a believer in anarchism. I have nothing more to worry about or regret. The only worry that had been hovering over my thoughts like a black cloud has dissipated completely. Everything is as bright and clear as today's sky.

I wrote letters to Koizumi Sakutarō, Katō Tokijirō, Nagae Tamemasa, and cards to Okano Tatsunosuke and Watanabe Yayoko.[31]

In the evening I received letters from our attorney, Hirade, and from Sakai. Hirade wrote:

> I knew what the verdicts would be before the judge finished reading ten lines of the argument. Like all lawyers who hope for favorable decisions, I had clung until then to the hope that five or six of the defendants would get off with light sentences. But it was in vain. Hard as it was to remain in the courtroom, I did not want the two men I was defending to lose hope. So even though I found it painful, I stuck it out until the end of the proceedings. I even said a few words of encouragement to them. There's nothing that can be done about the application of the law, so let us leave the question of the verdicts' justness to the judgment of history. I don't think that you're the sort of person that requires words of comfort. I am tormented, though, when I think about how those who were not prepared to face the

worst must have felt. I haven't been able to do anything since the eighteenth.

Even a lawyer feels this way. Is it any wonder that I feel tormented beyond endurance, me, their comrade, who is responsible for their plight? I wrote a reply to Hirade under the dim light-bulb.

January 23. Clear. I wake up every night at 2:00 A.M. when they come to change my hot-water bottle [used as a footwarmer in bed]. Though I am drowsy, I can't fall back to sleep for two or three hours. I lie there thinking about all sorts of things. Last night when I woke up, I thought about a number of things—Sakai who came to see me the day before yesterday, my fellow defendants, my younger sister's grave,[32] which is in Seishunji [in Yodobashi in Tokyo]. When Sakai or Yasuko delivers the money to take care of the grave, as I asked them to, I wonder what that monk whom I detest so much will say. I don't believe in the superstition that the dead will be saved by the power of the sutra, so I tended to neglect sending gifts to the temple. Whenever I visited my sister's grave, the monk always gave me a nasty look. As a result, I stopped going to her grave site to place flowers and incense and instead placed her favorite food and so forth before her photograph. This is just as silly, for, after all, the dead person's body has already turned to smoke or has decomposed and returned to its original atomic particles. I don't believe that the spirit survives and is pleased to receive flowers, incense, or other gifts. I did these things out of habit and for my own psychological satisfaction.

Given my current situation, however, I feel I ought to give the temple at least a little money to care for the grave. If not for me, then certainly for the sake of my younger brother, who is currently in America. When he returns to Japan one of these years and asks about our younger sister's grave, he would, without question, be crushed if he found that the grave had been neglected and allowed to deteriorate because it was looked on as the grave of a person without family.

Last night I thought about what should be done with my body after my death. After my last insignificant breath and when I have become a mere lump of flesh, I suppose it doesn't really matter what happens to my remains. But I hate the thought of being squeezed into a coffin in an awkward position with my legs bent under. I want a coffin in which my body can be laid out flat. The day before yesterday, when my friends visited me,

I asked Warden Kinose, who was present as an observer, to get me a full-length coffin. I expect the coffin will be finished before long. I had also wanted to be in my good clothes. If by chance someone were to dig up my coffin and expose my body, I didn't want to look too unseemly. Now, however, I've decided it would be more natural for me to be dressed in my ordinary clothes. It doesn't matter if my dress is torn or soiled.

I had also asked Section Chief Iizuka to let me take a bath on the morning of my execution, but this morning I told them to forget about that too. I don't care about the headstone. Truthfully, I really don't care if they burn me and scatter my ashes in the wind, or if they throw my body in Shinagawa River. But I suppose they couldn't do a thing like that. So if I am to be buried, I really want to be buried next to my younger sister. As I said, I don't like that temple, so I have arranged to be buried in the convict graveyard in Zōgegaya. This will be the least trouble. The day before yesterday when Sakai and Yasuko asked me if I had anything I wanted taken care of, I told them where I wanted to be buried.[33]

This morning I wrote cards to the Baibunsha and to our attorney, Hirade. I asked the people at Baibunsha to arrange to have a new wooden tablet set up by my sister's gravestone when they went to the temple.

Thinking about the grave, I was reminded of the prosecutor Taketomi Wataru.[34] I met him three years ago after the Red Flag incident. At the time, we clashed over my request to have the wording of my pretrial statement corrected because there were inaccuracies. We ended up getting angry at each other. Then the following year—that is, two summers ago when I was imprisoned and charged with a violation of the press law in connection with my work with the magazine *Jiyū Shisō*—the same prosecutor tormented me. He was extremely mean and devious in questioning me and pressed the case against me in a merciless fashion.

When the current affair broke out, I was initially examined by him, but I was determined not to say a word, since I disliked him so much. In fact, I even thought of killing him and bringing him along with me to the land of the dead if I got the chance. Later, however, he talked about his life—about his mother and how he had worked his way through school—and I began to feel sympathetic toward him and abandoned any thought of killing him. I, too, shared my feelings with him, and we parted amicably.

Several days later he came to me and said, "I find it interesting that you don't want to say a word to me about the affair. I won't try to make you talk about it. Instead, won't you tell me about yourself? Wouldn't it be a novel idea to have me, whom you detest so much, write your life story? I really would like to do it."

I imagined that this would be his way of repaying me viciously, but no matter who writes about me it's highly unlikely that anything good will be said. I have been a maverick and haven't followed any straight and narrow path. Thanks to my stubbornness and determination not to knuckle under, I succeeded in not becoming a prostitute or a textile-factory worker. But the story of my life would not elicit the sympathies of anyone except, perhaps, kindhearted people concerned with social problems. I have given up any hope of winning people's understanding. My story is bound to be told in a slanted way, and I might as well have it told as unsympathetically as possible. So, in the end, I told my life story to the prosecutor almost as if it were a novel.[35]

When we discussed things unrelated to the current affair, the prosecutor impressed me as a cheerful person, free of sinister intents. I didn't see anything hateful in him. I can vividly recall his face as he listened avidly to my story. He would say, "It really is like a novel," and kept repeating, "You and I must have had some strong ties in our previous existence." In the end, he told me, "If by chance you are executed, or if you happen to die before me, I promise to bring flowers and incense to your grave."

His eyes seemed to say that he was not merely flattering me. So I thought he might visit my grave at least once. When I mentioned this to someone, they laughed and said that he was probably just superstitious about the entire thing.[36]

If I could return as a ghost, there are so many people, beginning with the judge of the Court of Cassation, that I would like to terrify. It would be wonderful to scare them witless and make them grovel.

Early this morning, I had an interesting dream. I was with two or three people whom I can't recall now, and we were walking on a path in a field by a brook. When I looked up, I saw the sun and the moon, about three feet apart, vividly etched in the blue sky. The sun was the same color as the moon, and it was not fully round but was shaded by a third. The moon was about ten days past the new moon. I told my companions that when the sun and the moon appear together it means a great calamity is about to befall the nation. Then I woke up. Maybe my brain is somehow injured, but from way back I've often dreamed all night long. I've never had a dream like that, though. A crescent-shaped sun and moon. I wonder what all this means?

Nowadays, every morning when I get up I think in amazement, "Oh, am I still alive?" That I am still alive feels like a dream.

I heard from Tanaka, chief of moral instruction, that over half of the defendants condemned to death have been given a reprieve. Their sentences were probably reduced one degree to life imprisonment. The verdicts were so unjust that this came as no surprise. Still, it is delightful news. I don't know whose sentences were reduced, but it must be those who had very little to do with the affair; those people who, in my opinion, were completely innocent. They must be overjoyed, since, even though they were condemned unjustly and arbitrarily, they were facing the death penalty.

The authorities first hand down these harsh sentences, then reduce them, touting the action as an act of the emperor's benevolence. They try to impress the people of Japan, as well as those of other nations, that this is an act of justice and mercy. Are we to admire this kind of clever scheming? or condemn it as artful politicking? Still I am really happy that my comrades' lives have been spared. To be fully satisfied I would like to see all others saved except for the three or four of us. If I could take the places of all of them, I would be happy to be broiled to death by being trussed upside down or have my back split open and have molten lead poured into me. I am willing to suffer any kind of torture and punishment.

Someone told me an interesting story about Tanaka who was a samurai of Aizu-han.[37] Tanaka was captured and condemned to death in 1872. On his way to the execution grounds he was unexpectedly given a reprieve. It is a story that intrigues someone in my situation a great deal.

Tanaka is tactful in tailoring his talk to fit the person he is talking to. He does not say anything mentally upsetting but simply comes up with timely and appropriate stories. I am impressed. It is the fruit of years of experience.

Five letters arrived. They were from Sakai Mā-san, Koizumi Sakutarō, Minami Sukematsu, Kayama Sukeo, and Tomiyama.[38] Mā-san's is a beautiful picture-card of flowers and grass. She has written in pencil, "I understand you are giving me something. Thank you very much. Goodbye." I can just see her big eyes, fair face, and adorable figure. She is really a lovable child.

Koizumi wrote, "I am writing this as a farewell missive. On New Year's Eve when I got drunk at Chikushi-kan I wrote the following poem for [Kōtoku] Shūsui:

> Before I lift the sake cup, I think only of the relationship with
> beautiful princesses.
> After I am drunk I understand the bitter search.
> Tonight my dear friend is in prison.
> Where will the spirit that haunts his dreams be at the end of the
> year?

I also started to compose a poem for you, but I failed to do so and completed only one phrase: 'How pitiful. This enlightened age derails the talented lady.'"

He has been of great help to me during the past two or three years. I read his letter over and over, and was overcome with emotion. Please stay well. Live for a hundred years.

I am writing this under the dim electric-light bulb. I can barely move the brush, which is cold as ice. It is difficult. The call for us to go to bed was issued sometime ago. The lonely wind is blowing past the window. I guess I will call it a night.

January 24. Clear. I wrote to Messrs. Sakai and Masuda, and Ma-bō. I asked Sakai to send my younger brother in America some mementos from me.

The court's verdict, consisting of 146 pages, arrived. I plan to send it to my comrades in the United States. Yoshikawa sent me the *Suikodo-Kensō.*[39]

I feel distressed after reading the hyperbolic, twisted reasoning of the verdict. I cannot get my spirits up to write today.

A postcard from Yoshikawa arrived.

At night I wrote letters and cards to the four lawyers, Isobe, Hanai, Imamura, and Hirade, and to Messrs. Yoshikawa, Minami, Kayama, and Tomiyama. [In her letter to Yoshikawa she wrote]:

> Yesterday I heard that more than half of my fellow defendants were reprieved. When I heard the verdicts, which were completely unexpected, I was so bitter that the blood in my whole body flared up as if on fire. Now, I am very happy that some of the defendants have been saved. They must be the people who I was certain were innocent. After hearing the news I felt that half the burden on my shoulders had been lifted.

FOUR

THE ROAD
TO NIHILISM
Kaneko Fumiko

Kaneko Fumiko's life (1903–26) was conditioned by the social environment of the underprivileged sectors of two societies. In Japan she suffered privation and hardship before she was sent to Korea at the age of nine and after she returned to Japan when she was sixteen. In Korea she was thrown into a society where the entire indigenous population had been impoverished and oppressed by the annexation of Korea by Japan in 1910. Her life there with her grandmother—a member of the privileged, "carpetbagger" class—did not change her status as underprivileged, because of the abusive treatment she suffered at the hand of her grandmother. Her ultimate rejection of all authority must certainly have been based on the treatment she received from her parents and grandmother, but her observations in Korea undoubtedly reinforced her view of life as a struggle for survival in which the strong abuse and exploit the weak. She eventually embraced a thoroughly anarchist, nihilistic philosophy, and she made common cause with Pak Yeol (1902–74), a Korean anarchist.

When she arrived in Korea that country had just been brought under Japanese rule. Japanese rulers had imposed a military administration to keep Korean nationalism under control and had also confiscated large tracts of farmlands from Korean farmers, reducing them to tenancy and vagrancy. Koreans who went to Japan in search of work ended up laboring as miners or construction workers. In the late 1930s they were forcefully conscripted and dragooned into labor crews.[1]

The Korean nationalists on the peninsula struggled to resist the Japanese rulers, but to no avail. In March 1919, just before Kaneko was sent

back to Japan, a violent confrontation broke out between Koreans staging
a peaceful demonstration for independence and the Japanese authorities.
In the end, at least 2,000 Koreans were dead and 20,000 arrested.[2] Seeing
this, it was little wonder that Korean youths like Pak Yeol became anarchists and that Kaneko joined hands with him rather than committing
herself to the socialists that she had met. Instead, she and Pak Yeol, who
had become acquainted in Tokyo in 1922, organized a two-person anarchist society, the Futei-sha (Society of Malcontents). They were arrested on
September 23, 1923, two days after the Great Earthquake, when the entire
area around Tokyo was in a complete state of disorder and chaos. During
this crisis the authorities ruthlessly set out to crush communists and labor
organizers. Furthermore, wild rumors spread that disaffected Koreans
were taking advantage of the chaos to loot and kill, vigilante groups were
formed, and hundreds of innocent Koreans were massacred. An unofficial
estimate held that as many as 2,600 Koreans were killed.[3]

The authorities placed Kaneko and Pak under "protective custody,"
interrogated them, and charged them with high treason, specifically of
plotting to assassinate the emperor. When they were arrested, Kaneko
was twenty and Pak twenty-one. They were indicted in July 1925 and
brought to trial in February 1926. On March 25 they were convicted and
sentenced to death.

Kaneko Fumiko was born in Yokohama. Her parents were not married legally and did not register her birth. As a result, Kaneko was treated
as a person without any national identity and was not allowed to attend
elementary school except as an auditor. She grew up in extreme poverty,
often going hungry. Her father was unable to hold a job, drank heavily,
gambled, and had a violent temper, often beating his wife. He finally
abandoned the family for his wife's younger sister.[4]

The following years were rootless ones for Kaneko as her mother
drifted from man to man, hoping for some sort of economic security. It
was a life of insecurity and poverty. In desperation Kaneko's mother considered selling her to a brothel, but the plan fell through when the broker's
terms were insufficient.[5]

Kaneko's mother then became the common-law wife of a man who
came from an out-of-the way village in Yamanashi prefecture, and Kaneko began rural living for the first time. She was shocked at the primitive
conditions prevailing there. In fact, the meals were poorer and coarser than

the ones she was later fed in prison, where the cereal was 40 percent rice and 60 percent barley, whereas in the village the "rice" bowl did not contain a single grain of rice. Kaneko did note, though, that "unlike the rice in prison, the village rice-bowls did not have pebbles and worms in them."[6]

Kaneko's mother had a child by her Yamanashi husband. One night she overheard her mother and her husband pondering what to do with the baby and heard them mention the possibility of infanticide. Shortly after that her mother's family came to take her and her mother back to their home. Instead, her mother left with another man. The trauma of being abandoned by both her father and her mother had a profound effect on Kaneko. She remarks in her memoirs, "I want to cry out to the fathers and mothers of the world. 'Do you really love your children? Your love really lasts only as long as your primitive parental instincts. After that you pretend to love your children so long as they can serve your interests.'"[7]

When she was nine Kaneko was taken to Korea by her paternal grandmother, who was then living with her daughter and her husband in that country. Their original plan was to have the aunt adopt Kaneko because she and her husband were childless. Kaneko spent the next seven years with her grandmother and aunt in a small village in southern Korea, and they were grim years indeed.

Perhaps because Kaneko lacked the "refinement" proper to the family, her grandmother and aunt abandoned their plan of adopting her and began instead to treat her like a maid, an unwanted member of the family. Her grandmother was a sadistic person who castigated and beat Kaneko for the least mistake or infraction of the many stringent household rules. For example, she locked the little girl up in her room without food for a day and a night for having walked home with a girl friend from a "common" family. (Kaneko's community in the village was sharply divided into two classes, the "better" families and the "common" ones.) She stinted and scrimped as she sought to spend as little money as possible on Kaneko. At one point Kaneko contemplated suicide after having been deprived of food for three days. Just as she was about to throw herself in the river, she heard the sound of cicadas. "I looked around once more. How beautiful nature was! I listened carefully. What serenity!" When she thought that she was saying farewell to "the mountains, the trees, the stones, the flowers, the animals, and the cicadas, to everything," she concluded that no matter how cruel and mean her grandmother and aunt were to her, there were too many wonderful things in the world for her to renounce it. She decided to stay alive. "I mustn't die, I must join hands with others who are being tormented like me, and get even with those who are oppressing us."[8] Kaneko endured several more years of abuse. Finally, when she was fifteen, her grandmother decided to send her back to Kaneko's mother's family in Yamanashi prefecture. She would soon be approaching marriageable age, and evidently her grandmother did not want to have to defray the expenses of a marriage.

Besides her personal hardship, which left her with many bitter memories, Kaneko was also struck by the arrogant manner in which the Japanese occupiers treated the native Koreans. Her grandmother's family had underpaid their Korean servant, abused him verbally, and kept him and his family in penury. "As a result, Kō was very poor. No member of his family could eat a full meal. In the coldest days of winter Kō's children shivered in bed with only bedding made of hemp sacks."[9] And yet the abused Korean families showed the most compassion and sympathy toward Kaneko, which no doubt helps account for her sympathy with the Korean youths she later met in Tokyo and her involvement in their political ventures.

Her life back in Yamanashi was scarcely happier. Her maternal grandparents and her uncle and his wife had had a falling out, and family life was tense, a common occurrence in Japan. (The myth of the peaceful and harmonious Japanese family is belied by the lives of most of the women in this volume.)

Kaneko's mother had married and divorced several times more while Kaneko was in Korea and was still incapable of taking Kaneko back into her family. Her father's life was only slightly more stable. Kaneko lived with him briefly and attended a sewing school. He schemed to arrange a marriage between Kaneko and her mother's younger brother (her uncle), a young Buddhist priest whose financial prospects he thought could redound to his advantage. The plan fell through, however, when her uncle discovered that Kaneko had been seeing a young man (Segawa Hiroshi, who appears in her memoirs below) who was regarded as a delinquent. Kaneko was unhappy with her life with her father and left for Tokyo when she was seventeen. This is the point at which the translation from her memoir begins.[10] The portions translated constitute only about one-third of the memoir, the period after she went out to Tokyo. The earlier sections deal with her childhood, her years in Korea, and her return to Yamanashi. Her political thoughts are not revealed in her memoirs, but during her interrogation on November 22, 1923, she expressed her opinion frankly.

The views held by Kaneko Fumiko are remarkable for a young woman of her day. She was hardly twenty, had a limited education, and grew up in an atmosphere in which patriotism and loyalty to the emperor were the sine qua non of Japanese life. Not only is it remarkable that she formulated such a heretical political philosophy, but her refusal to grovel before authority is even more extraordinary. She refused to be mealy-mouthed and cower before her persecutors. Her candor, courage, and adherence to her convictions enabled the authorities to charge her with treason and gain her conviction. The records of her interrogation were not, of course, made available to the public until the end of World War II. The picture presented to the general public was that of a nefarious, degenerate woman. A photograph of Kaneko and Pak sitting close together with Pak's left arm over Kaneko's shoulders was passed on to right-wing military officers, not only to play up the immorality of the "traitors," but also to discredit the Wakatsuki government then in office for its lenient treatment of the two.[11]

Following their convictions and the imposition of the death sentences, Kaneko and Pak expected to be executed. Then on April 5 the chief of the Ichigaya prison, Akiyama Kaname, informed them that thanks to the benevolence of His Imperial Majesty, their sentences were being commuted to life imprisonment. He then handed the certificate of reprieve to Pak Yeol, who accepted it. When he handed Kaneko the certificate, she glared at him and tore the document to bits. Akiyama was shocked at this act of defiance, and got the other officials present to swear to secrecy about this because all the officials who had anything to do with the reprieve would have to resign. He made a public announcement that the two had accepted the commutation with gratitude. He did not reveal what actually happened until 1959.[12]

Kaneko was then sent to prison in Utsunomiya. There she refused to perform any prison work assigned to her. But about three months later she asked to be allowed to work on the task of weaving hemp ropes. The next morning, on July 23, 1926, she was found to have hanged herself with the rope that she had woven.[13]

Pak Yeol remained in prison until the end of World War II. He eventually returned to Korea and became active in the movement to unify the two sections of his country. He died in January 1949.

Kaneko was virtually ignored by her compatriots until the postwar years. The only person who seemed to consider her important enough to record in history in the prewar years was Takamure Itsue, who included Kaneko in her Japanese women's biographical dictionary published in 1936.[14]

What Made Me Do What I Did

KANEKO FUMIKO

For those who want to carve out an independent life, especially those who want to pursue learning and make a living as a scholar, there is no place as fascinating and as seductive as Tokyo. Needless to say, Tokyo is the place to go for children from wealthy families who can count on money from home. But even a person like me, with barely enough money to travel, is attracted to Tokyo. I didn't know whether life there was really as perfect as I expected, but for a girl like me, Tokyo seemed like a paradise on earth which would provide me with everything I desired. On to Tokyo, to Tokyo! Regardless of the hardships that you will impose on me, and the trials that you will put me through, I know that you will fulfill my hopes.

My life has been one misfortune after another ever since I was born. I was continuously abused and mistreated in Yokohama, Yamanashi, Korea, and Hamamatsu. Until now, I have not been able to take hold of my own life and identity. But now I am grateful for everything that has happened to me in the past. I am grateful to my father, my mother, my grandparents, my aunt, and my uncle. I am grateful to a destiny that did not let me be born into a wealthy family but that made me suffer as much as possible in all aspects of my life. Why grateful? Because if I had been permitted to grow up with my father, grandparents, and aunt and uncle, without experiencing any pain, I would undoubtedly have been molded by the thoughts and personalities of people whom I detest and hold in contempt. I would not have discovered my own identity. Now I am seventeen years old [the year was 1920].

I can stand on my own two feet. That's right. I must work out and create my own way of life. And Tokyo is the great unexplored land where I will be able to do that. So, on to Tokyo, to Tokyo!

As soon as I arrived in Tokyo, I went, as was planned, to my great-uncle's home in San-no-wa. Since we had never corresponded, I had not written in advance to ask for his help. However, I was convinced that he would help me. He would certainly let me stay with him the short while until I could become independent and work my way through school. Just as I expected, great-uncle's family welcomed me. But they did not agree with my plans. Every night great-uncle asked me to sit beside him while he drank sake and tried to persuade me to change my mind.

"Listen, Fumi. Think about this carefully. Right now you are determined to study. But what if, after a great deal of hardship, you did manage to get an education and become a schoolteacher. All you will be able to earn is about fifty or sixty yen a month. You won't be able to make a living with that kind of pay. Well, maybe when you are single it might be enough. But you can't stay single forever. Eventually you will have to marry. Then you are bound to have children. And if you get pregnant you will not be able to go to school with a bulging stomach. Then you won't be able to earn any money. That's why I believe that you should stay here and learn how to use the sewing machine. Then you should marry a hard-working merchant. You'll definitely be happier that way. No matter what you say, this is a world that runs on money. A bit of education is not going to make it possible for you to earn a living."

I could understand great-uncle's reasoning. It is only natural for him to think that way. And I was grateful to him for thinking about my future. But I no longer wanted to be under the care of anybody. I had already suffered enough in living that sort of life. I wanted to be independent and self-sufficient. This urge was too strong for me to resist. I appreciated great-uncle's advice but could not follow it. I simply told him, "Thank you so much, but I believe a woman like me can never become the wife of a tradesman."

But he was unrelenting and repeated his arguments night after night. Finally, though, I convinced him to let me go out into the city and work my way through school.

About a month after I arrived in Tokyo I managed to find a way to earn my own living. While scouting around the city, I saw a poster on a telephone pole which read, "Students working their way through school, Welcome. Keisetsusha." I felt as if I had hit the jackpot. I repeated the words on the poster over and over. I especially liked the name Keisetsusha (a society of those who study by the light of the firefly and snow). I headed straight for the Keisetsusha.

It was located in the back of the alley on Ueno Street near Ueno

Hirokōji. When I got there I found that it was a newspaper delivery agency, a sign there read Shirohata Newspaper Store. The glass door at the entrance was closed, but I could see two desks on the dirt floor inside. A young man was leaning over a desk, looking over what seemed to be a ledger.

"Excuse me," I called out, somewhat nervously, and opened the glass door. The young man looked up from the ledger and glanced at me without expression. "I am looking for a job, but is the master in?"

"Let me see," the young man said, tilting his head a bit, and went in the back. Then a big fat man with a reddish face came out. This was the boss.

I told him that I wanted to work my way through school and I wanted a job. The boss stared at me and then said without a smile, "It's tough work. It would be impossible for a woman." I told myself that no matter how hard it was I could take it. It would probably be difficult to find a better deal than this. I was determined to get the job.

"No matter how difficult it is, I can do the job. Please hire me." The boss did not answer right away.

"I've used a few women, but they really couldn't stick it out. And if I employ a woman, problems with the men tend to break out. . . ."

"I've had a rough life," I said earnestly. "When I think of that, I know that I can endure any sort of hardship. And as you can see, I'm more like a man than a woman. There's no chance that trouble would break out in my relationship with men."

He thought things over for a while and said, as if he were making up his mind reluctantly, "Well, let's try it anyway." In a positive tone of voice, he said, "Start anytime you want to." I felt that he had a good heart.

"Thank you so much. I shall count on your help."

He then went on to explain. "There are ten people working for us now, all men living together in the house across the street. As you are a woman, you can't live with them there, but you can live here. I will deduct fifteen yen a month from your earnings for room and board. I'll give you the Sambashi area; it's a good market. You'll easily be able to earn enough to go to school."

I felt as if I had gone to Heaven. I returned to my great-uncle's in San-no-wa, collected my belongings, and returned to the Shirohata Newspaper Store.

The next evening I went out to sell papers. The boss's wife, with her baby on her back, took me to Sambashi, and she taught me how to carry the baskets, how to fold the papers, how to call out to the customers, and so on. There was a ban against ringing a bell, so I had to shout "Evening papers! Evening papers!" in order to attract people's attention. At first I found this terribly hard to do. My voice would choke. It took me fully ten days before I could yell out without feeling embarrassed.

As soon as I started working, I borrowed money from the boss to pay for my entrance fee and other school expenses. My boss kept urging me to enroll in a girls' high school, but I was disillusioned with girls' schools. To simply attend a girls' high school would not be worth all the work. I was determined to study English, mathematics, and classical Chinese and then to take the high school equivalency test and go on to women's medical school. I looked over the newspaper clippings that I had saved when I was in Hamamatsu and chose my schools.

There were very few girl students in either the English or the mathematics school. I deliberately chose these schools because of that. I did not want to be in a situation where I would have to compete with other women in dress and appearance. Also my experience in Hamamatsu, where home economics is stressed instead of academic subjects, had taught me that the academic level in women's schools tended to be low. Neither the teachers nor the students took learning seriously. I was convinced that I would not make any progress in a women's school. Moreover, I felt that entering a men's school and studying with men would indicate that I was more capable than the average woman. I wanted to compete academically with men and win. In part, I wanted to get even with men, and I was also unconsciously motivated by a kind of vanity.

Our working day lasted from about 4:30 in the afternoon until 12:30 at night, roughly eight hours. We had to be on our feet the entire time, so we got rather tired. Many people were on my street until about 7:00 o'clock. Their interest in the news was strong until then, so we sold quite a number of papers. Keeping so busy, we tended to forget about how tired we were. But by 9:00 or 10:00 o'clock very few people passed by. Then the work became boring, and we tended to let up mentally too. By that time we were also exhausted. My legs were sore from standing for so many hours, and my whole body felt weak and limp. I would try to rest by leaning against a telephone pole. Sometimes I would doze off and barely catch myself before toppling down.

There were many street-corner meetings near where I sold my papers. Once a week, without fail, the Salvation Army arrived with their psalms and tambourines. Then there was a group of three or four dressed in traditional apparel and square hats. They carried a lantern on a bamboo pole on which were written the words Buddhist Salvation Army. They would sing Buddhist songs, like "The Color of the Banner of the Book of the Royal Way," and deliver Buddhist sermons. Occasionally a group of socialists would also appear. They didn't carry lanterns or anything else, but as soon as they arrived, they would post placards on the wall of a nearby restaurant. Then they would take turns exhorting the passersby. Their long hair would fly about as they gestured, and they would speak until they were hoarse. Sometimes the three groups would get into violent arguments, with one disputing another's claims. On these occasions, very few people bought papers, for they found it more interesting to listen to the groups castigate one another.

One night when I was feeling despondent about the lack of sales and was standing listening absentmindedly to the speakers, a young man approached me and said, "Aren't you from the Shirohata agency?"

I was taken aback but replied firmly, "Yes, that's right."

"I thought so. My name is Haraguchi. I used to work for them. Please say hello to the Shirohatas." The young man then handed me a leaflet on the Russian Revolution.

Four or five nights later the same group of socialists came and started their street-corner lecture. Then they each took a handful of pamphlets and set out to sell them to the people who gathered around to listen to them. The pamphlet was entitled "What Would It Be Like to Live in a Socialist Society?" I had no idea what socialism was all about, but I felt that I should buy a copy, so I said timidly, "Please give me a copy."

"O.K. It's forty sen," the young man said and handed me a pamphlet. Haraguchi, who had introduced himself to me the other night, seeing me buy a copy said, "Hey, this person is likely to become one of us. Give it to her at cost." The other man said, "O.K.," and charged me only twenty sen.

And I did become one of them before long. I believe the young man who sold me the pamphlet was Takao, who was later killed by Yonemura.[15] This group of young men later organized the Rōdōsha (Workers' Society) in Sugamo.

Early one evening it began raining so heavily there was hardly anyone on the streets. The papers did not move at all, and by ten o'clock I had sold only a few copies, and my basket was still half full. Though it had stopped raining by then, everyone had gone home earlier than usual and hardly anyone was around. But I had to sell the papers, so I kept calling out until I was hoarse. But no one was interested. I leaned against the wet telephone pole and kept my eye on the clock across the street. I wished I could quit and go home, but that night the time seemed to pass slower than usual. From time to time I called out, but I could not interest any customers. Occasionally, one or two people would buy a paper, not because they especially wanted one but, I felt, because they felt sorry for me.

By the minute, fewer and fewer people passed by. I was upset and felt tireder than usual. There seemed to be no point in trying to sell any more copies, so, even though it was a little earlier than usual, I headed for home. As I went into the alley from the main street and stepped on the wooden plank over the sewer, the boss heard my footsteps. He called out from the second floor, "Who is it that's come home so early?"

"It's me, it's Kaneko," I replied, looking up to the second floor. The boss was there with a guest, drinking beer.

"Kaneko? It's still early. It's not even eleven o'clock." He lowered his voice a little, but he did not let me off the hook. "No one else has come back yet. You have the choicest location. There is no reason for you to quit this early."

"I know, but the papers weren't selling at all. It rained earlier and there's hardly anyone out on the streets," I said, pleading for his understanding. But the boss refused to sympathize.

"Of course, there are nights when things don't go well, but you can't leave a choice spot like that unattended. Even if things are slow, you've got to stay there until the regular quitting time. Otherwise people will stop coming."

I felt miserable, but I returned reluctantly to my district. Now, there were even fewer people on the streets. I barely had the heart to call out "Evening papers!" I did so once or twice, but the only result was the sound of my voice echoing mournfully over the woods of Ueno. It seemed to symbolize my own pitiful state.

I leaned on the railing of the bridge, half in tears, waiting for quitting time. Two or three stars shone above the big clock. From the direction of the broad street, an empty rickshaw appeared and then stopped in front of me. The young rickshaw-man put down the handlebar and said, "Excuse me, but won't you give me two or three papers?"

"Oh, yes, what would you like?"

"It doesn't matter. Give me whichever ones are left. . . ."

I realized he was buying the papers simply because he felt sorry for me, and I looked at his face without handing him the papers. He had on a student's cap, but the insignia was covered over with a white piece of paper. He must be a student working his way through college, like me, I thought.

My own vanity about being a student lifted my spirit, so I asked him, "You must be going to school. Isn't it so? Which school is it?"

The young man simply smiled and didn't reply. I repeated my question. He finally said, "I'm in the same school as you, and in the same class."

"What? The same school and the same class?" I said in amazement.

"That's right. You may not have noticed me, but I have known who you are for quite some time. Because I often see you dozing off in class I know that you are working your way through school. I've seen you selling your papers here from time to time."

The young man's name was Itō, and he was a member of the Salvation Army, that is, he was a Christian. He had been a student at a veterinary school in Azabu, but he couldn't afford the tuition. Also, he was often sick and had to miss school, so he decided to take some time off. Now, in order to prepare to return to the veterinary school next year, he was taking an algebra course at the Math Study Institute. I was the only woman student there, so he noticed me, and what's more, he was among those who conducted street services for the Salvation Army, so he had noticed me selling evening papers. He had been keeping his eye on me for some time.

Seven days after I started vending papers I had been ensnared by a man who specialized in seducing working students. The boss had warned me to be careful, and I was wary of talking with strangers. But I was certain this young man was not dangerous. I felt lucky to have met someone like him.

Itō advised me, "This sort of work is really hard. It may be all right in the beginning, but as time goes by, your spirit will be broken too. You'd be better off finding something else. Don't ever hesitate to ask me for help. As you can see, I too am without resources, but I'll be happy to help you in any way I can." I was feeling lonely and depressed, and his words cheered me up. I felt like crying with joy, and was overwhelmed with a sense of gratitude when we said goodbye.

The longer I stayed with the Shirohatas the clearer it became that there was not much difference between Mr. Shirohata and my father. Mr. Shirohata may have behaved the way he did because of his personality, but mostly, I believe, it was because he was making too much money off the working students.

Mr. Shirohata had two wives. His former wife had been driven out when he brought the second wife into the house. I say "former wife," but they had not been divorced, and he was still supporting her. According to what I heard, he had met the current Mrs. Shirohata at a teahouse in Asakusa. She was a strong-willed woman, tough enough to drive the former Mrs. Shirohata out of the house. She was also abnormally high-strung. When she got hysterical, no one could control her.

Now Mr. Shirohata had another woman in Funabashi with whom he was intimate. Every three days or so he would douse himself with cologne and go visit her. On these occasions, no doubt to vent her frustration, Mrs. Shirohata would take as much as twenty to thirty yen of the money brought home by the paper vendors and go out and buy herself a kimono or an obi. Once, while I was working for them, they had a big fight. Mr. Shirohata got angry at her for something, and she struck back by castigating him about his relationship with the other woman. The argument must have gone to Mrs. Shirohata's head. She tied a satin obi to a second-floor veranda and climbed down. She then went out to the main street, hailed a rickshaw, and drove all around Mukōjima all night long. Then she went to a friend's home in Honjo. There, it is said, she knelt for two days and two nights, acting as if she were counting money, while mumbling something incoherent. For those days, I had to cook for the family and care for the three children.

While Mr. Shirohata was seeing these other women, his first wife was forced to live in a back-alley, tenement house in Shimoyazaka Honchō. Mr. Shirohata paid her rent, but she had to pay for all the rest of the living expenses for herself and her two children by selling newspapers from Mr. Shirohata's shop. However, her vending district was not very good, and even if she managed to sell her allotted one hundred copies, she made at most only two yen. And the incumbent Mrs. Shirohata deliberately made things difficult for her by delaying the delivery of the papers and so on. Moreover, she would treat her like a beggar to torment her.

Seeing this, I got depressed because the problems of my family were being repeated here. What was worse, these things were happening in a family that was affluent, and their money was earned penny by penny by the sweat and blood of working students. So it seemed to me all the more immoral.

[Kaneko's daily routine, while she was working as a newspaper girl, consisted of getting up at 7:00 and attending English class from 8:00 to 12:00 and math class from 1:00 to 3:30. Then off to her newspaper job from 4:00 to midnight. After she returned home she helped with household chores until 2:00 in the morning.]

When I was hired by Mr. Shirohata I told him I would bear any kind of hardship and not quit. Though I was still determined not to give up, my spirit was willing, but my body could not take it any longer. I finally decided that no matter how determined I was, I could not keep it up. Things had gotten so difficult that it made no sense to continue this way. So I decided to leave the Shirohata news agency. But I had borrowed about twelve or thirteen yen from the Shirohatas to pay for my tuition and clothing. I would have to repay them, but there was no way I could repay that kind of money.

Itō the rickshaw-man was trying to help me find a way to repay my debt and get a better job. But he had his own problems, and I could not count on him to solve mine. That would be like clinging to a dream. So I consulted Haraguchi, with whom I had become friendly after hearing him talk about socialism. I asked him if he could help me find a way to get some money. But Haraguchi was not sincere about helping me and said, "I can't think of any way to help you." So I had to resign myself to staying with the paper agency for awhile and bide my time.

I don't know how he found out—perhaps from my co-workers to whom I had talked about how difficult life was at the shop—but one day Mr. Shirohata asked me with a sour look on his face, "Kaneko, I hear you are planning to leave this place. Is it true?" I had intended to stay at the shop until I paid off my debts, but when I was asked about it point-blank I could not lie.

"Yes, I can't take the hard work any longer. So I have been thinking of leaving after I repaid the money I borrowed from you. . . ."

"Is that so? That's why I warned you in the beginning," Mr. Shirohata replied curtly. Then he said, "O.K., if you want to leave, go ahead. But we have to make other arrangements, so you can leave as of tomorrow."

Since that was his decision, I realized I could not stay at the shop any longer. But what was I to do? I did not have a single sen, and I did not have another job. I didn't know what to do. Furthermore, even though I was to leave the next day, that evening he sent me out to sell papers at the worst spot. As a result, I owed him fifty sen more.

Because I was being dismissed by the boss, I thought he was going to cancel the debt I owed him. Later, however, I found out that after I had left, he immediately went to my great-uncle's house in San-no-wa by rickshaw. There he poured out all sorts of abuse against me, and then pulled out an itemized bill and demanded that my great-uncle pay my debt. Great-uncle felt obliged to meet his demand and paid off my debt. Later when I visited my great-uncle's home, great-aunt made all sorts of nasty remarks to me and made me beg my great-uncle's forgiveness.

I left the Shirohata paper agency toward evening. I had no place to go and didn't know what to do. Then it began to rain. I stood on the sidewalk in front of the Matsuzakaya department store, despondent and dejected. I thought and thought, but I could come up with no way out of my dilemma. Then it occurred to me to go see Mr. Akibara, captain of the Salvation Army in Kuromon-chō. I had met him through Itō a few times. I decided to ask him to let me stay at his place for the night.

I didn't have an umbrella, so I pulled up the skirts of my kimono and ran along under the eaves of the houses, splashing mud about with my sandals. It was either Wednesday or Thursday. The Salvation Army building is usually closed at night, but there was a meeting of some sort being held, so it was lighted brightly and was crowded. I felt hesitant about going inside, and stood in front of the building for awhile. But I couldn't stand there forever, so I braced myself and went inside. About thirty people were seated on benches. Itō, who was sitting toward the front of the room, saw me and approached me.

"I've been driven out," I told him.

Itō took me to the corner of the room and said, "Tell me about it later. Tonight Major K from the headquarters in Kanda is coming to give a talk, so we are holding a special meeting. The sermon should begin soon. You came just at the right moment." He took me to the section of the room where women were seated and brought me a small Bible and a book of psalms. He opened the Bible to the page which the major's sermon would refer to and then returned to his seat. I was in no mood to read the Bible. I was full of anxiety and fear and felt as if I were about to fall into a dark hole.

Soon the proceedings began. Prayers were said and psalms were sung, but I was too preoccupied to pay much attention. I bowed my head mechanically with the rest of the congregation, got up when they did, and sat when they did. I hardly noticed when Major K began his sermon. Soon, however, I felt calmer. Perhaps I had gotten in tune with the atmosphere. But at about the time I had begun to take in what the major was saying, he ended his sermon.

After the sermon the congregation began to sing psalms again. It sounded as powerful as a huge wave surging and swelling, and I was overwhelmed with a feeling that I too could be swept forward and transported to some wide open space. The singing was followed by a prayer led by the major, who seemed to have been overcome with emotion and had difficulty speaking. His prayers offered on behalf of troubled souls and their salvation made me feel that I must listen to him reverently. After the invocation, the faithful's testimonies began. One young man, who looked like a store clerk, testified that he had been mired in the depths of anguish and suffering, but he was saved when he gained faith in Jesus Christ.

An old woman sitting next to me got up and said, "I am really fortunate that I was saved by Jesus Christ." Everyone began to shout "Amen! Hallelujah!" Some shouted emotionally, "Yes, yes, O dear God!"

Itō moved to the front of the room, knelt by the lectern, and began to pray. I felt as if he were praying for me, praying for my salvation. I felt that I could sit still no longer. It was as if a power that I could lean on was present in the room and was beckoning me to come forward. An unknown power was forcing me to move to the front of the room. When I came to, I found that I had marched up to the captain, and, kneeling on the floor by his foot, I was crying hysterically.

The captain shouted "Amen!" and grabbed my arm. He then pulled me up and began to ask me all sorts of questions. Still crying, I answered him timidly. The captain wrote everything down in a notebook and said, "Everyone, please pray for this sister who has been saved." He then got on his knees and in a quaking voice began to pray for me. I was overwhelmed with gratitude and was in a state of euphoria. I forgot all my worries and began to pray to God and sing of his glories with the rest of the congregation. So I had joined the Christians before I was fully aware of what I was doing.

Itō found me a room in Shimbana-chō in Yushima. He then bought from an acquaintance who owned a soap store several yen worth of powdered soap for me. And so I became a vendor of powdered soap. I opened my soap-stand in Nabe-chō in Kanda. I collected a small lamp, several sheets of newspaper, about thirty packages of powdered soap, and put them in a small pan that Itō got for me. I wrapped the pan in a striped cotton-cloth wrapper and set out on my career as a vendor. I would begin selling at about four or five in the evening, just about the time the tofu vendor went about tooting his little horn.

[Finding that she could not sell enough soap at her "shop," Kaneko began to peddle from house to house.]

Eventually I got used to peddling, and it no longer pained me to approach a house. But I still did not sell many packages. If I succeeded in selling thirty sen worth a day I was doing well. Thirty percent of thirty sen comes to only nine sen. There was no way I could stay alive on nine sen a day. I did not have enough money to go back to the dealer for more soap packages. My geta had worn down because I was constantly on my feet walking about town, but I couldn't afford to buy a new pair. So I would scavenge for some women's geta, or even men's geta, that had been thrown out by some wealthy family in the suburbs.

I had time to attend the two schools I was enrolled in, but I lacked the money to pay for the tuition, so I dropped out of the math class and attended only the English class at Seisoku. I was in the second-level class then. It was summer, so I was enrolled in the special summer session, which began at seven in the morning. I got up early in the morning, read some passages in the Bible, then knelt by the wall and prayed for a moment before I set out for school. Since I had sold my washpan, I stopped by at the public toilet in Yushima Park and used the water fountain to wash my face. When I had some money, I would breakfast at the cheap restaurant under the Shōhei Bridge.

One good fortune befell me after I started summer school. Among the few women students attending the session was Kawada. She would bring me a lunchbox filled with rice every day. Kawada, who lived in Tozuka, was the younger sister of a socialist.

Occasionally I ran into Itō at the cheap diner. He was still pulling a rickshaw at night, but his earnings were meager too. Nevertheless, he would give me twenty or thirty sen from time to time. Sometimes when we ran into each other on the way back from school we would go to dinner together. On these occasions Itō talked only about religion.

"How is your religious faith coming along these days?" were his first

words whenever he saw me. Whenever I consulted him about some serious matter he would get on his knees and pray earnestly. It didn't matter
where we were, on the roadside or in a public building.

He used to advise me to always attend Sunday morning services. In
time of stress or hardship, one must always pray, he told me. "Prayers give
one strength," he insisted. Acquiring a little bit of strength would not have
helped my situation, though. But I took his advice and went to church and
prayed. Itō and Akibara kept telling me to have faith. As long as one has
faith everything will become clear, they insisted. I had confidence in Itō, so
I went to church, prayed, and in order to serve others, got up early in the
morning and cleaned the toilet of my rooming house. I did all this at the
insistence of Itō.

I served God and served others, but I received no reward. I had not
eaten in three days. I had not been able to find some other way of earning a
living, and moreover my rent was again due and the landlord was insisting
that I pay him. But I had no way to pay him. I finally decided to become a
maid, something that Mr. Akibara had suggested earlier. I packed what
was left of my belongings and left the rooming house. Just before I left I
put my bundle down by the entrance and bowed down courteously and
bid the owners farewell, saying, "Thank you so much for taking care of
me for such a long time." The landlady was having supper with her husband in the room by the entrance. She merely glanced at me indifferently
and, without even putting her chopsticks down, said, "You're welcome.
Goodbye."

All the consideration that I had showed them, such as sleeping outdoors
when I returned, so as not to wake them up, cleaning the toilet for them
despite my busy schedule, seemed to have meant nothing to them. Were
the teachings of Christianity true or not? Was it merely an opiate to delude
the people and allay their misery? Christianity was nothing but falsehoods
if it did not enable a person's sincerity and love to rouse similar feelings in
others and help make this a better world.

With Mr. Akibara's help I found a job as a maid with the Nakagi family
in Seitenchō in Asakusa. The Nakagis owned a sugar store. There were
eleven members in the family: the older couple, their son and his wife,
their two children, two younger sons of the older couple, a maid, a store
clerk, and me. The old household head had turned over the store to his son
and did not bother at all with the family business. He was away from home

most of the time and only came home every five days or so. I later learned that he spent all his time at a "teahouse" near Asakusa Park. He spent his time with his friends, gambling and drinking day and night. He also kept a mistress in a house near the park and spent much of his time there. [Kaneko found working for the Nakagi family trying because of the conflicts among the family members and their willful behavior.]

I became a maid out of necessity, but I deeply regretted having to quit school. Moreover, the life-style of the Nakagis depressed me. I wrote Kawada a letter soon after I started working as a maid and told her about my frustrations. Kawada came to see me as soon as she received my letter. I was overjoyed when she came, and I asked the Nakagis for some free time to walk about the city with her.

Listening to the things that I could not explain fully in my letter, Kawada sympathized with my plight and said, "My older brother is planning to come to Tokyo soon and start a print shop. Why don't you come and work for him? Then you'll be able to go to school. . . ."

Naturally I would have loved to do so. But that would have meant joining the socialists' circle. Itō would feel hurt about this, and I went on to explain my friendship with him.

"It would mean turning against Itō. I couldn't bear to do that to him. . . ."

"You're right," Kawada said. But after reflecting for a moment, she said cheerfully, "But it'll be all right. The moral obligation you have to him cannot be repaid, but the material obligation can. I will help you repay the material debt."

In truth, I had been wanting to break away from Christianity. Kawada's suggestion was too good to ignore. I felt a bit guilty, but I agreed to leave everything up to Kawada. Two days later she sent me a money order good for twenty-five yen. I went to the old mistress and told her that though I was grateful to them, I now wished to take leave of my job. She had just had surgery to remove a boil from her hand, and as she stared at her bandaged hand she told me that this would cause them some inconvenience. She said pleadingly, "Well, Fumi, if you leave us right now we'll be in a terrible bind. As you know, the young mistress is not in good health. On top of that she is pregnant. The other maid, Kiyo, is incompetent and unreliable. And my hand is in this kind of shape. . . ."

I was able to understand her predicament, but I was now obligated to Kawada too. So I told her, "I understand the situation, but I don't think I'll have another chance to get a job as good as the one that is being offered me, so. . . ."

The old mistress seemed determined not to let me go. She persisted, "Please stay until my hand gets well. Please do me this favor."

Finally, I could not refuse her pleas and agreed to stay with the family for the remainder of the year. I was unhappy not to be able to accept Kawada's offer and felt that I should at least return the money she had sent me, but she refused to take it back.

Itō came at least every three days or so to talk about religion with his fellow Christians, Yamamoto, a clerk in the Nakagi store, and members of the Nakagi family. He was worried about the approaching examinations, fearing that he would not have enough time to study for them because of his work. So I decided to give Itō the money that I had gotten from Kawada without making a point that it was repayment for his many favors. I wanted him to have it so that he could pursue his studies in a less harried fashion. I waited for him to visit me so that I could give him the money, but he did not show up as usual. I felt that I couldn't wait much longer, so I sent him the money by postal money order. I inserted a note stating, "I will explain how I got this money later, but since I acquired it, I am sending it to you. This should be enough to sustain you for a month, so why don't you take some time off and study hard for your examination?" I wrote my name on the envelope in masculine style, Kaneko.

A couple of days later Itō came to visit me, and, as usual, I saw him off to the trolley when he left. When we were alone Itō said, "Thank you for the money. That really was a surprise. However, when you have something to say to me, tell me when I come to visit you. In the future please don't write me. If people were to find out that I had received a letter from a woman, my reputation would suffer and they would not have faith in me. . . ."

"I understand. But I couldn't wait any longer, so I wrote to you. I made sure that my name would look like a man's."

"Oh, yes. I appreciate your kind thoughts, but please don't send me any more letters. . . ."

"I am sorry," I said, feeling disappointed. But I didn't feel annoyed at Itō at all. On the contrary, I felt that I could trust him all the more and was ready to see him whenever he came to visit me. When I saw him off I kept going farther and farther, chatting with him. I would say, "I'll see you off to the lamppost, to the telephone pole." But the members of our household trusted Itō and me, so they did not regard our relationship with suspicion at all.

During this period I did not go to school. I was not busy, so I had a fairly easy time. Now I could help Itō for a change. When I saved one or two yen from tips and gifts, I gave it to him. When I didn't have any money to give to him, I tried to come up with other presents.

One evening when I was seeing Itō off, I was carrying a fairly heavy bundle. Itō saw it and asked in a puzzled voice, "What in the world is that?"

"This? Since it is getting cold, I made a cushion for you to sit on. And a pillow too. You don't have any cushion, do you? And your pillow must be worn out and soiled."

Itō was astonished. "How did you know that? That my pillow is dirty?"

"Remember the other day our head clerk went to your place and took a nap? When Yamamoto returned he said that your pillow was dirtier than the straws in a pig pen. He also told me that you don't have a cushion." Itō expressed his gratitude over and over, and I felt truly happy and pleased.

November 30. I shall never forget that date. That night Itō, who had not come to visit me for some time, suddenly came to the house. Unlike himself, he was downcast and looked pale. I was concerned, so I rushed through my work and got the mistress's permission to see him off. We walked for a while, but Itō didn't say anything. He merely nodded as I spoke. When we came to a dark, quiet spot, he abruptly stopped walking and began to speak in a deliberate fashion.

"Kaneko, I must make a confession. I was wrong about you. Frankly, I've been under the impression that you were a loose woman. Only recently have I realized the truth. You are really an altruistic person. I have known our group commander for quite some time, and I have known numerous Christian women in our group, but I have never known anyone as kind, thoughtful, and gentle in a really feminine way as you."

I was taken aback by what he said and stared at him. He looked sincere and earnest, and I did not believe he could be lying. "A loose woman"— when he said this I felt as if I had been pricked by a needle. But I felt extremely shy and pleased when he said "the kindest woman I have ever known." I was simultaneously elated and melancholy. I merely listened to him without saying a word. We had resumed walking, had walked past Kaminarimon and had come to Kikuya Bridge. The station clock indicated that it was past eleven o'clock, and the stores were getting ready to close for the night.

I stopped walking and said, "It's past eleven. We must say good night."

"That's right. It's rather late," Itō said calmly. Usually he told me to hurry back before it got too late, but this night he didn't seem to want to say goodbye. "There's something else I want to talk to you about, though. Shall we walk on toward Ueno? We can take the trolley back."

"All right. Let's walk for a little while longer," I said without hesitation. My emotions swept aside any hesitation.

We walked in silence, each of us deep in thought. When we got to Lake Shinobazu in Ueno we stopped walking. It was a quiet night and no one seemed to be around. Itō knelt down by the willow tree on the lake and began to scratch out some words with a twig that he had picked up. He then said, "As I mentioned earlier, I had to restrain myself time and time again ever since you came to live in Yushima. But recently it's gotten so that I can't control myself. It's gotten so that I am no longer content to look upon you simply as a neighbor. . . . You understand me, don't you? . . . Even when I am reading at home, my thoughts flee to you. When I don't see you for one day I feel unbearably miserable. So, I can't study and my faith is getting shaky. I've been experiencing so much agony that I wish I were dead. . . ." His words were certainly what I had been wanting to hear. I tried to calm my pounding heart and listened in silence to what he was saying.

"I thought and thought about this and I finally decided that I must go back to being my former self and part with you. . . . I have made up my mind about this. I am convinced that this is the best way for both of us. . . . We must not act impulsively when there is no assurance that we will be able to spend the rest of our lives together. To do so would be a serious sin. Don't you agree with me? It would be wrong, wouldn't it?"

Itō continued in a more forceful manner as if he were trying to shore up his courage. "I have decided to say goodbye to you tonight. From now on I shall not see you or think about you. Today is the last day of November. I came to see you today to make this a memorable day for our farewell. You understand how I feel, don't you? . . . I shall never go to your home any longer. I shall subdue my own feelings. . . . Well, this is goodbye, then. I shall pray for your well-being." Saying this, he got up.

Inwardly, I was disappointed, and I thought, "What a cowardly messenger of love." I wanted to say something, but since he was getting ready to leave, I could only say, "Is that so? Well, goodbye, then."

Itō walked away without looking back as if he were escaping from someone trying to cling to him. I felt lonely and sad, and yet the scene struck me as deliciously touching. With mixed emotions I watched him disappear from sight.

After I left the sugar shop I became a hanger-on at a couple of places where a number of "socialists" lived. Then I ended up once more with my great-uncle in San-no-wa. My great-uncle admonished me, "Didn't I tell you? There's no way you can go to school selling newspapers or selling things on the streets at night. Maybe a man can do that, but not a woman. You'd be better off if you forgot about studying." But he seemed to have given up trying to fight me and did not try to force me to give up my schooling. So I was able to go to school while helping with household chores at his home.

I would get up at five in the morning, cook rice, make miso soup, and try to study. After I prepared breakfast for the family I ate breakfast by myself and went off to school while the family members were still asleep. I returned from school a little past noon. Then I did the washing, cleaned the house, prepared supper, and so on. I was almost as busy as I was at the sugar shop. But this was after all my relatives' home, so my schedule was more flexible. They agreed to give me five yen a month for spending money. I had to pay two yen for tuition and spend 2 yen 30 sen on trolley fare. That left only seventy sen, but it was enough to buy pen and ink. But I was eager to read, so I felt bad about not having any money to buy books.

At school I got to know two socialists. One was a Korean name Seo. He was taciturn with a rather leaden look. Whenever he had time in class he quietly read *Kaizō* magazine.[16] Seo was not sent by a wealthy family to study in Japan. Like me, he was trying to study while struggling to earn his living. It must have become impossible for him to continue his studies, for he soon stopped coming to class.

The other socialist student was named Ono. I heard that he used to work for the Tokyo Municipal Tramway System but was fired for taking part in a strike a year earlier. He sat right in front of me and read from his book in a squeaky voice. At that time he was a member of the Shinyūkai (Fraternal Society) or some such organization, but he did not seem to have a strong personality. He belonged to a circle of lukewarm socialists. But he used to bring his union paper as well as pamphlets and leaflets with him, so I managed to borrow or receive outright reading materials put out by his group. This helped me to gradually grasp the concepts and spirit of socialism.

Socialism did not really supply me with fresh ideas. Its theories simply underscored and validated the beliefs that I had developed from my own experiences. I was poor then and I am still poor. And because I was poor I was used ruthlessly by the rich. I have been abused, castigated, oppressed, denied my freedom, exploited, and dominated. Deep in my heart, I'd been harboring hostile sentiments toward the people who held power over me. At the same time, I felt strong sympathy for those who were in the same situation I was in. I wanted to fight for the members of the pitiful class to which I belonged, even if it meant sacrificing my life.

Even with these strong beliefs, I did not know how to put my sentiments into practice. I was helpless. I had no training and no connections. I was simply a rebel full of discontent, dissatisfaction, and defiance. [That summer she returned to Hamamatsu to visit her father.]

It was the end of August when I got back to Tokyo. Four or five days later I was out on some errands and got caught in a rainstorm at the tram station in Kasuga-chō. I decided to visit Segawa, who lived nearby. As usual, I just walked up the stairs without calling out and opened Segawa's sliding door. He was leaning over a desk, evidently writing a letter. When he saw me, he smiled and said, "Oh, it's you. You took me by surprise."

"I got caught in the rain and got soaking wet. See, I'm dripping from head to toe," I said, showing him my wet clothes. I then glanced at his desk and asked, "What are you doing?"

Segawa became flustered and quickly put the letter away in his desk drawer. Then he leaned on his desk and said, "Why don't you sit down?" I was not a well-bred young lady so I pulled up my kimono and sat down, crossing my legs.

"When did you get back?" he asked.

"Four or five days ago," I replied.

"You were away a long time, then. Where were you wandering around for fifty to sixty days? I couldn't write to you, because I didn't know where you were. You should have written me at least one letter."

"Well, I didn't have anything special to write about."

"Nothing to write about? Do you mean that you don't write a letter unless you have some special reason to write? So when you're away from me you forget about me, just like that?"

"I wonder. Maybe so . . . just like you. . . . I'm hungry. Why don't you order something for me?"

It was past suppertime at the boarding house, so Segawa had some buckwheat noodles delivered from a noodle shop for me. By the time the lights came on the rain had stopped, but I decided not to go home and settled down. We chatted about many things. Then a couple of men came in the room, saying "Excuse us," when they saw me.

Both of them were about twenty-three or twenty-four years of age. One was light-complexioned and tall. The other was of medium height and had a thin face. His hair was combed back and he wore black horn-rimmed glasses. Segawa introduced me to them. The long-haired one was Hyeon, a Korean socialist whom Segawa had mentioned before. He usually used his Japanese name, Matsumoto. The other person was Hyeon's friend Cho.

Segawa had told me earlier, "There is a Korean socialist called Hyeon in this boarding house. He is being tailed by a couple of policemen. He's big time." I looked at Hyeon carefully. He didn't seem all that special, and he didn't say anything that would lead one to believe he was a socialist. Since I was visiting Segawa, they must have felt that they were intruding and left after saying a few words.

That night I slept with Segawa, as I often did. The next morning the man of the boarding house brought in a breakfast tray for one. Segawa didn't bother to order anything for me. He started to eat by himself and said, "Fumi-chan. Do you want to eat? If you do, I'll leave some of this for you."

I was let down, but simply said, "That's all right. I'll go home and eat." I leaned on his desk and read a magazine while he ate. After Segawa finished eating he went to his window and looked outside.

"Fumi-chan, come and see. It's a beautiful day."

"Is that right?" I replied, without much enthusiasm.

Then I spoke to him about a matter that had been bothering me for some time.

"Hiroshi, what would we do if I got pregnant? . . . Carrying on like this." I'd been thinking about this question seriously. I was afraid of the consequences, but I also imagined myself as a mother holding in my arms the yet unborn baby.

Segawa seemed completely unconcerned. He glanced at me, then yawned and stretched out his arms. He answered wearily, "What if you got pregnant? Don't ask me about it."

I suddenly felt as if I had been pushed into an abyss. Despite what he said, I expected Segawa to think seriously about the question and say something further. But he said nothing more. He merely took down the violin that was on the wall, sat down by the ledge of the window, and began to play it as if he didn't have a care in the world. I had always known that we were not bound by true love. So I had no intention of blaming only Segawa for our relationship, but if I did get pregnant I expected him to take some responsibility. His attitude revealed that he was totally irresponsible. I realized for the first time that I was being toyed with and taken advantage of.

I was dizzy with anger and anguish. I got up abruptly and left the room. Segawa said something to try to stop me, but I went downstairs to the washroom without answering him. In the room next to the washroom I saw Hyeon. He had on a broad-striped summer gown (*yukata*) and was reading a book by the table near the window. I wanted to go into his room and talk to him. But because I had just met him briefly I hesitated. Instead, I went into the washroom. While I was drying my face I looked toward Hyeon's room again. He had put down his book and was looking at me.

"Good morning. I was pleased to meet you last night," I said.

"Well, the pleasure was mine. . . . Even though it rained last night, it's nice today, isn't it?"

I went to the entrance to his room and said, "Your room is nice. You can see the garden. . . ." I could see the plants in the garden beyond his room.

"Please come in. I'm not doing anything right now. . . ."

Hyeon placed another chair by his table. Without hesitation I went into his room, sat on the chair, and looked around. Photographs and portraits of famous revolutionaries were hanging on the wall. What looked like propaganda leaflets were also plastered all over the wall. I got up and took a good look at them. I pointed to one photograph and asked Hyeon, "Oh, isn't this a photograph of the people in G Society?"[17]

"That's right. Do you know these people?" Hyeon took the photograph off the wall and put it on the table.

"Yes, I know three or four of them," I said and leaned over the photograph and pointed out several figures. "This is T, this is S, and this is you. Isn't it so?"

Hyeon leaned over the photograph too. Our faces almost touched. "That's right, that's right. . . . Well, I was right. When we met last night, I thought you were one of us, but I thought it would be awkward to ask you, so I didn't say anything."

Concluding that I was one of his comrades, he became much friendlier. I too felt close to him because he was a Korean. It was as if I had been reunited with a close friend after a long separation, and we talked candidly. I told him that I had lived in Korea for seven years. Hyeon talked about his family there.

Hyeon was born the only son of a family in Seoul. His family was fairly prominent and wealthy. He was currently a student at Tōyō University, studying philosophy. But he was not attending classes regularly. Much of his time was spent wandering about with his friends.

"So, you are spending most of your time working for the movement?"

"No, they call me a petit bourgeois and an intellectual and do not allow me to become a bona fide member of the movement," and he laughed sadly.

I too was not a member of any group at that time and was not involved in any political activity, so I could sympathize with his plight. I was happy to become friends with someone who shared my feelings and was in a similar situation so far as political action was concerned.

Then I heard the sounds of slippers in the corridor, and Segawa appeared at the entrance to Hyeon's room. "Fumi-chan, you can't go barging into other people's room like this. Come on back," he said.

At this, the anger that was smoldering inside me exploded, and I shouted back, "It's none of your business. I can go wherever I want to. What's wrong with that? I can do as I please. Don't butt in!"

"But you're disturbing Hyeon. . . . So early in the morning."

"Shut up!" I screamed, getting angrier. "Hyeon isn't objecting to my visit. What right do you have to complain? Don't interfere in other people's business. Just take your lunch and be on your way. That's about all you're good for."

"You just remember this," Segawa shot back and left in a huff. He probably didn't feel much pain or shame as he went off to work. After my outburst he stopped coming to see me.

While I was railing against Segawa the maid stood in the hall listening with astonishment. Even this did not upset me. By then I had decided that what other people thought didn't matter. I had to do my own thing. I spent another hour talking with Hyeon. Exhilarated for having told Segawa off, I jabbered away excitedly.

When I left Hyeon's room it was after nine. A couple of blocks away from the boarding house, someone called my name. It was Hyeon. He had changed his clothing and was wearing a suit and a Bohemian necktie. When he caught up with me he asked, "Have you had breakfast? . . . I haven't eaten yet. The meals at the boarding house are not very good, so I'm on the way to have breakfast out. Why don't you join me. It won't take too long. . . ."

"Well, thank you. I haven't had breakfast yet either."

"Fine, let's go then."

We walked away from the main street where the trolleys ran and walked up the slope. When we got to the post office, Hyeon asked me to wait a moment and went to the money order window, probably to get some money. He came away stuffing something in his vest pocket.

Near the Tenjin Shrine we went upstairs to a neat little Western-style restaurant. Since it was still early in the morning, no other customers were in the restaurant. Hyeon and I were now like old friends.

The next day when I got back from school a letter from Hyeon was awaiting me. The words Special Delivery were stamped on the small white envelope. Inside, there was a neatly written note on fancy stationery—"Please come to the Kangetsukyō," a bridge in Ueno. So I went. It was late summer but it was still hot. Many people were on the bridge to cool off. I carefully looked over the crowd. I couldn't see Hyeon. I was sure he would not trick me about meeting him there. I walked past the bridge. There I found Hyeon standing at the far end of the bridge.

"Oh, Fumiko, thank you for coming," he said and grabbed my hand. We walked about in the park. "I've fallen in love with you," Hyeon told me.

"I like you too," I said. We then went to a small teahouse. And once again I talked to Hyeon about my aspirations and my current situation.

"Well, I'll find a place where we can live together," he promised me.

After that I felt increasingly drawn to Hyeon. Whenever I didn't see him for a few days I was unbearably lonely. Then I would go looking for him. Often I failed to find him and came home completely exhausted.

Family members began to keep their eyes on me. So it became more difficult for me to step out.

Whenever I saw Hyeon I asked him, "Haven't you found a place for us yet?"

"I've been looking every day," he would say and pull out rental ads from his pocket and show me. I was preoccupied with finding a place to live with Hyeon and leaving great-uncle's place as soon as possible.

One evening after nine o'clock when I was sewing some winter clothing in the sitting room I got a phone call from Hyeon. He said, "Fumi-chan, do you know that Kunō is seriously ill? No? Well, I didn't either. I just heard that she is in critical condition. I'm planning to go and see her right away. Would you like to come along too?"

Kunō was a socialist about thirty-five or -six years old.[18] I had heard that she was married to an intellectual and had two children, but that she had abandoned her husband so that she could devote all her time to the cause. I had met her a number of times. She lived in poverty with some young socialist and was working tirelessly to carry on the struggle. I did not know that she was ill. I had to go and see her.

I told Hyeon, "I'll go too. I'll be right over, so please wait for me."

"I'll be waiting. Hurry."

I took leave of the family and rushed out. When I was getting ready to leave I heard Hanae (the young wife of the family) say, "All lies. She wants to go and see that young man, so she had him call her."

Of course, I was happy about the chance to see Hyeon but this time all I could think about was Kunō. I didn't care what Hanae said.

Thirty minutes later I arrived at Hyeon's friend's boarding house, where he was waiting for me. When I went into his friend's room, three or four men were lying or sitting on the floor with their legs sprawled out. They were idly chatting away.

"Good evening. I'm sorry to have kept you waiting, Matsumoto. Let's get going." I stood by the threshold of the sliding door nervously and tried to get Hyeon to hurry. He made no effort to get up but simply grinned. One of his friends got up and came to me and said, "That was a lie. Come in." He took my hand and showed me in.

"How can you? A lie?" I said angrily. But I was also pleased. "What's up? Calling me out like this. What do you want?"

"Well, Fumi-chan. A little while ago a blind flute player came by.

While we were listening to him play we all began to feel melancholy and sad. I cried when he finished playing. So come in. We're all really distressed. . . ." Hyeon did sound forlorn and sentimental.

"What are we going to do with you spoiled rich boys?" I said and went in the room. They all welcomed me.

"It really is a melancholy night. But now that you're here I feel much better," Hyeon's friend said. He ordered many Western and Chinese dishes and set a feast before us. The men drank beer and ate some fruit. They then chatted away, sang some songs, and laughed uproariously.

I knew that I had to leave before it got too late and was nervous about being present at the party. But I couldn't bring myself to leave and go home. Ten o'clock came and went, and then eleven o'clock. The men gave no indication of leaving. They began to play cards. Since I was fond of cards, I was easily persuaded to join them. Soon the sound of the trolley could no longer be heard. I ended up staying overnight with Hyeon in a room that his friend had rented for us.

When I got up the next morning I began to worry about what to say when I got home. I recalled what Hanae said when I was getting ready to leave the house. Even though I had not lied, the fact was, I did not go to visit Kunō. Great-uncle's family members would surely be mad and look down on me. Thinking about this left me feeling nervous and worried.

Hyeon and I went back to his friend's room. The others ate the Western-style breakfast they had ordered and then went back to playing cards. I did not feel like eating breakfast or joining them in the card game. I sat by the window, sunk in despair. From time to time the others called out, "Come over here, Fumi-chan. Aren't you feeling well?" When I didn't answer them, they turned back to their card game. I could not bear it any longer and told Hyeon, "Matsumoto, can you leave the game for a moment? I'm going home, but I want to talk to you for a minute."

Hyeon left the game reluctantly. We went back to the room where we had slept. As soon as we sat down I said to Hyeon, "You know, Hyeon, we've been going out together and sleeping together like this often. It's getting very hard for me to stay at my great-uncle's, so what about our plan? What are we going to do? You've got to decide on something soon."

Hyeon had been saying from the beginning of our friendship that we should rent a quiet place in the suburbs and live together. But lately he had not shown any signs that he intended to follow through with the plan. I had begun to wonder if he was really sincere. But the more I worried about this, the more I felt drawn to him. I had stayed out a number of nights with him, and now it had gotten difficult for me even to go home.

"Oh, that plan," Hyeon replied, clearly upset. "Well, I'm still looking for a place, and I do have some places in mind. In fact, there's a house in Ueno which a friend has rented. But he's gone back to Korea for the time being and I can't close the deal. But I think we can get it settled soon. I'll take care of it." As usual, he was ambiguous and evasive. It was clear that he was ducking the issue.

I decided that it was pointless to press him about the matter further. I just had to wait and believe that he meant what he said even though he was being equivocal. But I still had the problem of making some sort of excuse to Hanae about the night before.

"This is another matter, but remember I came out last night saying that I was going to visit Kunō. I just can't go home without some sort of excuse. I need some sort of evidence that I visited Kunō. This past spring I pawned a kimono to help Kunō out. To prove that I have been at Kunō's I'd like to take the kimono out of the shop and bring it home with me. . . ."

It was as if I were asking Hyeon for money. But for two people in love it was not an extraordinary request. If, however, Hyeon was toying with me and taking advantage of me, he could justify his actions by saying that I was asking him to give me some money in return for sex. That I was, in effect, selling my body. I did not want to ask him for money. But I felt that it was absolutely essential that I go home with the kimono so that I could justify my absence. Without thinking carefully about whether it was a wise idea to ask him or not, I just blurted the request out.

"Oh, is that so? I understand, I understand. That's the thing to do," Hyeon said cheerfully and complied readily with my request. He began to look in his pocket but he said, "Wait here for a moment," and left the room. Just then two maids passed by our room with brooms in hand. They peered into the room, whose door was left slightly ajar by Hyeon. As they passed by I heard them whisper, "Sumi-chan, what kind of woman do you think she is?"

"She must be a whore who makes the rounds of the boarding houses."

Then Hyeon came back and handed me a five-yen bill. I fought back my tears and took the money.

When I left the boarding house the men were still playing cards raucously. It was already past ten. It was raining slightly, but I could not buy an umbrella or geta with the money Hyeon gave me, because I had to go to the pawnshop to get the kimono. I sloshed through the rain to Kunō's home in Sugamo.

"Excuse me," I called out at the entrance of the Kunō house.

"Yes?" someone answered and came out. It wasn't Kunō.

"Ah, is Kunō in?"

"Kunō? I don't know anyone by that name."

I was baffled by this and headed to the Rōdōsha (Workers' Society), which was nearby, to ask if anyone knew what had happened to Kunō. I didn't know anyone at the society, but they knew the whereabouts of Kunō. One of those present said, "Kunō? She left for the Osaka area with Mikimoto."[19]

"Is that so? I'm in trouble," I said.

"Did you have some business with her? May I ask who you are?"

The person who spoke to me asked me to stay and visit for awhile, but I left without telling him my name.

I knew the pawnshop that Kunō patronized, so I went there. When I told the proprietor that I had come for the kimono, he said, "Oh, yes, I definitely remember that kimono. I am sorry. The time was up last month, so I sold it. I got in touch with her many times but she refused to pay the interest. Not even once." My last strand of hope had snapped. I couldn't even cry. Not that I wanted to get the kimono back for myself, but at the moment I needed it badly. And Kunō's behavior made me wonder about the kind of person she was. I used to believe that those who adhered to certain isms were a special kind of people, that they were outstanding. Now I felt that I had been a fool to indulge in such a fantasy. I felt disillusioned, as if I had just awakened from a beautiful dream to find myself dumped in a sewer.

My uncle from the Buddhist temple came to visit great-uncle in Sanno-wa. He was ill and looked to be completely debilitated. In the past, he had humiliated and insulted me, and I could not forgive him for that, but seeing him in this condition, I could no longer harbor any anger toward him. I took him from hospital to hospital. But wherever we went they were unable to assure us that he would recover. He returned home without any hope that he would get better. I saw him off at the Iida-machi Station.

"Goodbye, take care of yourself," I said when he left.

He responded, "Thank you. Study hard."

He did not know that he did not have much longer to live. But I knew. When I thought that this was the last time I would be seeing him I was distressed. The train left at a little past six. The city streets were brightly lit. I wanted to shake this sense of forlornness. I stood there watching several trains go by and began wishing desperately to see Hyeon, even though I could no longer regard him as my lover. I went to the nearest booth and called several places until I finally tracked him down.

Hyeon said, "I'm glad you called. I've been wanting to talk to you about something too." He told me to come to Cho's place in Hongō. Hyeon had gotten there a few minutes ahead of me when I arrived.

"What do you want to talk to me about?" I asked.

"Well, what I have in mind is . . ." Hyeon began to talk in his usual roundabout fashion. In effect, what he told me was that he and Cho were going to Germany to study.

I had already given up on him, so I said, "Is that so? Well, that's wonderful."

"Let's have a farewell party. Let's have some fun," Cho said and ordered some Western dishes and sake.

I didn't feel sad or bitter, but I began to despair, and drank whiskey recklessly. I drank until I couldn't stand up.

I also could no longer stand staying at great-uncle's place. I left his house, with a broken heart.

I left great-uncle's home and ended up in a little restaurant in Hibiya. The place was known as Socialist Oden's. The owner was a supporter of socialists, and he acted as if he were a socialist himself. His restaurant became a gathering place for newspaper reporters, socialists, office workers, literary figures—that is, a place where intellectuals congregated.

I served the customers during the day and went to school at night. The owner promised to pay for my tuition and trolley fare. Until then I had been attending school only during the day. After I started night school, I found a woman friend. Her name was Niiyama Hatsuyo.

Hatsuyo was the only woman that I got to know well in my entire life. I not only learned a great deal from her, but I learned for the first time what it means to have a warm, strong friendship. Later, when I was arrested, I was told that the police asked Hatsuyo who her closest female friend was. She answered without hesitation that it was me. For me, too, Hatsuyo was my greatest friend. But Hatsuyo is no longer in this world. Having reached this point in the story of my life, I want to reach out to Hatsuyo. But she can no longer grasp my hands.

Hatsuyo was about two years older than I, about twenty-one when we met. She was a brilliant person, but she also had masculine qualities, in the best sense of the term. She had a strong will and was not one to be dominated by others.

Her family was not rich, but she did not come from a lumpen proletariat family like mine. Still, she did not live a life of ease and comfort. Her father was a drunk and paid no attention to his children. He died when Hatsuyo was in the second year of high school. Soon after that Hatsuyo developed tuberculosis and had to return to her home village in Niigata prefecture. She had to rest there for over half a year. It was then that she began to think about life and death and turned to the study of Buddhism. Her affliction, however, was not serious. She returned to Tokyo and graduated with special honors from one of the prefectural schools.

Those who knew how brilliant Hatsuyo was urged her to go on to college. But she felt she could not continue her education when her mother was working to support the family. To earn her own living, Hatsuyo enrolled in a typing school and became a typist. She got a job with a firm run by an Englishman and began studying English at night.

I can't remember exactly how we became friends. In night school, we women students—there might have been four or five of us then—were required to sit together in the front of the classroom. At first we hardly spoke to each other and merely nodded as a way of saying hello. One day I heard Hatsuyo arguing with a male student about death. I interjected something. This was, I believe, the beginning of our friendship.

From the beginning, I was drawn to Hatsuyo. Whatever she did and said interested me. I was hoping to become her close friend, so whenever I saw her at school I used to hug her.

As I think about it now, I don't think I was influenced directly by Hatsuyo's thoughts. But I learned a great deal more from the books she owned. For a long time I'd been wanting to read more books, but I lacked the money to buy them. After I became Hatsuyo's friend I borrowed many of her books and read them. Thanks to her I was able to read *Worker Sergiev*, a book that impressed me most profoundly. She also loaned me *Night before Death*. She was the one who exposed me to the thoughts of, or at least made me aware of the names of, thinkers like Bergson, Spencer, and

Hegel. I was influenced most deeply by the nihilistic thought that was in the books owned by Hatsuyo. I learned about Steiner, Artsybashev, and Nietzsche through her.

One cloudy evening when it looked as if it might start raining right away, I left the restaurant at four and, since it was a couple of hours before class, dropped by at the nearby boarding house of Hyeon's friend.

"Welcome," Cheong said as he greeted me. "I've been wanting to give you something good." He handed me a letter from Hyeon which he had mailed to me on his way to Korea. It said that he had received a telegram saying his mother was critically ill and that he had rushed off for home. He apologized for not having had time to say goodbye. All this was a fabrication, for he had made plans to return to Korea sometime before.

"Well," I said and threw the letter down, but I was not especially upset. Cheong didn't say anything either.

Almost as if he were waiting for me to finish the letter, he quickly brought out several printed sheets. They were the proofs of an eight-page octavo of a monthly magazine that he was planning to publish. He had spoken about his plan earlier. "Oh, is it ready?" I asked, sharing Cheong's joy. I took them and looked at them. The content was familiar because it was a collection of Cheong's writings, and I had already seen the manuscript. One thing caught my eye, however. It was a short poem inserted in the corner of one of the final page-proofs. I read the poem and was impressed by its forcefulness. Each stanza made a powerful impression. After I finished reading it, I felt my blood coursing through my body as a powerful emotion boosted my spirit.

I looked at the author's name. It was Pak Yeol, a Korean, one that I had not heard before. I thought perhaps it was a pseudonym of someone I knew, then realized that none of my Korean acquaintances was capable of writing such a powerful poem.

"Who is this Pak Yeol?" I asked Cheong.

"Him? He's my friend. He's a poor fellow who is not very well known yet."

"Is that so? But he seems to possess something very forceful. I've never read a poem like this before." Cheong didn't seem to take the author seriously. I almost felt contempt for Cheong, who seemed incapable of appreciating the poet's talents. Cheong was less than pleased with my comments. "Is that so? Which part of the poem is so good?"

"Which part? The whole poem is good. Good is not the right word. It's very powerful. Reading this, I feel as if I've at last found what I've been searching for."

"You're really impressed by it, aren't you? Would you like to meet the poet one of these days?"

"Oh, yes!"

It had started to snow. The snowflakes were making a light sound. The clock struck six in the corridor downstairs. The students living in the house went downstairs, talking loudly.

"Hey, how about your school?" Cheong asked.

"School? It doesn't matter," I said casually.

Cheong looked at me incredulously. "How come? Aren't you working your way through school?"

"That's right. I used to be serious and hardworking, used to eat only one meal a day so that I could go to school. But no more."

"Why?"

"No particular reason. Mostly it's because I feel it's pointless to try to become a success in the kind of society we are living in today."

"Well, then. What do you plan to do after you quit school?"

"I've been thinking seriously about that. I want to do something, but I don't even know what. I only know that it's not to continue working my way through school. But there is something that I have to do. Something that I can't help doing. Right now, that's what I'm searching for."

Until now, full of ambition, my only goal had been to work my way through school and become a successful, prominent person. Gradually, though, I'd come to the realization that there was no way I could succeed by working my way through school. Moreover, I'd come to realize that there was no one as worthless as the so-called successful, "great" person. What value was there in others' opinions? I was not living to please or impress other people. I had to satisfy my own true needs and be true to myself. In the past I had served as a slave to others all too often. I had been a plaything for too many men. I had not been the master of my own life. I had to find work that was meaningful. That's right. My own work. But what was "my own work"? That's what I had to discover and pursue.

I began to develop these ideas after I became friends with Hatsuyo and was influenced by the books I borrowed from her. Also, without question, I was influenced directly by her character and her behavior. Cheong agreed with me earnestly, and we talked about all sorts of problems with an intensity we had not shared until then.

At about this time I began to understand what society was all about. I had gradually learned to perceive the social patterns present under the veil that covered them. I came to understand why a poor person like myself could not study in school or become "great." I also began to understand just how the rich got richer and the powerful could get away with anything. I began to realize that socialism had its validity. But, at the same time, I could not accept socialist thought in toto. Socialism claims that it wants to transform the society for the benefit of the oppressed, but I was not convinced that socialist measures would really bring about the happiness and the well-being of the masses.

Undoubtedly, advocates of socialism will trigger social upheavals for the "sake of the masses," and the masses will probably rise up in rebellion with those who act on their behalf, even put their lives on the line with them. But suppose that a social revolution did take place, what would the masses have really won? Leaders would gain power and create a new order—and the masses would again be enslaved by the powerful. So what does xx (deleted) [revolution] mean? It simply means replacing one authority with another.

For the most part, Hatsuyo held the leaders of socialist movements in contempt; at the very least, she regarded them with cool detachment. She once remarked, "I cannot embrace any idea whatsoever when it comes to human society. Rather, I believe that the most practical and most meaningful way of life consists in joining together with friends and living together in harmony." One of our friends said that such beliefs were a form of escapism. But I do not agree. I, like Hatsuyo, believe that it is impossible to change today's society into one where everyone is happy. Like her, I can not embrace any one idealistic vision. But I do disagree with her on one point. Even if we cannot embrace any social ideals, every one of us can find some task that is truly meaningful to us. It doesn't matter whether our activities produce meaningful results or not, for the real significance of our existence consists in simply devoting ourselves to something that we believe is truly meaningful. This would enable us to bring our lives immediately into harmony with our existence. It would not be like working for some distant goal.

One cold, cold night I skipped my conversation class and visited

Cheong's boarding house. As usual I opened Cheong's sliding door without announcing myself and entered, saying "Good evening."

Cheong and a stranger were sitting by the brazier, talking quietly. The stranger was on the slim side and not very tall. He was about twenty-three or twenty-four. His rich hair reached his shoulders, and he wore a blue-cotton worker's uniform and a brown overcoat. The buttons on his overcoat were dangling, about to fall off. His sleeves were in shreds, and the knees of his trousers were worn and full of holes.

"Come in," Cheong greeted me.

The stranger glanced at me and then looked down at the charcoal in the brazier without speaking.

"It's really cold, isn't it?" I said as I entered and sat by the brazier.

"You didn't show up for a couple of days. Was anything wrong?" Cheong asked.

"No," I said as I turned and asked the guest, "Weren't you at the benefit concert for Russian famine relief at the Chinese youth center the other day?"

"Maybe," the guest said but did not say whether he was there or not. He then got up to leave.

"Oh, don't leave. Why don't you stay and visit? I'm not here for any particular reason," I said, trying to persuade him to stay.

He still remained silent and stood with his legs planted firmly on the tatami mat. He looked at me coolly through black, horn-rimmed glasses perched under his thick eyebrows, and for some reason I felt intimidated. A moment later he said, "Well, I must go," and left the room.

"Hey, where are you going to sleep tonight? You can stay here with me," Cheong got up and called after him, following him into the corridor.

"Thank you. I'll stay with my friend in Komagome tonight," the guest said, in a calm but bleak tone of voice.

I was upset and nervous about his leaving. "Cheong, what's his name?"

"Oh, him? He's the author of the poem that impressed you so much a while back."

"Oh, that was Pak Yeol?" I exclaimed and blushed.

"That's right. It's him," Cheong said quietly.

I peppered Cheong with all sorts of questions about Pak Yeol. According to him, Pak Yeol had worked as a rickshaw-man, a sandwich-board man, a mailman, a day laborer, and so on, but right now he was out of work and drifting from friend to friend and staying overnight with them.

"Then he is like a stray dog. But he exudes confidence and power. He has a majestic bearing."

"Well, as long as he has friends to feed him, . . ." Cheong said and sounded a bit scornful. But seeing that I was upset at his comment, he continued, "But he is a great man. There aren't too many people in our circle who think and act as seriously as he does."

I said to myself, "It must be so." Something was stirring within me, coming to life in my heart. I wondered what made him so powerful. I wanted to discover that and make it my own.

I left Cheong and returned to the restaurant. On the way back I thought, "This is it: the work I want to begin will be found in him. He himself is what I've been looking for." A mysterious sense of happiness danced in my heart. That night I was too excited to sleep.

The next day, early in the morning, I visited Cheong and asked him to introduce me to Pak Yeol. Cheong replied, "He drifts around here and there and it's hard to get in touch with him."

"That's all right. Just ask him to come to my restaurant. Just give him the message," I told him, and Cheong agreed.

But Pak did not show up. So four or five days later I went to see Cheong again.

"Did you tell Pak about what I asked?"

"Yes, I saw him two or three days ago and told him."

"What did he say?"

"Well, all he said was, 'Is that so?' Nothing more. He didn't seem to be too interested."

Did this mean that he was not interested in meeting with someone like me? I was disappointed and worried, but I didn't give up and kept waiting for Pak to show up. Ten days passed and then twenty, and still no Pak. "There's no hope," I thought and fell into despair. I felt that Pak's reaction confirmed that I was a worthless person. There was nothing I could do. I would have to go my own way. I thought there was nothing else but to become a typist like Hatsuyo and take a job.

Then, about a month after I had asked Cheong to give Pak my message, he showed up at the restaurant. It was the fifth or sixth of March. When I saw him my heart began to race. When he came I was entertaining two groups of customers who were drinking sake.

"Oh, so you finally decided to come," I said in a low voice as I led him to a table in the corner of the room. "Why don't you rest for awhile here. I'll be going off duty soon." I acted as if he had come to eat and brought him some tofu and daikon.

When it was time for me to go to school, I went upstairs to get ready. I asked Pak to leave first and wait for me outside. Carrying my school bag as usual, I left the restaurant. Pak was waiting in the alley. We walked together to the main street where the trolleys ran. When we reached the street Pak stopped suddenly and said, "You're going to Kanda, aren't you? I have to go to Kyōbashi, so I'll say goodbye here." He then started to walk away.

"Wait a minute," I said, running after him. "Come back tomorrow. I'll have something good prepared for you to eat."

"Thank you. I'll come." However, he left without even looking back, and I was disappointed.

The next day he showed up at about noon. I sat at his table and said in a low voice so that no one else could hear me, "Can you come and meet me in front of the school tonight? I have to talk to you about something."

"Where is your school?"

"It is Seisoku in Kanda."

"All right. I'll be there," he said.

Finally, I felt at ease and waited for evening. As he promised, Pak was waiting for me by the leafless tree in front of the school.

"Thanks for coming. Let's walk awhile." We strolled to a secluded spot, but we didn't say anything. I was looking for a quiet place where we could talk at leisure. When we came to Jimbō-chō I saw a large Chinese restaurant.

When the waiter delivered the food we made some small talk and ate. I wasn't very hungry, but Pak ate as if he were famished. I wanted to talk to him about what I had in mind, but I was tense and found it difficult to begin. Finally, overcoming my discomfort, I said, "You must have heard from Cheong that I want to get to know you. . . ."

"Yes, I heard something like that."

Pak took his eyes off the food and looked at me. Our eyes met and I began to feel nervous again. But I had to tell him what I had in mind so I continued.

"I would like to ask you bluntly. . . . Are you married or have someone? . . . Do you have something like a sweetheart? If so, I would like to be allowed to associate with you just as a comrade. . . . What do you think?"

What an inept way of making a proposal. And what a comical scene. Even now when I think about it I can't help bursting out in laughter and blushing. But right then I was all seriousness and sincerity.

"I'm single."

"Is that so . . . ? Then I would like both of us to speak frankly and openly."

"Of course."

"Now, I'm Japanese, but I don't think I have any prejudice toward Koreans. Do you harbor any antagonism toward me?"

Because I felt that I fully understood how the Koreans felt about the Japanese, I thought I had to ask this first. I was afraid that he too might feel antagonistic toward all Japanese.

But Pak said, "No, I feel hostility toward only the Japanese ruling class, not the ordinary people. I feel quite friendly toward someone like you who is free of prejudice."

"Thank you." I felt more at ease and smiled. "May I ask you one more thing? Are you a member of the Korean nationalist movement? . . . In fact, I lived in Korea for a number of years and I think I understand how those active in the nationalist movement feel. Needless to say, I am not a Korean, so I have not experienced abuses at the hands of the Japanese the way Koreans have. So I do not feel right about joining the Korean movement for independence. If, by chance, you are a member of the independence movement I will not be able to join you."

"I am in sympathy with the Korean nationalist movement, and I did try to join the movement in the past. But I am no longer part of that movement."

"Then you are completely opposed to the nationalist movement?"

"No, not at all. But I have my own way of thinking and my own work. I cannot join the front line of the nationalist movement."

All the obstacles were removed. I was relieved. But it was not the right time for me to mention what I really had in mind. We talked about all sorts of things after that. The more we talked, the more I felt the great strength within him, and I was drawn to him more and more.

"I have found what I've been looking for in you. I would like to work with you," I finally said.

He then said without enthusiasm, "I am an unworthy person. It's as if I continue to survive because I am unable to die."

It was after eight, so I said, "Let's meet again." I asked the waiter for the check, which came to a little over three yen.

"I'll pay for it. I have some money today," Pak said, and he took out from his overcoat pocket several cigarettes, and two or three crumpled up yen notes along with seven or eight copper and silver coins and put them on the table.

"No, I'll pay," I said. "It looks like I'm richer than you."

We met often after that and ultimately reached the point that we could talk to each other without strain, almost as if our hearts were linked together. We were completely at ease, and we came to a firm understanding. We made our decision on the second floor of a small Western-style restaurant in Misaki-chō. It was about seven o'clock, too late to go to school and too early to go home. We walked along the path by the imperial moat toward Hibiya. It was still cold. We held hands and stuck them in Pak's overcoat pocket and strolled on without any destination. We were alone in the park. Only the sound of the creaking trolleys broke the night's silence. The stars above and the street lamps illuminated the park.

Pak chatted away in an unusually animated manner. He had been born in the rural area of Kyong-sang-pukto. His family belonged to the lower class; they had been farmers for generations. Among his ancestors, however, had been some learned and fairly important men. His father had died when Pak was four, and his mother was a warm, kindly person. When Pak was a young child he was so attached to his mother that he couldn't go to sleep unless his leg was tied to his mother's. At seven he began school at the village temple, and at nine he started going to an elementary school that had recently been built in the village. He was a good student and wanted to continue his schooling, but his family's economic situation worsened, and Pak's older brother asked him to work on the farm, so he had to quit school. But Pak couldn't suppress his desire for education; when he was fifteen he went to Taegu without his family's permission and took the entrance examination for secondary school. He passed with flying colors, and his older brother then agreed to let him attend and aided him financially even though the family was in dire financial straits. Pak also enrolled in the Waseda University correspondence school and started to read Japanese literary works.

It was also at about this time that he became interested in the Korean independence movement. Soon, though, he realized that the movement was grounded on false premises. Even if the ruling powers changed, the masses would not benefit at all. At the age of seventeen he left Korea and came to Tokyo.

His life in Tokyo was a continuous struggle to stay alive, and he became increasingly absorbed in his own problems. He lost all interest in movements that were merely empty talk and empty words and decided to pursue his own independent goal.

Pak did not explain all this to me in one sitting. He didn't like to talk about himself, and these facts of his life came out in bits and pieces. This account is based on both his fragmentary comments and what I heard from others later. In fact, Pak and I talked more about the future than the past. We discussed the course of life that we should follow, realizing too that there was but a faint hope of achieving our objectives.

"Fumiko, I am planning to go live in a cheap rooming house so that I can work for the realization of our goal in earnest. What about you?"

"A flophouse. That's a great idea," I replied.

"But it's going to be unsanitary. Are you sure you can take it?"

"Of course. If I can't stand something like that, I shouldn't be involved in any sort of movement."

"You're right," he said and remained silent for a moment. Then he said, "You know, Fumiko, I hear that members of the bourgeois class go on a honeymoon when they get married. To commemorate our decision to live together, why don't we start an underground press?"

"That's a great idea. Let's do that," I agreed almost gleefully. "What should we publish? I have a stencil version of Kropotkin.[20] Shall we translate that together?" I suggested.

But Pak rejected this idea. "A translation of that is already in print. And I don't want to publish things that have been written by other people. Even if it is insignificant, it's better to publish something that we've written ourselves."

We talked about our plan excitedly. Before we knew it we had left the park and were in the boulevard. It was late.

"I wonder what time it is. I have to be home by nine," I said ruefully.

"Wait here for a moment, I'll go take a look," Pak said and went to the police box at the intersection of the trolley tracks and checked the time. Neither one of us had ever owned a watch. When he came back he said, "It's about a quarter to nine."

"Well, I have to go home now."

"But you have about thirty minutes more. If school lets out at nine, it'll take you another ten minutes on the trolley, so you'd be getting home at about nine ten. That gives you twenty-five or thirty minutes more."

"Thank you. You're right." So we went back into the park, holding hands. We found a bench by a tree and sat there quietly with our cheeks pressed together. Finally, we had to leave. When we got to the park exit, I asked Pak, "Where are you going from here?"

"I think I'll drop by at my friend's place in Kōjimachi," he replied without enthusiasm.

"Aren't you insecure, not having a regular place to live?"

"Of course I feel insecure," he said, looking down at the ground. "When I am healthy like this it doesn't matter, but when I get sick I really feel helpless. Even people who are kind to you ordinarily don't want you around when you're sick."

"People are heartless. You look frail too. Have you been seriously ill since you've come to Tokyo?"

"Yes. Last spring I caught a bad flu. But I had no one to nurse me, so I suffered in a flophouse in Honjo for three days without food or drink. I thought I was going to die. It was really frightening."

I was overcome and tears filled my eyes. I gripped his hands firmly. "If I had only known you then . . ."

A moment later Pak said firmly, "Well, good night. I'll be seeing you soon." He let go of my hands and hopped on a trolley headed for Kanda.

I stood there watching his trolley leave and said to myself as if in prayer, "Please wait a little while longer. Once I finish school we shall be together. I will always be with you from then on. I won't let you suffer alone when you are sick. If you die, I shall."

I am ending my account here. From this point on I am not allowed to write about anything except my life with Pak. But I have completed what I had intended to write about. Why did I do what I did? I shall not offer any explanation, for here I wanted to tell the story of my life. Sensitive readers will no doubt understand the reason for my activities. I am certain of this. Undoubtedly my life here on earth will soon end. But even if an individual physical being is erased from the world, I am convinced that the essence will survive in the reality that is eternal. I am ending this crudely written account with perfect composure and serenity. May all the people and things I love be blessed with good fortune.

[The following excerpts are from Kaneko's interrogation on November 22, 1923.]

Question: Why did you embrace nihilism?

Answer: Because of the circumstances of my family and the ensuing social oppressions.

Q: What about your family?

A: I have no family in the true sense. . . . I was abandoned by my parents and separated from my brothers and sisters. I had no family life. My birth was not recorded, so I was oppressed by the society. It is the fault of the social system. . . . [After coming to Tokyo] I read the writings of Sakai Toshihiko and socialist magazines. Observing this, my parents seemed to be concerned that I was inclining toward socialism. In about 1922 I became acquainted with a Korean, Pak Yeol, who was unknown and propertyless. I decided to live with him and informed my parents about this. . . . After I started living with him my father wrote me a letter, in May of that year, contending that I was a descendant of a Chancellor of the Realm, Fujiwara-no-Fusamae [681–737], who lived over a hundred generations ago. I was besmirching this illustrious Saeki family line by living with a lowly Korean. He was disowning me and henceforth I was not to think of him as my father, he wrote. So I was disowned by my father, who had already abandoned me. Mother too had abandoned me. . . . She even considered selling me to a whorehouse. . . . My parents bestowed no love on me and yet sought to get whatever benefit they could out of me. Theirs is a truly selfish love, a form of greed. So I, an object of greed, fail to understand the meaning of filial piety. The so-called morality is based on the relationship between the strong and the weak. That morality is always manipulated to serve the convenience of the strong. That is, the strong insists on preserving his freedom of action while demanding the submission of the weak. From the standpoint of the weak, morality means an agreement that calls for one's submission to the strong. This moral principle is common through all ages and all societies. The primary aim of those in power is to preserve this moral principle as long as possible. The relationship between parents and children is also based on this principle. It is only coated over with the attractive-sounding term "filial piety."

Q: How did you come to associate with socialists and eventually arrive at nihilism?

A: Three intellectual groups influenced me while I was peddling newspapers. . . . One was a Buddhist salvation group, the second was the Christian Salvation Army group who beat their tambourines, and the third, the long-haired socialists who cried out in desperate voices. . . . I first approached the Salvation Army group.

[She then relates her experience with Saitō—identified in her memoirs above as Itō. She explains she grew disillusioned with Christianity when he said he had to end his friendship with her because he had fallen in love with her.]

What an extraordinary contradiction for a Christian to preach love on the street corner then fail to follow through on a pure, unblemished love. Christians have become fettered to the concept of God which they created. Theirs is a cowardly faith of slaves. The virtue and beauty of human beings is to live naturally, ungoverned by external forces. I decided that I could not embrace Christianity, which preaches the doctrine of life that conflicts with the ideals of beauty and virtue. So I abandoned Christianity. . . .

[She was then befriended by a socialist, Hori Kiyotoshi, but she became disillusioned with him also because Hori, she claimed, was a hypocrite. He concealed his relationship with his geisha wife, fearing that it would hinder his chances of getting ahead in the world. He also made all of those under him do all the work in his printing business while he idled his time away.]

I was also introduced to another socialist, Kutsumi Fusako [see Kunō above]. Her family life and principles were no different than Hori's. Kutsumi took care of her own personal needs but paid no heed to her children's needs. She would find some excuse to go out with a young man and stay out all day long. I heard her remark that all she had to do was to get on the platform and make a speech about socialism and say "The present society must be destroyed" to get the police to intervene. The next day the papers would report that Kutsumi Fusako made an extremist speech, and so the police prevented her from speaking. I got disgusted with the widespread desire among the socialists to get their names in the papers. At this time Kutsumi had no money even to buy food, so she pawned my clothes. She then let the redemption period expire and allowed the pawnshop to sell them without my permission. I am not complaining about losing my clothes, though she knew that I needed them because winter had come. She showed no sense of responsibility. I detested her attitude, a socialist who gives no thought to other people's needs and thinks only of feeding herself.

I had imagined that socialists were people who rose above the meaningless customs and morality of the society. I envisioned them to be courageous fighters with no interest in so-called fame and honor and social reputation. I thought they were warriors fighting to destroy the perverted society of today and striving to create an ideal society. However, even though they denounce the irrational and hypocritical aspects of the society, and pretend that they are indifferent to social criticisms and to fame and reputation, they in fact are governed by and are concerned about the standards of the mundane society. They seek to adorn themselves with conventional ornaments and take upon themselves conventional values. Just as generals take pride in the medals on their chests, socialists covet records of arrests in order to earn their bread. They take pride in this. When I realized this fact I gave up on them.

I also came to be appalled at the somnolence of the peasants, who are mired in pain but feel no pain, and the ignorance of the workers, who work diligently while they are being devoured to their bones. If the chains that bind them are removed, they are likely to go to the wielders of political and economic power with their chains and beg them to chain them up again. Perhaps they will be happier if they are allowed just to sleep in ignorance. So I got disgusted at all currents of thought and from the spring of 1922 tightly embraced the nihilistic beliefs I hold today.

As for the significance of my nihilism . . . in a word, it is the foundation of my thoughts. The goal of my activities is the destruction of all living things. I feel boundless anger against parental authority, which crushed me under the high-sounding name of parental love, and against state and social authority, which abused me in the name of universal love.

Having observed the social reality that all living things on earth are incessantly engaged in a struggle for survival, that they kill each other to survive, I concluded that if there is an absolute, universal law on earth, it is the reality that the strong eat the weak. This, I believe, is the law and truth of the universe. Now that I have seen the truth about the struggle for survival and the fact that the strong win and the weak lose, I cannot join the ranks of the idealists and adopt an optimistic mode of thinking which dreams of the construction of a society that is without authority and control. As long as all living things do not disappear from the earth, the power relations based on this principle [of the strong crushing the weak] will persist. Because the wielders of power continue to defend their authority in the usual manner and oppress the weak— and because my past existence has been a story of oppression by all sources of authority—I decided to deny the rights of all authority, rebel against them, and stake not only my own life but that of all humanity in this endeavor.

For this reason I planned eventually to throw a bomb and accept the termination of my life. I did not care whether this act would touch off a revolution or not. I am perfectly content to satisfy my own desires. I do not wish to help create a new society based on a new authority in a different form.

Q: What is your opinion concerning the Japanese state and social system?
A: I divide the Japanese state-social system into three levels:

The first class is the royal-clan members.

The second class is the government ministers and other wielders of political power.

The third class is the masses in general.

I regard the first class, the royal clan, as pitiful victims who live like prison inmates whose comings and goings are strictly regulated, just as they are for the imperial regent. I think they are pitiful puppets and wooden dolls who are being manipulated by the second class, the real wielders of power, in order to pull the wool over the eyes of the masses. The third class, the masses, as I mentioned earlier, are ignorant beyond salvation. The second class, the wielders of political power, are the ones who have the real power to persecute the weak, like myself. For that reason I feel nothing but bitter hatred toward this class. Whereas in reality the second class is the actual wielder of power, the first class is the formal wielder of power. So these two classes go hand in hand. Consequently I place the second class on the secondary level and direct my rebellious sentiments against the first class. I also contemplated throwing bombs at both classes. Pak Yeol and I talked about this.

I am keeping a journal of my days in prison. On November 6 I wrote: "The rights of the people are being tossed about by the wielders of power as easily as if they were handballs. The government officials have finally thrown me in prison. But let me give you some sound advice. If you wish to prevent the current incident from bearing fruit, you must kill me. You may keep me in prison for years but as soon as I am released I will try the same thing. I will destroy my own body and save you the trouble. You may take this body of mine anywhere you please, to the guillotine if you wish or to the Hachiōji prison. We all have to die eventually. So you may do as you please. You will only be proving that I lived true to myself. I am perfectly happy with that." You expect me to compromise with you people, change my way of thinking, and live in conformity with the ways of the society? If I could compromise with you now, I would have compromised with you when I was out in society. You don't have to preach to me about that. I have enough sense to understand that. I am prepared for whatever you may do to me. So do as you please. Don't hesitate. To tell the truth, I would like to go out into the world once more. I know that all I have to do is make my bid by saying "I have undergone a change of heart," and bow my head. But I cannot destroy my current self so that my future self can survive.

Officers, let me proclaim courageously to you once more: "Rather than prostrate myself before the wielders of power, I prefer to die and be true to myself. If this displeases you, you may take me anywhere you wish. I am not afraid of anything you may do to me." This is the way I have felt in the past and it is the way I feel now.

Q: Did you become acquainted with Pak Yeol after you developed this manner of thinking?

A: That's right. After I met Pak we talked about our ideas and found that our views were similar. So in order to work together we began to live together.[21]

[During the course of the interrogation Kaneko revealed her opinion about the emperor system candidly]:

Even before I met Pak Yeol I believed that the emperor was a useless entity. Pak and I got together because we agreed about this. We joined hands as comrades to overthrow the emperor system. By nature human beings should be equal. And yet human beings who are equal by nature have been made unequal because of the presence of an entity called the emperor. The emperor is supposed to be august and exalted. Yet his photograph shows that he is just like us commoners. He has two eyes, one mouth, legs to walk with, and hands to work with. But he doesn't use his hands to work and his legs to walk. That's the only difference. The reason I deny the necessity of the emperor system rises from my belief that human beings are equal.

We have been taught that the emperor is a descendant of the gods, and that his right to rule has been bestowed upon him by the gods. But I am convinced that the story of the three sacred treasures [the sword, the mirror, and the jewel, which came down from the age of the gods as emblems of imperial authority] is simply a myth plucked out of thin air. If the emperor were a god, then his soldiers would not die. Why were tens of thousands of royal subjects killed by the Great Earthquake in his immediate presence? We have in our midst someone who is supposed to be a living god, one who is omnipotent and omniscient, an emperor who is supposed to realize the will of the gods. Yet his children are crying because of hunger, suffocating to death in the coal mines, and being crushed to death by factory machines. Why is this so? Because, in truth, the emperor is a mere human being. We wanted to show the people that the emperor is an ordinary human being just like us. So we thought of throwing a bomb at him to show that he too will die like any other human being.

We have been taught that the Japanese national polity consists of an unbroken lineage of the imperial family throughout the ages. But the imperial genealogy is really fuzzy. And even if the genealogy is unbroken through the ages, it signifies nothing. It is nothing to be proud of. Rather, it is shameful that the Japanese people have been so ignorant as to acquiesce in having babies foisted upon them as emperors.

Under the emperor system, education, laws, moral principles were all devised to protect the imperial authority. The notion that the emperor is sacred and august is a fantasy. The people have been led to believe that the emperor and the crown prince represent authorities that are sacred and inviolate. But they are simply vacuous puppets. The concepts of loyalty to the emperor and love of nation are simply rhetorical notions that are being manipulated by the tiny group of the privileged classes to fulfill their own greed and interests.[22]

FIVE

THE SEKIRANKAI

The Red Wave Society

Though the Seitō circle started out as a literary group, it became increasingly involved in social issues, especially those dealing with women. Only on rare occasions such as *Seitō*'s publication of Fukuda Hideko's article on socialism did Hiratsuka Raichō and her colleagues take up broader political or economic questions. It was not until Itō Noe took over the journal that a greater emphasis was placed on broader social questions. Itō Noe was one of the few Seitōsha members to become directly involved in political or social action. She serves as a bridge between the literary-minded, more elitist group of Seitōsha members and the more activist group of socialists and communists who emerged in the early 1920s, the group of women who came together in the Sekirankai, the Red Wave Society.

After the execution of Kōtoku Shūsui, Kanno Sugako, and others, the socialists and anarchists maintained a low profile. The Japanese entry into World War I brought about a wartime boom, and initially there were fewer economic difficulties and social tensions. But the end of the war brought an economic downturn that led to increasing labor disputes and social unrest. In 1918 riots broke out throughout the country over the enormous increase in the price of rice. The violent suppression of the rioters created great social tensions and raised the hopes of those aspiring to stage a revolution in Japan similar to the one that had just occurred in Russia. The Bolshevik Revolution had had a tremendous impact on the thinking of the Japanese socialists and communists. In its wake, the radical elements among both groups, as well as among labor organizers, grew increasingly militant. This resulted in a split in 1925 between the moderate labor leaders, who had emerged from the Yūaikai, and the more militant elements, who turned to Bolshevism. Until they too split with the communists, who toed the Moscow line, Sakai Toshihiko and Yamakawa Hitoshi also derived their inspiration from Moscow.

At this point there were a number of socialist "study" groups, such as Yamakawa Hitoshi's Suiyōkai (Wednesday Society), Takatsu Seidō's Gyōminkai (Enlightened People's Society), Ōsugi Sakae's Rōdō Undōsha (Labor Movement Society), the Hokufūkai (North Wind Society), which consisted of union members of a watch factory, and the Hokkō Jishukai (Self-Rule Society of the Northern District). In late 1920, these groups came together and formed the Nihon Shakaishugi Dōmei (Japanese Socialist Federation). However, because of Article 5 of the Police Security Regulations, women could not participate in the organization. As a result, in 1921 a group of women organized the Sekirankai, a separate socialist women's group. Among the organizers were Sakai Magara, Kutsumi Fusako, and Hashiura Haruko. Itō Noe and Yamakawa Kikue served as advisers.[1]

There were about forty-two members in the society, but only about seventeen played an active political role. The others were interested in the organization mainly as a study group. In its policy statement, the Sekirankai proclaimed: "We forthrightly declare war on all oppressive systems that keep our brothers and sisters in a state of ignorance and poverty." In calling upon women to participate in the May Day march of 1921, Yamakawa Kikue drafted for the society the following manifesto:

> May Day is the day for the proletarians, for us workers who are oppressed. For centuries and centuries, women and workers have endured together a history of oppression and ignorance. But the dawn is approaching. The morning gong that was struck in Russia signals the first step in the victory that will minute by minute banish the darkness of capitalism from the face of the earth. Sisters, listen to the power of women that is embodied in that sound of the gong. Let us exert the utmost of our strength and, together with our brothers, strike the gong that will signal the liberation of the proletarians of Japan. Women who are awake, join the May Day march!
>
> The Sekirankai is a women's organization that plans to participate in the enterprise to destroy the capitalist society and build a socialist society. The capitalist society turns us into slaves at home and

oppresses us as wage slaves outside the home. It turns many of our sisters into prostitutes. Its imperialistic ambitions rob us of our beloved fathers, children, sweethearts, and brothers and turn them into cannon fodder. It forces them and proletarians of other countries to brutally kill each other. It is a society that, for the sake of its greedy profiteers, crushes and sacrifices our youth, health, talents, all chance for happiness, even our lives, and feels no compunction. The Sekirankai declares all-out war on this cruel, shameless society. Women who wish to be liberated, join the Sekirankai!

Socialism offers the only way to save mankind from the oppressions and abuses of capitalism. Sisters who love justice and morality, join the socialist movement![2]

On the second May Day march staged in Japan (in 1921), the Sekirankai marched with its banner. The police charged on them, and many of them were arrested. Kutsumi relates her experience on this occasion in excerpts from her memoirs below.

The Sekirankai did not survive the arrests of its leaders following the May Day demonstration. It was dissolved in 1925, and a few women (including Sakai Magara, Kutsumi Fusako, and Yamakawa Kikue) regrouped and organized the Yōkakai (Eighth-Day Society).[3] Itō Noe had been murdered in 1923, and soon after a few other members died of illness. By 1925 most of the other Sekirankai members, including Hashiura Haruko, drifted away from the movement, because of political oppression or social and family pressure or disillusionment with the unprincipled behavior of some of their male comrades, especially the anarchists who turned to shakedown activities to get money for their own benefit.[4]

Sakai Magara (1903–1983)

Although she was only eighteen, Sakai Magara was one of the key figures in organizing the Sekirankai and in staging the May Day demonstration. She was the daughter of Sakai Toshihiko, a pioneer socialist, and was caught up in the revolutionary movement from early childhood. Her father's frequent confrontations with the police and the government were part of her life from childhood. She recalled catching a glimpse of her father when he was in prison.

It was when I was about seven. My mother [stepmother] told me to hang on to one end of a towel and wait for her while she grabbed hold of the other end and went inside the door. It was as if we were holding hands even though we were separated by the door. After a number of quiet, chilling minutes she came out. She took my hand and rushed me toward the exit. She then pointed to some people who were walking along the corridor enclosed with iron bars in the building across from us. There was a man in Japanese attire sandwiched in between policemen in black uniforms. That man was my father. During the Red Flag incident [see chapter 3] of 1908, which is viewed as a prologue to the Great Treason incident, Father was sentenced to two years in prison for defying the police officers. When we went to see him, he was then in Chiba prefecture. Children were not allowed to visit prisoners, so that a short glimpse was all I had of him. My memory of the Great Treason incident starts here.

When I was eight Father was released from prison and started the Baibunsha. . . .[5] One day when I stepped out of the house I came across a policeman who was assigned to keep an eye on Father. He was pacing back and forth, watching the house. I went past him and ran toward the Tennō Shrine in Yotsuya to look for some playmates. A boy came after me shouting, "Hey, Maguro." I had this odd name Magara, so he mixed up my name with the name of the fish, maguro. The boy was older than me. He poked me and said, "Hey, your family tried to kill the emperor, you know." I did not fully understand what he meant, but I felt that my parents had been involved in some sort of dreadful business. The word "kill" upset me. I felt as if I were a member of a diabolic clique. I was ashamed and went home downcast. . . . [Magara recounts her own incarceration]: In December 1921 Nakasone Sadayo and I passed out handbills to soldiers billeted in civilian homes during the army maneuvers that were being held in the Kantō region. The handbills called on the soldiers to oppose wars and rise up in mutiny. Arrested for allegedly trying to convert the soldiers to the Red cause, we were indicted for having violated the publication laws and were incarcerated in Tokyo prison.

Fukuda, who was in Osaka prison in 1889, Kanno Sugako, who was sent to prison in 1908 in the Great Treason incident, and Takatsu Tayoko, who after being charged in 1921 for writing a poem that was interpreted as advocating the assassination of the emperor had gone to prison with her baby on her back, were the only women who had been charged and arrested for harboring dangerous thoughts before we went to prison. Other women had been detained for short periods, but it was very unusual for women to be imprisoned.

The two of us spent New Year's in jail, and on January 9 we were released on bail. The following year [August 1923] we were sentenced to four months in prison, so we went to jail again.

There were only five cells, so Sadayo and I, both charged with the same crime, were assigned the left and right sides of the same cell. It appeared that Takatsu Tayoko, who was in cell 3, was released on bail at just about the time we came in. I believe Kanno had been in cell number 1. I was not in the same cell that she had been in, but the cells were constructed in the same way, so I sat in my cell and imagined how my predecessor had spent her time in the cell. I knew that Kanno, who had been here all alone from June to the end of January, had attained a state of serenity, and I too tried to attain that kind of serenity.

Just before Kanno was strangled, she sent me the following postcard. I was six then.

January 24. Mā-san: Thank you for the beautiful postcard. You seem to be doing well in your studies. Your handwriting is very good. I am impressed. Have your mother make a tunic out of the upper garment that I am giving you. Also, I want you to have the doll, the pretty boxes, and the cute needles in the drawer. These are with my belongings. Have your parents pick them out for you. I would like to see your adorable face just once more. Goodbye.

I don't recall getting the doll and the boxes, but I do remember the formal upper garment of silk, greyish blue with chrysanthemum designs. When I was in girls' school, I used it as my formal wear. After I graduated from school, I had it dyed purple and used it as a half-coat. I was wearing it at just about the time I went to prison.

Mother told me that when I was in prison Father walked down the street at the end of the year and struck down with his cane the decorative pine wreaths that were placed on the corners, shouting, "What is there to celebrate?" Of course he had had a few cups of sake, but he was not drunk. People may have laughed at him for being childish and wild, but I never realized how much he loved me till I heard that story.

In 1908 Father spent two years and two months in prison for the Red Flag incident. I was four then. He wrote me from prison, saying:

February 2, 1909. Magara, Father will not be able to come home for awhile yet. Mother will be busy with all sorts of business, so you stay with Auntie Katō and wait for me. Don't be selfish, and listen to what Auntie tells you. She will take good care of you. And have Mother come and see you from time to time. I am sure you are well and your cheeks are red like apples. Father is well too.

After my mother died [when Magara was a year and a half], I was left in the care of my father's cousin. After Father married Nobeoka Tameko, he brought me home. But then the Red Flag incident took place, and I had to be turned over to Mr. Katō Tokijirō. My mother too was taken care of by the Katō Hospital before she died.

My stepmother Tameko's younger sister told her that it was shameful to have Sakai's child taken care of by someone else. As a result, while Father was in prison I was sent to stay with my stepmother, who was working as a hairdresser. Father had consulted Kōtoku about this.

Because I do not have any brothers or sisters I am indebted to many people for taking care of me. Presently, I am the mother of three girls. I do not expect them to be especially filial; all I want of them is not to die before me.[6]

Magara's first confrontation with the authorities occurred in November 1920 when she was arrested for taking part in the Book Day sponsored by the socialists. Magara and her friends went out in the streets of Tokyo to sell socialist tracts. She was arrested and detained overnight. In early 1921 Magara, Kutsumi Fusako, Hashiura Haruko, and Akizuki Shizue took the initiative in organizing the Sekirankai. Then the second May Day incident took place, and she spent another night in prison. After she was released, she continued her activity in the movement, making her first speech at a conference on women's concerns in June of that year. After that followed her arrest with sixteen other members of her circle for distributing handbills to soldiers.

She was released on bail and continued her activities on behalf of socialism. In July 1922 the Communist party was organized illegally under the leadership of Magara's father, Sakai Toshihiko. The membership was small; half a year after its establishment there were only fifty-eight members, three of whom were women: Magara, Nakasone Sadayo, and Yamakawa Kikue. Magara and Nakasone returned to prison when the final judgment on the handbill incident was handed down. Meanwhile, the authorities discovered the existence of the Communist party and arrested its leaders, including Magara's father. As a result, both Magara and her father were in prison during the Great Earthquake of 1923, and unlike many of their fellow socialists and communists, were not victims of the right-wing and military lynchers and assassins.

Two years after its dissolution by the government, the Communist party was revived, but Sakai Toshihiko and Yamakawa Hitoshi opposed this move and eventually parted ways with the Bolsheviks. Magara also followed her father's lead and left the Communist party to join the socialists who broke with Moscow.

In 1922 Magara married Takase Kiyoshi,[7] a fellow communist. They were divorced in 1937, and she then married Kondō Kenji, who had been active as an anarchist in the days when Magara was involved in the Sekirankai. In 1933 her father died, just as the wave of ultranationalism and militarism was cresting. Perhaps for this reason Magara remained relatively inactive during the 1930s and the war years. In the postwar years, she refused to join any political party but played an active role in the League of Women Voters. She did not abandon her socialist philosophy, however. She remarked in her old age, "It is not important whether it is based on Marxism or not. I believed that the goals of socialism were equality between men and women, peace in the family, and elimination of poverty. My life was founded on these beliefs. I still believe this to be true."[8]

Hashiura Haruko (1898–1975)

Hashiura Haruko was born in a small village in Tottori prefecture in 1898. As her recollections below indicate, she came from a progressive family, beginning with her father. Two of her brothers, Tokio and Yasuo, were active socialists and were harassed by the authorities. Tokio's wife, Riku, was also active in the Sekirankai. When Haruko was seventeen, she moved to Tokyo and joined the socialist circle there. She became a member of the Sekirankai and participated in the May Day demonstration of 1921. She was arrested there, and as she was being led away, escorted by the police, newspaper photographers snapped her picture. The photo that appeared in *Yomiuri Shimbun* showed her with her head held up high in proud defiance. This image caught the public's attention, and Hashiura won the admiration of supporters and sympathizers of the left. Interestingly, it was not until the postwar years that the public knew the identity of the girl in the photograph.

Soon after this incident Hashiura drifted away from the socialists and turned to religion. She became a believer in Konkōkyō, a popular cult founded by a peasant in 1855, which had come to be regarded as a religion that would enable one to gain material well-being. Haruko believed Konkōkyō to be more effective in helping those in need. In 1923 she married a man who remained indifferent to the idea of working to support his family. She finally left him after thirteen years and earned a living as a housemaid and later as a housemother in a social service institution.

During World War II Hashiura went to work in north China as a housemother in a youth corps. She returned to Tokyo after the war and worked in a social service institution, caring for orphans and juvenile delinquents. In 1955 she quit work because of ill health and lived alone in poverty. She caught pneumonia in 1975 and died shortly thereafter. It almost seems as if she willed her death. She refused to eat, saying, "I find no pleasure in staying alive."[9]

Interviewed in 1971, Hashiura said, "I have failed to accomplish anything at all since the days of Sekirankai. I have been overrated by people ever since I was identified as the girl in the photograph. I've been wanting to tell everybody the truth and let them know the kind of life I've led since that incident."[10]

The following are excerpts from an interview with her conducted by Makise Kikue in November 1971.[11]

On the day before the parade [Sakai] Magara handed me a piece of black satin cloth as well as some red cloth and told me, "Make a banner with the black satin and use the red cloth to sew on the characters for Red Wave Society (Sekirankai)." I was then living in Takinogawa [in Tokyo] with my older brother Tokio [Tokio was one of the founders of the Communist party]. I asked Wada Kyūtarō to write *seki-ran-kai* in large characters on paper. I then used these to form the characters for Sekirankai and sewed them on both sides of the black satin. It had to be done carefully, and I worked at it all night with the help of my niece.

The next morning we got ready to leave the house. My brother's house was located on a dead-end alley. There was a community well just beyond the house, and the trolley line ran on the other side. Three policemen were guarding the entrance to the house to prevent us from leaving. My older brother's wife, Oriku, hid several small flags, with the characters for May Day written on them, in her sash. Then she left the house as if she were going shopping. I was wondering how I could get out. Then my niece went out to the well with a pan to wash her hair, which gave me an idea. I let my hair down, carried a pan with me, and stepped out of the house, telling the police, "Because you're watching the house I can't go out, so I guess I'll wash my hair."

The three guards didn't follow me and began to relax in the sun. When I was sure that they were not watching me, I jumped over the ditch and took off running. Others were waiting for me in front of the barbershop on the main street. I attached the banner to the bamboo pole and headed off.

During the march, the police moved to take the banner away from me. I tried desperately to hang on to it, but a horde of police came at me and I lost it. In the melee, one of the police grabbed my hair from behind. This made me angry, and I lashed out with my arms, slapping one of them across the face. The policeman yelled at me, "How dare you hit a policeman. You hit a policeman!"

I said, "You grabbed my hair."

He yelled back, "It wasn't me! It wasn't me!"

I felt sorry for him and said in a politer tone, "I don't know who it was, but somebody grabbed my hair from behind."

By this time he looked embarrassed and crept away, staring at the ground. He was just a young officer. Then an officer who seemed to be the leader yelled, "Arrest her! Arrest her!" They all rushed to apprehend me. I told them, "You don't have to grab me. I'll go with you," and marched along with them. Photographers kept clicking their cameras. I was arrested near the Shinobazu Pond in Ueno. The azaleas were in full bloom, and many people were out looking at the flowers. Some of them yelled, "Socialists, don't give up!"

I was taken to the Yanaka police station. One person, evidently a pickpocket, was being slapped around and beaten, and I thought they were going to beat me. However, they didn't do anything; they even permitted my friends to bring me things from the outside. Soon the police came and said, "Here, we brought you your friend," and led Magara in. We were put in the same cell. Many men were arrested too, but Magara and I were placed in a cell separate from them.

I had been arrested once before during Book Day [so named because on those days they went out to sell socialist "books" or tracts], but on that occasion I was released the same day. This was the first time I had been detained overnight in jail. The cell's window was high up the wall. I thought I would go mad if I had to stay there any length of time.

The photograph of my arrest appeared in the papers because, it was said, I kept my composure when I was arrested. The photographers didn't get my name, so I was not identified in the papers. *Yomiuri Shimbun* printed one of the photographs. Magara told me, "The photograph in the *Yomiuri Shimbun* is great. I saved one for you." That photograph was then reproduced during the post–World War II years in the *Asahi Graph* [a pictorial magazine published by a liberal newspaper] with the heading "May Day. That Day, That Moment." This was the issue of May 1, 1964. I was identified as the girl in the photograph for the first time because Magara told them. Until then the photograph was merely identified as "a woman arrested on May Day." Later Takatsu Seidō [organizer of the labor group, the Gyōminkai] praised me. "Look at you. Striding courageously forward with your head held up high." Ōsugi said, "I didn't realize there was a girl like this among us."

At that time I was attending a sewing school. When they saw the photograph at the school, a big commotion erupted. I always did a meticulous job of sewing, and my teacher used to praise me, saying, "Your sewing shows your inner spirit." When the teacher saw the photograph, she exclaimed, "Oh, Hashiura is in the paper. It must be a mistake. You must go to the paper and have it corrected." The uproar got out of hand, and I quit the school. I then enrolled in a school that taught sewing with sewing machines.

After the May Day incident, I attended a number of meetings with Magara. Once when we were singing revolutionary songs a man grabbed my hand and began to abuse me. Magara stepped in to help. Things remained tense for awhile following the May Day affair.

At that time, Itō Noe was living with Ōsugi Sakae in Zushi and was doing some Western-style sewing. She used to tell me to come and sew with her because I was learning to use the sewing machine. But I didn't visit them, because I didn't like how Ōsugi kept changing wives. Already married, he had turned to Kamichika Ichiko and then to Noe. My father had been especially strict about relations between men and women, and I was influenced by him. I had met Ōsugi before, but I didn't work with him in the movement.

I was born in Ōiwa-mura in Iwami county, which is located a little inland from the Japan Sea, about sixteen kilometers from Tottori city. I was the youngest of a family of six boys and four girls. Our family business prospered under Grandfather. He made sake and sold miso and soy sauce. There was also a two-story building with three large rooms where silkworms were raised. Grandfather was a good business manager. He regulated materials, time, and labor in a military fashion. He was very strict about time. Breakfast was at eight on the dot, lunch at twelve, and supper at five. If we turned up even a minute late, he would not allow us to eat. We might be playing in the hills, but as soon as the sun had risen to directly overhead, we would rush home. None of us was allowed to be choosy about food.

Whenever he started a new project or when it was necessary to correct mistakes, he called together all the servants and workers and talked things over with them. Once a decision was made, everybody had to abide by it rigidly. If anyone failed to do so, he would beat them up with his abacus. Grandmother, on the other hand, was very gentle. People used to say she was like the Buddha. Father too was a gentle person and did not like business. At the end of every month, he used to get into an argument with Grandfather. Grandfather would order his chief clerk to go and collect money that was owed the shop. He would tell him not to leave the premises of those who owed him money until they paid up. Father would say to Grandfather, "It's unreasonable to insist that a person who has no money should pay up." This was what they usually argued about. By the time I was old enough to understand what was going on, Father had quit the sake business.

Father was dedicated to religion. He used to study the Confucian *Analects* in order to become a better person. At first, he turned to Buddhism, but he disapproved of the priest's personal conduct, so he turned to a new religion that emerged about then, the Kurozumikyō.[12] When people came to buy soy sauce or miso, he would ignore them and keep reading the newspaper. But when they came to ask him to pray for them to cure one ailment or another, he would jump right up and begin praying.

Father was puritanical about sexual relations. He used to say, "We cannot insist that women remain chaste while men need not be." The villagers considered him an oddball. He did not get along with them and felt isolated. That is probably why he became more deeply involved in religion. Mother had absolute faith in him. When I was about six she used to tell me, "If someone does something wrong, even if it is the emperor, Father will speak up." When my older brother Tokio went to Waseda University and became a socialist, was arrested during the first roundup of communists (in 1923), and was sent to prison for two years, Father said, "Tokio is right. Yoshihito [Emperor Taishō] is wrong."[13] Father refused to recognize hierarchical differences. I think my older brother became a socialist because of Father's influence. I believe I too inherited his beliefs.

Father knew nothing about socialism until he heard about it from my older brother. Then he began studying it and concluded that socialism was in tune with what he was seeking in life.

Our oldest brother, Masuo, used to subscribe to a socialist magazine. The younger brothers read the magazine too and began to turn to socialism. Brother Masuo used to help any villager who was in financial trouble. Consequently our family property was slowly depleted. I read a book of poems by Mushanokōji Saneatsu [a prominent writer, 1885–1976] entitled *The New Village,*[14] which was in Masuo's room. Our storeroom was full of our older brother's books. There were books on the emancipation of slaves, folktales by Tolstoy, a book about Joan of Arc, poetry books, and so on. As soon as I learned to read I used to go into the storeroom, pick a book that I could read, and dig into it. I later realized that the book on the emancipation of slaves was a translation by Sakai Toshihiko. Brother number six, Sueo, graduated from Hokkaido University and was befriended by the author Arishima Takeo.[15]

My brother Sueo became a devout Christian. When brother number five, Tokio, discussed social problems or made sarcastic remarks about the government, brother Sueo used to keep his peace and pray. Tokio, my socialist brother, used to say, "He really puts me in an awkward position when he prays." He used to say, "Socialism calls for the nationalization of everything. Then everybody will be equal and be well-off." What he said seemed like a wonderful idea to me. That's the way it should be, I concluded.

When I was eighteen [seventeen by Western counting] I went to Tokyo to be with older brother Tokio. We were accompanied by Nishio Toshizō [later general and commanding officer of the Japanese forces in China during the war with China that broke out in 1937], my cousin, who had just returned from studying in Germany. I went to Tokyo to study, and I enrolled in the Seika girls' school in Yodobashi as a second-year student.

After I graduated, I entered the Watanabe Girls' School to study sewing. The May Day incident took place when I was enrolled there.

In Tokyo I was impressed by the magnificent imperial palace surrounded by a large moat, and by the people, dressed in splendid clothes, riding in cars. In contrast, the workers repairing the streets were dressed in plain work clothes. The sharp contrasts were striking. Despite the differences in status in the countryside, the bonds of personal relationships were strong. In Tokyo, however, human relationships hardly mattered. There, the smart, the strong, and the cunning were taking advantage of the weak and the good-natured. The rich were enjoying the fruits of the land. I began to feel a strong sense of outrage.

I mentioned the Book Day incident earlier. While selling some socialist books I was arrested and taken to the Kisagata police station. The police chief looked at me with contempt and spoke to me roughly. Evidently, he regarded me as a tomboy. I glared at him quietly until he began to speak to me more politely. I was by nature stubborn. Socialism made me even less docile.

[After the May Day incident] my brother Tokio told me, "I have to live my own life. I can't live with you indefinitely." Because I was convinced that I wouldn't be able to make a living by sewing alone, I decided to get married. Influenced by my idealistic brother number four, Yasuo, I decided to marry a man from the most unfortunate of people. In our Hashiura family, male-female relations were regulated in a strict, puritanical manner, and so I had no awareness of the unsavory side of life. I married a person from a totally different family environment. I was a fool.

My husband used to come and visit my brother Yasuo. I knew he painted Japanese-style paintings, and I thought he was a very kind, gentle, good person. My brother Yasuo opposed the marriage. He told me, "That fellow listens to what I have to say, but he never expresses his own opinion. I have no idea what he is thinking about. When I visited his family I found out that his older sister is someone's mistress and she sent him through high school. He is already twenty-nine, but he is still being supported by his older sister. His mother is also being supported by his older sister. This shows you the kind of man he is. At twenty-nine he should get a job and make his sister quit being a kept woman. He wants to marry you because he thinks you can help support him." I went ahead and married him against my brother's advice. I was twenty-five then.

After our marriage my husband still refused to do a lick of work. He didn't earn a penny, and I had to pawn my possessions, my clothes, and everything else. I had no time for the [socialist] movement. I was busy enough trying to earn money to feed us. After I heard Wada Kyūtarō's talk, I was convinced that capitalism was wrong and that socialism was the answer, and that to work for the happiness of everybody was a good thing. But I did not agree with the idea of sacrificing some people to attain that goal. I believed in a peaceful approach, and I decided that even if it took longer to reach the goal, I should rely on religion to get there. I was influenced by my father's religious zeal.

I heard Yamamuro Gumpei [founder of the Japanese Salvation Army] speak on the street corner and was deeply impressed. I began to read his book and visit the Salvation Army. Once when I went there, an old woman came up to me and said, "Surely, you must have committed some sin. You must repent." I didn't think I had committed any sin, and what she said turned me off. I stopped going there, but none of the other established religions interested me, because they all seemed too rigid. What appealed to me was the magnificence of nature.

When Mother died, I felt that the forces of nature could not be challenged. The grandeur of nature was stupendous; in the face of it human beings were helpless. If there was a God, I decided, it was nature itself. Then I found [through my husband] that there was a religion embodying these beliefs, the Konkōkyō.[16] I do not go to their church any longer, but I still approve of their teachings. They say that when you sit and rest on a tree stump, you must thank it when you get up to leave; that women are the farmland of the world; that the natural world is magnificent.

At one time, I opened a missionary station in Meguro [in Tokyo]. Even then the Special Higher Police [in charge of controlling "dangerous" or "subversive" thought] used to come and check up on me. Whenever any socialist did anything, they would come and investigate me. I told them, "I still believe that there should be equality for everyone so that everyone might be happy. I am no longer interested in working for the movement. I am going to work for the happiness of everyone through religion." They asked me, "Then should we take your name off the blacklist?" I replied, "It makes no difference to me. But the number of socialists is increasing all the time. Aren't you wasting your time keeping track of someone like me? If you like, take me off the list." After that they stopped coming around to check up on me.

Kutsumi Fusako (1890–1980)

Kutsumi's life story is told in considerable detail in her recollections below.[17] She was born into a samurai family in Okayama prefecture and as a child was exposed to Christianity. Eventually, however, she turned to socialism. She was an admirer of Fukuda Hideko and, at the age of sixteen, left for Tokyo to join her. There she helped Fukuda with the publication of the magazine *Sekai Fujin* (Women of the World). During this period she met a number of militant socialists, but at this time her political philosophy was more in tune with Christian socialism.[18]

In 1913 Kutsumi married a Christian evangelist and pacifist, Takada Shūzō. Takada was unemployed and did not seek work, declaring his faith in the providence of God. This left Kutsumi with the task of supporting the family. She eventually had two daughters by Takada. In 1920 she left Takada and drifted away from Christianity. She turned to socialism and joined Sakai Toshihiko's circle. She joined Sakai Magara in organizing the Sekirankai and participated in the May Day march.

After the May Day incident she accompanied Mitamura Shirō, a leading communist, to Osaka, where they worked with a tenants' alliance. She also worked with Mitamura in organizing labor unions and workers' strikes.

Kutsumi's children suffered because of her devotion to Mitamura and her work with the unions. Moreover, they also suffered persecution. When Kutsumi was arrested in Hokkaido, her older daughter, Hitoko, was also jailed for forty days. Years later, Hitoko expressed her bitterness about what she perceived as her mother's lack of concern for their welfare.

Mother did not take care of us at all, she just let us shift for ourselves. When it was convenient for her, she would let us stay with her. Otherwise she would leave us here and there. At times she even sent us off to our father, from whom she was divorced. She did not care whether the people she left us with took good care of us or not. Usually they did not. Those who were asked to take us in found themselves saddled with a thankless task. I had to change schools seven times. I never even graduated from elementary school. For Mother, her work and her man came first.... She retained the old-fashioned ways of the Meiji woman. She always insisted that we obey her, and she would not allow us to assert ourselves at all. Mother also had a mean streak in her. When she left us with some family, she would say to me, "I may never see you again."[19]

Her daughters were not Kutsumi's only critics. Kaneko Fumiko bitterly resented Kutsumi's lack of consideration in dealing with her. (See chapter 4.)

Regardless of her behavior toward her children, Kutsumi was absolutely faithful and submissive to Mitamura and attended to him like an old-fashioned, self-effacing wife. The contrast between her politics and her behavior is intriguing.

While Mitamura and Kutsumi were immersed in the labor movement, a split occurred between the moderate Sōdōmei and the radical Rōdō Kumiai Hyōgikai. Mitamura and Kutsumi joined the latter. During this period, Kutsumi met Tanno Setsu, whose memoirs are in chapter 6.

It was the Hyōgikai that led the Hamamatsu musical-instrument manufacturer's strike. Mitamura and Kutsumi played active roles in the strike, but in the end it failed. They then returned to Tokyo and joined the Communist party, which had been revived in late 1926. In 1928 Mitamura was sent to Hokkaido to take charge of the Communist party there. As Kutsumi relates below, while they were there the mass arrests of March 15, 1928, took place, and eventually Kutsumi was arrested, beaten up, and sent to prison. Mitamura was in Tokyo at that time and escaped arrest for a year. He then began a relationship with another woman. When he was finally discovered by the police, he shot and injured one of the arresting officers. (See Tanno memoirs in chapter 6.)

Kutsumi was released in June 1933 and returned to Tokyo. She expected to continue her work with the Communist party, but Mitamura, together with other leaders, like Sano Manabu (chairman of the central committee of the party) and Nabeyama Sadachika (central committee member), had defected from the party. At the time, Mitamura insisted that he was not abandoning the revolutionary cause but was merely severing ties with Moscow. The public's perception and the perception of his comrades, however, were that he was a traitor. Kutsumi, ever loyal to Mitamura, followed suit and devoted her time to helping the families of the defectors. Then she got involved in the Sorge spy ring.[20] She was recruited in 1936 by Miyagi Yotoku, an Okinawan Marxist artist who had returned to Japan in 1933,[21] after organizing workers in the United States. Despite the danger, Kutsumi decided to work with Miyagi in order "to defend the only socialist country in existence, the Soviet Union."[22] In September 1941 the spy ring was uncovered and the entire group was arrested. Kutsumi was imprisoned until the end of World War II. It appears that the material she gathered was of no great importance.[23]

In the postwar years, Kutsumi refused to join the revived Communist party, though she was invited to do so. Because of his defection, Mitamura was ostracized by the Communists. In 1946 he organized his own right-wing socialist group and began to take an anticommunist stance. Kutsumi continued to follow Mitamura's lead and supported his work. Even when he began an affair with another woman and had a child by her, she remained loyal, even maintaining friendly relations with the woman and the child.[24] To the very end she was a selfless follower of her husband.

Kutsumi Fusako's Recollections

My mother was born in 1863. She was a very strict person. My father married into Mother's family, since she was the only child. . . .[25] They got divorced when I was five. When Mother was pregnant with me, she went to the midwifery and nurses' training school of the medical school to study to become a midwife. Before that, she had applied to the all-male normal school that had just been established in Okayama. However, she was told that she had failed the physical examination. Okayama Women's Normal School was not established until 1902, and at that time no woman would have been admitted to the men's normal school. Evidently, it was only through some error that Mother had been allowed to take the entrance examination. When they found out she was a woman they rejected her. . . .

I was born on October 18, 1890. Mother used to practice midwifery near a church. I was a young child then, so it was probably in about 1892. I was influenced by Christianity early in life. There was a French Catholic church in front of our house. A girls' school was attached to the church, and nuns from France ran the school. It was in the old samurai district of Okayama. . . . The church had constructed a chapel on one of the old samurai lots. When I was five, I began first grade there. I liked going to this school. The sisters were called *dōtei-sama* (Miss Virgin), but we children used to call them Mother. The "mothers" were very kind to me.

When I was seven I caught dysentery. I suppose there were isolation wards then too, but I was kept at home and our house was quarantined.

The front of the house was roped off, and we could have no contact with the outside. The sister who was good to me would crawl under the rope and visit me. One day she told my family, "Fusako will die soon, so in order for her to join Jesus she must be baptized." My grandmother, who was steeped in the samurai spirit and was a strict adherent of Buddhism and Shinto, was infuriated and told the sister, "That's an outrage. Please leave our house!" The sister refused to yield and insisted, "I will not leave." Then Grandmother told her, "If this child goes to the Christian heaven, we will not be able to get together in the Buddhist paradise." They got into a terrible squabble. As a result of this argument, our family severed all relations with the church. I was no longer allowed to go to the church or the kindergarten, and I was sent to the elementary school affiliated with the Okayama normal school.

Another influence on my thinking was Fukuda Hideko. Fukuda was an Okayama native and was about my mother's age, so I knew about her. My mother probably scoffed at her as "that woman who committed a crime against the state." As for myself, that someone like Fukuda came out of my home community of Okayama greatly impressed me. I was also influenced by the young men in our family who were interested in socialism.

My mother's cousin, who had been in Tokyo, talked to me about attending some socialist meetings. Also when I was in the first year of girls' [high] school, a young relative, Ōmae Shinzō, lived with us. He was the son of the head accountant of the Ogata Hospital in Osaka, and he owned a copy of *Society a Hundred Years from Now,* which had been translated by Sakai Toshihiko, a reporter for the *Yorozu Chōhō.* I believe that the book was a translation of Edward Bellamy's *Looking Backward.* I also borrowed from this young man *New Family Flavor,* edited by Sakai. All these things aroused my interest in socialism.

Maybe because he was interested in socialism, Ōmae used to support the *buraku* people [the outcastes].[26] This was before the *buraku* liberation movement had started, so he was acting on his own. There was a *buraku* section in the outskirts of Okayama. He knew that the *buraku* people were impoverished and living under pitiful circumstances, and he used to go there to do volunteer work in education. Because he was also a medical student, he used to provide medical assistance too. He bought an organ for the community and asked me to come on Sunday and help him teach the children songs and games. I went with him, for I did not feel that it would be shameful to work in the *buraku*. . . .

Ōmae used to bring the *buraku* people to our home. Mother didn't say anything, but Grandmother was an old-fashioned woman. She told us, "When the *buraku* people come, you may serve them tea, but be sure to use a separate set of cups. And don't let them touch the water jug, and be sure to purify the ladle after you use it." She probably thought they were unclean because in those days people were ignorant about sanitation and because their eyes were sore with infection. . . .

In order to go to girls' school I used to pass through the grounds of Shōkakuji, a Buddhist temple. One day—it was right after the Russo-Japanese War, so it was probably 1906—I saw a notice posted on the main building of the temple announcing a lecture on socialism. The lecturer was Zama Shisui, who at that time would go on "missions to spread the word," lecturing on socialism. Yamakawa Hitoshi was living in Okayama, and he sponsored the lecture. Because Ōmae had introduced me to socialism, I decided to stop by and listen to the lecture on the way home from school.

Arriving at the lecture, I was dressed in my formal skirt, and when I tried to enter the hall, the police stopped me and said, "You can't come into a place like this." I ran home, took off my formal skirt, put on an apron, and went back to the lecture hall. I told the police, "Can you let me in? I want to find out what the lecture is all about." This time they were less touchy and let me in. I was the only woman in the audience. By the time I entered the hall, the lecture had already begun.

Yamakawa was about twenty-five or twenty-six then. He had already published a tract called "Good News for Youths." He was charged with lèse majesté because of this and was sent to prison for about three and a half years. At the time of the Zama lecture, he had just come out of prison. His home was in Kurashiki city. Yamakawa's older sister was married to Hayashi Genjūrō, a Kurashiki pharmaceutical merchant, the largest in the prefecture. They had a branch store in Okayama in Kamiya-chō. Yamakawa lived on the second floor of the store and ran the business.

I met Yamakawa at the lecture. He invited me to come to an inn in front of the Okayama railroad station the next morning because Zama Shisui was staying there. I went there early the next morning. Yamakawa had left me a note addressed to "Miss Socialist" which said, "Zama had to leave earlier than expected. In the future please contact me at the branch store of

Hayashi Genjūrō's." He told me, "We must all concentrate our efforts at the center and work hard," so I decided to go out to Tokyo. A school friend, Shimoyama Umeno, wrote me a letter of introduction to Fukuda.

My mother found it hard to sympathize with my activities. She had separated from my father early in their marriage, and she had to work as a midwife to support us. I did not tell her about my contacts with Yamakawa. I believe she used to go to the Hayashi store. I heard her say, "I asked the chief clerk at Hayashi's to deliver some things for me, but he hasn't done so." By the chief clerk she meant Yamakawa. Yamakawa had no idea about the situation in our family. He just told me I had to go out to Tokyo and work.

I left home because the question of my marriage came up. In those days, if the family had only daughters, the eldest one had to take a husband into the family. The person selected for me was a farmer's son. He was then a student at the Okayama junior college. He had the backing of Yamamoto Jōtarō, a high-ranking officer of the Mitsui firm, and was working his way through school delivering newspapers. My mother had hoped to help him through school and adopt him into our family to carry on the family line. However, he did not approve of socialism. So my decision to leave home was based on my wish to avoid marrying him and also to work for socialism. I was in the fourth year of girls' school then. . . .

In December 1906 I went to Fukuda's home. The *Heimin Shimbun* was about to be published. They had purchased a building in Shintomi-chō and had installed a printing press there. In the following year, 1907, the first issue of the new daily paper appeared. Almost simultaneously, Fukuda's *Sekai Fujin* appeared on January 1, 1907. I helped Fukuda with her publication, reading proof, running errands, and so on. . . .

My father died on March 25, 1907. If he hadn't died at that time and I had stayed in Tokyo, I probably would have been involved in the Red Flag incident and arrested with Arahata and the others.

On April 20, 1911, my mother died of kidney trouble. . . . I then moved in with a family friend of Mother's. . . . By this time the authorities had me under surveillance. Undoubtedly it was because of my ties with Yamakawa and with the Iroha Kurabu [a socialist organization in Okayama]. The people with whom I lived were in a tricky situation. If they allowed someone like me to live with them, it was likely that they would get into trouble too. Ultimately, they decided to marry me off to someone in America. As a result, I left and went to Osaka to live with Takada Shūzō.

Takada's thoughts were a mixture of Buddhism and Christianity. He was a close friend of Nishida Tenkō,[27] who was greatly influenced by the Zen master of the Nanzenji in Kyoto. Takada, however, belonged to a progressive faction of Christianity. Earlier he had been married to a teacher at the Wilhelmina Girls' School. Later, when Takada, influenced by Buddhist thinking, ceased being an orthodox Christian, his wife left with her mother and two sons while he was on the road. When I moved into Takada's place, he was living with his younger sister, who had just been divorced.

In 1913 we were married. He was thirty-six and I was twenty-four. Initially, I had been attracted to Takada by his ideas. Also, he was from my hometown and we were related. The church in Osaka objected to his having incorporated Buddhist elements into his religious thought, saying that he had deviated from orthodox Christianity. Ultimately, he left the church. Takada's thinking was close to Uchimura Kanzō's [1861–1930], who believed in noninstitutional Christianity. Takada, however, was not Uchimura's disciple, though he agreed with him about noninstitutional religion. Takada did not work at all, because he believed that a person should live naturally in accordance with God's will. A person should not strain himself by working. Takada wasn't lazy and would go out on the road and roam about. When he went on the road, I had no idea where he had gone. In 1914 our older daughter, Itoko, was born, and in 1916 our second daughter, Jiuko, was born.

Takada had his own printing press and types. He printed and mailed a small newspaper out to people. His thinking was based on the notion that "the wind will provide me with enough fallen leaves to start a fire and cook my meals." He believed that if God so desired, he would be able to stay alive and continue his work. If it became impossible to continue his work, it only meant that it was no longer necessary. I decided that Takada's life-style, his dependence on the offerings of other people, was too self-indulgent. I could not abide by it. In order to eat, I had to work. So I sold his press and everything else and came out to Tokyo in 1918. Takada's thinking was founded on the Buddhist notion that one should visit a friend who shares one's beliefs and rejoice in their common faith. He was like a monk of the Tokugawa era, Ryōkan,[28] who roamed about paying no thought to the needs of his family.

In Tokyo I got a job with the Matsuya dry-goods store and was assigned to the regional business section. I helped edit a popular magazine they were publishing. I was paid twenty-five yen a month. . . . It was impossible to support the three of us on twenty-five yen, so I worked at night too. . . .

Then Takada came back from his travels. He scolded me, saying I had rebelled against him, the husband, by moving out of the house while he was away. The husband must be revered as much as one reveres Heaven. Women must not take any independent action, he told me. During his wanderings, he began a relationship with another woman, but he had no intention of parting with me or breaking up the family. I implored him to help me pay for the family's needs. He argued, "You are essentially a socialist. That is the course that you chose of your own free will. If you aren't being paid enough to feed the family, why don't you fight and demand a pay raise, enough to sustain the family?" I decided he was right. [She then quit her job with Matsuya and worked at a few other places, including a temple in Kanazawa.]

I then came back to Tokyo and got in touch with Sakai Toshihiko to see if he couldn't help me find a job. . . . I had met Sakai when I was living with Fukuda. I had done some work for him before, so he must have thought I could be of use to him. The first job he gave me was to make steno copies of the *Communist Manifesto*. This was completely against the law. . . . He must have translated it himself. I was prepared to face the consequences of doing this sort of work. Whenever I had any problem, I used to go and see Sakai. He used to greet me more warmly and openly than his wife did. He was that kind of person.

My thinking is not founded on dialectical materialism. It will be obvious to other people that I am full of contradictions. I guess I was most heavily influenced by humanitarian sentiments. I was not governed by logic, but by a desire that wells up from the bottom of my heart. I started out being influenced by Catholicism, then Protestantism, and then by socialism. . . .

I often behave in a completely illogical fashion. Taguchi Ugenta,[29] with whom I worked in the Sorge affair, used to laugh at me, saying, "Auntie, you are really silly. . . ." I guess I do behave in a peculiar way.

In about 1920 the Naporutsu Watch Factory labor dispute broke out. That was the first time I was beaten and knocked down. I can remember how mad I was, and my crying. Wada Kyūtarō was also attacked. They beat his head on the ground and dragged him around by his feet. The next day, the police came to apologize and brought a box of candy for my children. Since then I have experienced all sorts of incidents and have built up my ability to endure much physical abuse.

In those years, women were not allowed to join the Socialist League. So to participate in the second May Day celebration we hurriedly decided to form an all-women's organization, which we named the Sekirankai. This was April of 1921. Sakai Magara, Nakasone Sadayo, Takatsu Tayoko, and I decided to organize the society and went to Yamakawa Kikue to get her support. The members were wives, sisters, and daughters of socialists.

Magara wrote the manifesto for the society, and we passed out flyers to publicize its formation. Akizuki Shizue, the wife of the anarchist Naka-nomio Kōriki, his younger sister, Ine-chan, and Shindō Kyūzō went to the Bureau of Government Monopolies in Yodobashi and passed out the fly-ers. Two of them were arrested. I can't recall what the charges were. I was summoned to the prosecutor's office as a witness. When I was getting ready to go to the prosecutor's office, Ōsugi Sakae advised me, "Don't say anything more than you have to. When you are summoned to a place like that you mustn't say anything except 'I don't know. I forget.'" It was simple advice, but I kept this in mind and stuck to it. It served me well all my life.

The second May Day celebration of 1921 was the first one to include women. The night before, we shortened our long sleeves and prepared for the parade. We women joined the parade at the entrance to Shiba Park and marched on to the moat, passing in front of Chiyoda Castle. Police on horseback stood guard. The printers' union came after us, and the Yūaikai brought up the tail end. The union men shouted "Defend the Sekirankai! Defend the Sekirankai!" We paraded past the moat, singing the song of the revolution. Near Matsusumi-chō, Asanuma Inejirō, Asō Hisashi, and others were arrested.[30] At the foot of Ueno hill, Hashiura Oriku, Tanaka Mari-chan, and others were arrested. As we passed near the foothill and approached Tōshōgū Shrine, Hashiura Haruko and Sakai Magara, who was carrying the Sekirankai flag, were arrested.

Some thugs were waiting for us on top of Ueno hill, so we could not march up there. Many people were arrested at the foot of the hill. Ma-tsuoka Komakichi,[31] who was in charge of the parade, said, "We shall dis-band here." So we began to leave with Akita Ujyaku and others. Then the thugs shouted "Here's the woman!" and grabbed me and dumped me in the sewer ditch. I was soaked from the waist down in the mire and was dragged on to the Kurumazaki police station in complete disarray. People

on the way yelled at me, "Look at that crazy woman." I guess I did look
like a madwoman.

Somehow Hashiura Oriku managed to bring a pint-sized bottle of
whiskey in with her. She drank the whiskey in her cell and then began
yelling and screaming. Usually the police strip and search those arrested,
but because there were more than thirty men in the compound they didn't
check us very carefully.

At about the time we organized the Red Wave Society and through
1923 or so, the anarchist movement was on the upswing. The anarchists
organized a group called the Spartacus party and went among the workers
delivering lectures. The right-wing gangs tried to disrupt the lectures, and
there were many scuffles.

I was hired by Ōsugi to help in his labor movement. I did odd jobs for
him. . . . Yoshida Hajime and others were hostile toward Ōsugi and used
to say, "We're conducting a movement to oppose leaders. Why are you still
hanging around Ōsugi's place?" The movement to oppose leaders spread
to Osaka and became a movement to oppose Kagawa Toyohiko.

[Kutsumi began to live with Mitamura Shirō, who was two years her
junior. They moved to Osaka in December 1921. By then she was carrying
Mitamura's child. She worked as a maid for two years in Osaka before
finding work with a printer.]

Kagawa Toyohiko had organized the Osaka printers' union, but by the
time I arrived in Osaka the union was gone. The antileadership group
insisted that they, the workers themselves, must run the union. This sentiment grew until Kagawa was driven out. I went to Osaka after the May
Day celebration in which the Red Wave Society had participated. A person
named Sugiyama, who used to be a member of Kagawa's printers' union,
had taken over the printing firm, and I got a job there as an apprentice
printer. I learned the trade and became a type-picker. In those days
women were used primarily as type-decomposers. There were no women
type-pickers. Mitamura also came into the printing plant later and learned
the trade. But he concentrated mainly on the workers' struggle. . . .

At that time, experienced male type-pickers were paid 2 yen 60 sen a
day and type-setters were paid 2 yen 70 sen a day. As a type-picker, I was
paid 2 yen 35 sen a day. For a woman worker of those days, I was getting
good pay. Mitamura became a type-picker too and got paid 1 yen 50 sen a
day in a factory in Amazaki.

At about the time of the Great Earthquake, Mitamura started a strike at a small factory. He overturned the type cases and fled. Not only was the pay poor, but the owner, although he was a Christian, used to turn the clock back so that the workers had to work longer. Mitamura was sent to jail for about three months for his actions. On the day of his trial, Ōsugi was killed by the military police in Tokyo [September 16, 1923].

Initially Mitamura had intended to join the Sōdōmei and organize a printers' union, but Nishio Suehiro and others said they did not want socialists [i.e., Communists] in the confederation. As a result, Mitamura learned the trade, went into the printing factory as a type-picker, and organized a union. Now that we were union members, Nishio could not refuse to let us in the confederation.

Mitamura believed that the main force of the revolution must consist of workers, which is why he organized a union and joined the Sōdōmei. The Sōdōmei's policy was designed to curb anarchism. At that time, the workers were bent on getting rid of leaders, and antileader sentiments were volatile. They had driven Kagawa out, insisting that they were going to run the union themselves. The end result was the demise of the Osaka printers' union, which Kagawa had worked so hard to create.

After I went to Osaka, I moved closer to the Bolsheviks. Until then I had been in favor of anarchism. The anarchists continued to engage in armed robbery and violent threats. Furuta Daijirō killed a bank employee in Osaka. The socialist [i.e., Communist] alliance consisted of both anarchists and Bolsheviks. When I went to Osaka we didn't make any distinction between anarchists and Bolsheviks, so both factions used to come and stay with us frequently. Three anarchists, Konishi, Yamada, and Ōnishi, used to live on the second floor of our house, which was referred to as "the pillagers' house." Only after the Great Earthquake, from 1923 or so, did the anarchists and Bolsheviks split.

Times were really hard for us in those days. There were days when we had nothing to eat. When word got around that somebody had some rice, the whole group descended on the place and ate. And we also worked together. Nowadays the leaders are all intellectuals and paid officers.

The Osaka city tram-workers' strike occurred in 1923. . . . The Osaka labor alliance supported the strikers, so the printers union served as liaison for the striking workers entrenched in Kōyazan. The signboard of the printers' union was posted by our house. We lived on the second floor, and the union office was on the first floor. . . .

There were left- and right-wing groups in the Osaka labor movement. . . . In Tokyo, too, Watanabe Masanosuke was the leader of the left-wing labor group. The leftists got strong support from the amalgamated labor unions; there was even a move to remove the Sōdōmei from the group.

In those days, workers who went out on strike were not allowed to go back to work for the same company. So the young strikers all trained to become professional strike organizers. Some became agitators. . . . Mitamura used to conduct study sessions for them. That's the way things were in about 1923 and 1924. As the unions got stronger, Nishio Suehiro and Kanemasa Yonekichi, men who were all-out supporters of the Sōdōmei, must have come to feel threatened by Mitamura.

I began to participate in labor disputes in May 1926. First there was the united printers' dispute with the printing firms and then the Hamamatsu musical-instrument manufacturer's strike. These were followed by the Noda soy-sauce manufacturer's dispute. Then came the struggle over the leadership of the Hyōgikai (Labor Union Council).

In the Hamamatsu strike, we had posted a sign about three meters long reading "Strike Headquarters." The right-wing gang raided us there. There was a big scuffle. One of the attackers grabbed an iron pot filled with boiling water and threw it at Mitamura. His shoulders were badly scalded. They caught hold of me too and twisted my arms. Because of these attacks, the strike leaders stayed out of sight. We rented the upstairs of a textile-worker's house and directed the strike covertly from there. Mitamura, myself, Minami Kiichi from Tokyo, and Yamabe Kentarō from Osaka lived there and printed and circulated a "daily report."[32] We used the "daily report" as a flyer to publicize the strikers' case. This was one of the unique features of the strike. "Daily reports" had not been issued by strikers before this.

Minami's daughter got sick during this strike, and Mitamura urged him to go home to visit her. Minami wept, saying, "How can I go home when everybody else is struggling so desperately here?" But Mitamura persuaded him and he rushed back to Tokyo. Minami's home was in the back streets in Tama-no-i. He just caught a glimpse of his daughter, who had gotten up to go to the toilet. He then returned to Hamamatsu without even speaking to her. Soon after that, his daughter died. When his second daughter wanted to marry a young activist in the Proletarian Youth League, Minami opposed it. She too died, just before the March 15 [1928] roundup of socialists. So Minami had no heirs.

The company tried to lure the strikers away. They transported non-striking workers on trucks from their homes to the strike headquarters. They set up tents for them and had them demonstrate in front of us. Because we continued to issue "daily reports," the company officials began in earnest to try to quash our activities.

One day, Mitamura went out to Mie prefecture to the *burakumin* peasant union to get some rice. We had to feed over a thousand strikers, so we needed a lot of rice. While he was in Mie-ken, the other strike leaders were arrested. I was arrested too, but an acquaintance in the mediating committee told me they would release me if I agreed to leave Hamamatsu. I agreed and told them I would go to Tokyo. They asked me my reasons for going to Tokyo, and I told them my daughters were there with Sakai.

When I got to Tokyo I contacted the Hyōgikai and then went to Sakai's place. I put up my hair in Japanese style to disguise myself, and Sakai did not recognize me. . . . The policeman who was tailing me stayed there day and night. Sakai would open the second-floor window and shout, "I'm going to dump a bucket of water on you. . . ."

At that time, there were a number of student groups to study socialism, and many students supported the strike. After I arrived in Tokyo, I told Tanno Setsu, "Many women work in the harmonica division. It would be good if we could get some women to support the strike." She suggested that I bring along Itō Tatsue, a female printer, so I brought her with me and sneaked back into Hamamatsu. . . .

The company president, Amano's son, was a right-winger, so right-wing groups would descend upon the strikers and beat them up. The authorities intensified their search for the strike leaders in hiding. I was told [by the strike leaders] to go back to Osaka, so at the end of August I returned there. Three days after I left, the strike leaders were arrested. The strike headquarters staff was wiped out. We lost the strike.

The company had sent in thugs to beat up the strikers and shed blood. It was a violent dispute, but after more than a hundred days of struggle, we lost the battle. Mitamura was arrested for having published the "daily reports." He was charged with violating the press laws. Minami and others were also arrested. In order to crush the strike, the authorities had arrested all the activists, but in the end they were cleared of the charges.

After Mrs. [Margaret] Sanger came to Japan in 1922, interest in birth control increased. The primary reason for this was financial circumstances. Unlike those of today, unions then were not recognized by the companies. People were fired just for belonging to unions. As a result, many people were unemployed.

We were then living in the labor district in Konohama ward in Osaka. Families there had many children, so it was necessary to practice birth control. . . . I had met Yamamoto Senji[33] through a student at Dōshisha University. . . . Yamamoto was then a lecturer at Kyoto and Dōshisha universities. He had just returned from America and served as Mrs. Sanger's interpreter.

In the fall of 1922, Mitamura, myself, and two others visited Yamamoto in Uji. He did not know many labor union workers, so he was delighted and asked us to come and see him from time to time. We invited Yamamoto to Osaka and had him lecture to the Sōdōmei labor school that we had instituted. He came to lecture for us once a week. He also took part in May Day demonstrations. He wrote a pamphlet called "An Evaluation of Mrs. Sanger's Birth Control Plan." In those days, it was illegal to discuss birth control, so the pamphlet was published surreptitiously. We decided that it would be better for Mitamura and me to remain behind the scenes, so we used Noda Ritsuda's home as the office. We got his wife Kimiko to serve as the president of the Birth Control Study Society, which we had organized. We limited the membership to those with more than five children or those who suffered from certain diseases. The *Asahi Shimbun* reported on the society, and it became well known. A large number of people applied for membership. It was clear from the application forms that many applicants were residents of back-street tenements, people who were poor. . . . We posted a sign reading Society for Birth Control Study by Noda's house. Many people came to join the society. Kimiko was unable to discuss the issues with them, so she would send them over to me. It became my job to deal with these people.

We distributed rubber diaphragms manufactured by the Dunlap Company in Kobe. Birth control societies were located in both Osaka and Kobe. In Kobe, the society used the home of Aogaki, the executive secretary of the Kobe Labor Union League. In Tokyo, Ishimoto Shizue, who had become acquainted with Mrs. Sanger while she was in America, became the leader of the birth control movement. . . .

The Labor Union Council's headquarters were in Osaka. The head of the organization division was Kawada Kenji. This division opposed the creation of a women's department. They argued, "If you establish a women's department in the union, will you establish a men's department too?" Mitamura also opposed the idea.

I argued that women had special problems that had to be dealt with. A women's department was necessary. The opponents asserted that "all we need is policies to deal with women's concerns. The only issue that is unique to women is the period of pregnancy." The question was heatedly debated in the second general conference of the Labor Union Council, but it was tabled. Tanno was terribly upset about this. "I was asked by Watanabe to deal with this question, but look at what happened," she moaned.

There were many women in the metal workers' unions, but these units opposed the plan. I was a printer and helped to organize a printers' union and knew that women workers' pay was low. Initially, I had not given much thought to the idea of establishing a women's division. But once I started to work in the factory, I found that we did not get paid on time and we were not paid for overtime. I had used an alias when I got the job, so I was fired when they found out. Whenever I saw a poster recruiting women workers, I applied and got a job. But whenever there was a problem in the plant, I would speak up and then be fired. They would fire me without advance notice, and I would protest. They would then bar me from the plant. When I came home from work, others would come to me with their troubles. Sometimes I had to leave my children in the care of other people. There were all sorts of problems. I decided that it was essential that a women's department be created. But the men opposed the idea.

At that time I was concerned primarily about wages. I began to call for equal pay for equal work for men and women. But socialist leaders like Takahashi Sadaki, Kawada Kenji, Nabeyama Sadachika, and Mitamura all opposed the idea. When women's problems were mentioned, they would ridicule them, saying, "It's a matter of pregnancy or hysterics." They argued that the creation of a separate unit would cause friction with other groups. All we needed was women's policy. . . . In Tokyo they created the Kantō Women's Alliance [which was affiliated with the Communist labor movement].

While we were in Hamamatsu supporting the strike there, we had to let the printers' union business go unattended. Then the controversy over Fukumotoism broke out. The Osaka printers' union complained, "All of you are only interested in theoretical disputes. You are doing nothing to defend our interests. We want to leave the alliance."

Proponents of Fukumotoism insisted, "We must carry on to victory the political battle for the proletariat." When they were asked, "How are you going to win this battle?" they responded that it would be achieved through theoretical struggles. I was in the union office then, but the theoretical questions were too abstruse for me to understand. Eventually, people stopped coming to the office. . . .

My older daughter was living with the Sakai family in Kōjimachi [in Tokyo] and was commuting to the Banchō elementary school. She was sent from Osaka to Tokyo and had to change schools often. She never received an elementary school diploma. There are children who give their parents trouble by participating in the kind of activity that I was involved in, but in our case we parents caused trouble for our children. This was our situation in the early 1920s. Then we got arrested in the mass arrests of March 15 [1928]. And in 1941 I got involved in the Sorge affair. I always saddled my children with trouble.

In 1927 Mitamura and I came out to Tokyo. . . . Party headquarters were in Akabane. . . . When we were in Osaka, we were active in union work, so when we were desperate for money we could borrow money from people. Now, however, we were engaged in illegal activities, and borrowing was impossible. As a result, when we ran out of money we found ourselves in a terrible fix. In late 1927, just before Watanabe Masanosuke went to Moscow to discuss the 1927 Thesis, he visited us in Akabane, but we had only eleven sen. I could only buy some fried tofu, devil's tongue paste, and carrots. We didn't have any charcoal, so we used charcoal bits to heat the footwarmer. Then the party gave us sixty yen. Ichikawa Shōichi brought the money to us.[34] Suddenly we felt rich. We never knew where the money would come from or who would bring it to us. I did not try to find out.

After Watanabe Masanosuke went to Moscow to participate in the conference on the 1927 Thesis, Ichikawa Shōichi, Shiga Yoshio, and Mitamura made up the core of the party headquarters. . . . After Fukumoto Kazuo went to Moscow and was criticized for his position, everybody made a U-turn. They say Tokuda Kyūichi beat up Fukumoto with his slippers.[35] Fukumotoism was too difficult for me to understand. Mitamura said, "I've been told that it was designed to expand the party structure."

We spent 1927 engaged in "illegal activities." In January 1928 Mitamura was sent to Hokkaido to organize Communist cells there. I went with him and took my older daughter with us. When I say I have fond memories of Hokkaido, people laugh at me because I went there in January and in April we were arrested. I stayed in prison until June 1933. So I spent only a bit over three months on the outside in Hokkaido.

Before we went to Hokkaido, we had planned to send our older daughter to Moscow to attend the KUTV [Kommunisticheski Universitat Trudyashchikhaya Vostoka, a Communist college for Asian workers]. But we were arrested in the March 15 mass arrests and so we had to give up the idea.

In Hokkaido we did not find out about the mass arrests of March 15 because Hokkaido was isolated from Honshu. After March 15, communication from Tokyo stopped. Mitamura said, "Something must be wrong." Then Takeuchi Kiyoshi sent a young woman called Kawabata Yoneko to tell us what happened.[36] The newspapers were forbidden to write about the arrests. [The ban was not lifted until April 11.] . . . Then a few days later Takeuchi came to stay with us.

We were publishing a tabloid called *Hokkaidō Rōdōsha* (Hokkaido Workers). Takeuchi and I went out to mail the papers, but when we could not mail the papers from Sapporo, we went to another station. Then on April 2 Mitamura left for Tokyo to make contact with the party leaders.

On April 8 I received a letter from him. He wrote, "We are all well here. The cherry blossoms are in full bloom, so why don't you come to see them?" I burned the letter. My daughter, who was out looking at the snow in the yard, came in and said, "Something is funny. Somebody is looking this way with binoculars from a house about thirty yards away. The landlord is pacing up and down."

I realized something was wrong, but kept on washing the things that had gotten soiled with printer's ink the previous night. Then the police came bursting in. They asked me a series of questions. My family's name, my husband's name, my name and place of birth. I asked, "What is this all about?" One of them said, "I am sure it is a mistake, but can you please come to the police station with us?" I asked them to wait a moment while I changed my clothes. I then went in the back room where Takeuchi was. We had a membership list of party members in Hokkaido. They were numbered, and the list was rolled into a small stem. I gave Takeuchi the list and told him, "Please get rid of this," and pointed to the container of kerosene near the brazier. I said, "I probably won't come back."

When I got ready to go out of the house with them, the police said to my daughter, "You come too, please." When we had walked about a hundred yards the police hollered, "What is this, you old hag! You've got Takeuchi hidden in your house." I looked back and saw Takeuchi in ropes. He got caught while attempting to get rid of the material we had printed the night before by dumping it in the latrine. I had told him to burn it, but he did not have the time. "What are you up to, you old hag!" the police screamed, but I didn't say a word. We had only been at the new hideout five days. When we got to the police station, they beat me up relentlessly. But I didn't say a word. I remembered what Ōsugi had told me several years back.

Many people were arrested in the March 15 roundup. In Hokkaido, workers and peasants around Otaru, Hakodate, and Asahigawa were arrested. They had never been arrested before, so they told the authorities everything. It couldn't be helped. I don't blame them at all.

I was detained in the police station for two nights and then was sent to the prison in Sapporo. My face was swollen purple, and the area of my body where I had been stripped and whipped with a rope had swollen into welts. I looked a sight. The police taunted me, "Look at what you get for pretending you don't know anything." There was nothing I could do, so I let them proceed with their routine of interrogating me.

In May the prosecuting officer told me, "Because you refuse to talk, we don't know what to do with your daughter. We can't keep her in the police station. It looks like she's been active in the movement too. No matter what we ask her, she refuses to answer. Looks like you did a good job of training her. We don't know what to do with her. Who shall we turn her over to?" I told him, "As long as you let her out, she'll manage on her own."

It appeared that the police had our residence under surveillance. After the three of us were arrested, Kamei Katsuichirō went to the house.[37] It was like a moth flying into a flame. He was sent there by Mitamura to find out what had happened to us, because I did not reply to his letter. Kamei had come with sixty yen for our travel expenses. Twenty yen was for our daughter's travels. She later got in touch with her father [Takada Shūzō] and evidently turned the money over to him. She was fourteen then.

The authorities wanted to release her right away, but they felt they just couldn't turn her out when she had no place to go. So they kept her in the police station for forty days. Later, I found out from her that she had worked on a bus while I was in prison in Hokkaido. Because she was too young, she used a friend's niece's name and claimed to be two years older than she was and got the job. She also worked as a mannequin. She experienced much hardship.

In the fall following my arrest, I was tried in court. . . . I revealed during the trial that they had stripped me and tortured me. Yamamoto Senji came from Sapporo to see me and publicized the fact that the police had tortured a woman. So it became a public issue.[38]

Taguchi Gentarō, the son of a big landowner, who was known as the king of the Itami district, was in the same Sapporo municipal trolley-workers' cell with me until he was arrested on March 15. Later, he and I were arrested together again in the Sorge spy affair.

The prosecution asked for a five-year prison term for me. The judge sentenced me to four years. They condemned me as "a person who shows no remorse." The court of appeals upheld the verdict. Taguchi's father was a member of the district assembly and had a great deal of influence, and so, though the prosecution asked for a four-year prison term for him, he was given two years. He served his term in the Amibashiri prison. After he served his term, he was married and went into the fishery business in Sakhalin. His wife had been an admirer of Taguchi's. When he was arrested, she indicated to him that she wanted to marry him. Three other persons were given four-year prison terms. They were Hokkaido University students. Mitamura was in Tokyo, so he escaped arrest. Because I was in prison in Sapporo, I knew nothing about Mitamura and the shooting incident with the police. [See Tanno Setsu's account of this incident.]

After five years and three months in prison, I was released. This was on June 24, 1933. I arrived in Tokyo on the twenty-fifth and went to see Mitamura in prison. He had been arrested in the April 16, 1929, mass arrests. I came out of prison expecting to join the battlefront again, but what awaited me was the controversy over defection by some Communist leaders. It was immediately after Sano Manabu and Nabeyama Sadachika had issued their statement on defection on June 8. Mitamura then came out with his own statement. His was a criticism of the Communist party of that time. He stated:

> Sano and Nabeyama have criticized the Communist party from the standpoint of the superiority of the Japanese people. I fail to understand their point about the superiority of the Japanese people, but I believe the Communist party is mistaken about the direction toward

which the labor unions should be led. . . . I am not satisfied with the tactics being used by the Communist parties of other countries. Unless I take advantage of this opportunity, I will not be able to make my views known to the outside world. For that reason, I am issuing this statement. The tactics being used by the party are designed to glorify Soviet Russia. My aim is to stage a revolution in Japan. So I believe that we must adopt tactics that are suited to the actual state of affairs in Japan. At present, there is no one who will assist me in carrying out my plans. If I make my opinion known to the public, I am sure those who share my views will support me.

Kaizō magazine said they would like to publish an article explaining Mitamura's views, and so we published an article in the September issue under my name.

What struck me when I came out of prison was the persistence of bitter feelings that followed the vicious struggle. I got all confused. There was talk of someone shooting someone, of somebody being shot. Nothing but sinister incidents. After this, the party began to go downhill very quickly. I came out of prison at the worst point in the party's history. Lots of people came to visit me, but I failed to understand the issues that were being discussed. . . . I believe the party had made some mistakes in its policies. And it is possible that spies had infiltrated the party. Nobody could speak frankly with anybody during this time. I was friendly with Sakai Magara, but I couldn't consult her about party matters.

The only person I could talk with was Yasuda Tokutarō.[39] I was under severe strain then. Sano and Nabeyama were gentle people, but Mitamura was hot-tempered. He would scold me and tell me to go and find out what was happening in the outside world. The critics ignored Mitamura's criticism of the party and simply regarded him as a turncoat. Even though I wanted to find out what was happening in the party, no one was around; they were all in prison. I was in a fix. Mitamura admonished me not to go and see "Minami Kiichi or Mizuno Shigeo. Those guys have abandoned the struggle." He kept asking me to find out all sorts of things, but I could not come up with a solid answer for him. I was all alone and was in a terrible quandary. . . .

All the defectors were not the same. I was told how to deal with those who had recanted and promised the authorities they would abandon the movement. But there were scores of people who had defected following the Sano-Nabeyama defection. These people were shunned by the Worker-Peasant Aid Society that was being managed by Watanabe Masanosuke's mother. They had no one to help them. The legal-assistance society also refused to defend them. So I took it upon myself to find lawyers for them, supply them with food, and keep them in touch with their families. Perhaps what I did could be seen as the actions of a turncoat. But I asked myself, "If I don't help them, who will?" So I helped them. That's the way I am. It wasn't easy, but I also went to Watanabe Masanosuke's mother's group to get help. I went out to Ichigaya prison almost every day to do errands for the prisoners.

I went to Hanakawado [burakumin district] to get help for Takahashi Sadaki and Iwao Iesada [who was trained in KUTV]. The people flocked around me. They said that they were angry at Takahashi. "Takahashi Sadaki is not even a product of the Suiheisha, but he wrote about the buraku and participated in the Suihei movement. He was merely trying to drag the Suiheisha into the Communist party. It's an outrage." "As for Iwao, we will think about it further, but we will not agree to help you."

Matsuo Naoyoshi was in prison in Kosuge in Ibaraki prefecture.[40] He became seriously ill, and his sentence was suspended. He was sent to Nakano Sanitarium. He asked to see his wife, a beautiful woman. She had married someone else while he was in prison, but Matsuo did not know about it. People didn't want to tell him about it when he was on his deathbed. I went to visit him, and he died soon after. Many people needed help.

When I was helping the defectors I went to see Kazama Jōkichi.[41] He asked me if I had ever met M. I said I had not. He then said, "Yamamoto Masami has just come back from the Soviet Union, so go and see him and ask him when M came back from Soviet Russia. I don't know where he is." But at that time Yamamoto Masami was not allowed to have visitors.[42]

In 1932 the party leadership was held by members of the peasant division. M was in the peasant division at that time. Ōizumi Kenzō and Takakura Teru were also in the peasant division.[43] Takakura was active in the peasant movement in Bessho in Nagano prefecture. She was arrested but released. So her path and mine crossed often. At about this time Takakura had gotten linked with Miyagi Yotoku of the Sorge spy affair.

It would probably not be fair to call those who favored "socialism in one country" traitors [to the Communist cause],[44] but I believe there were problems with this movement. The Soviet Union itself had been bureaucratized at that time, so the Comintern had become an agency to defend

Soviet interests. Mitamura used to say when I went to see him in prison, "I don't like the idea of having the Japanese Communist party serve as a low-level agency of the Comintern. The Japanese workers wouldn't support the movement." I guess these difficulties arose because of the immaturity of Communist theories.

I was told by Mitamura to organize a party that would stand for socialism in one country. I wasn't bright, so I couldn't tell whether the proponents of socialism in one country were right or not. But when we set out to organize such a party, the authorities, anxious to take advantage of any movement that would help in destroying the Communist party, seemingly facilitated our efforts. Nakao Katuso [chief of the Labor Union Council's Kantō regional division] came out of prison and called for the establishment of such a party. We were supported not only by the defectors but by others as well. . . . Watanabe Taeko was also released from prison with a suspended sentence and joined our group. She was put in charge of the Kansai region.

The group held regular meetings and was just about ready to make public its policy and objectives when the February 26 incident of 1936 [when young army officers attempted a coup d'état] took place. The group panicked. They buried documents relating to policy statements in the yard of the home of one of the members, Hiroshima Sadakichi. . . . But three days later everybody was arrested. I was arrested too. . . .

Watanabe Taeko's father was in the Osaka court of appeals, so she went back to Osaka and got a job with the Ōhara Research Institute on Social Problems. But she kept in touch with Tokyo. Then about two months later she severed all relations. She told Nabeyama Utako, "Nabeyama is a world-class revolutionary. I plan to work with him, so from now on I shall provide Comrade Nabeyama with his necessities in prison." Utako was infuriated and asked Taeko, "What in the world are you talking about?" She drew Nabeyama's older sister into the dispute; the situation got messy.

Shiga Yoshio, who was in prison, said he disagreed with Nabeyama's statement on defection.[45] If Taeko supported Nabeyama, he would divorce her, he told her. It was rumored after that that Taeko became friendly with Ryū Shintarō,[46] at the Ōhara Research Institute.

I had, in the meanwhile, been cut off from the socialism-in-one-country group. I was not aware of exactly when they decided to cut me off or why. They didn't even inform me that they had drafted a policy statement. I devoted my efforts to helping the prisoners prepare for the second hearing and to providing them with food and other necessities and serving as their liaison with the outside world. This was as much as I could do to help them.

Just before the opening of the second hearing, in about September, the lawyer for the labor-farmer faction, Nakamura Kōichi, and other young lawyers were arrested. So my efforts were fruitless. After the second trial, the sentences of the defectors were reduced. Mitamura's sentence for life, handed down in the first trial, was reduced to fifteen years. The prison terms of Sano, Nabeyama, and others were reduced too. Sano, Nabeyama, Mitamura, and others were all sent to the Kosuge prison. Once the final verdict was handed down, it was no longer necessary to bring the prisoners food and other necessities, so this aspect of my relief work ended. I asked Takase Kiyoshi to help me publish Sano and Nabeyama's "On Socialism in One Country, a Criticism of the Japanese Communist Party and the Comintern." Sakai Magara was the publisher, but it was banned by the government as soon as it appeared in July 1934. Copies were hidden here and there, but so far as I know Magara's copy and the one my older daughter kept are the only ones extant. To publish that book at that time was a major undertaking. Sano and Nabeyama were released from prison in 1942. Nabeyama entered the army's Cherry Blossom Agency. Mitamura served his term in Kosuge prison and was kept under preventive detention until the end of the war.

In 1936 the Thought Criminals' Protection and Supervision Law was enacted. Kawasaki Natsu became my "protection" officer. When I mentioned this to Yasuda, he said, "I think she'll be all right." When I went to the Protection and Supervision office in Sendagaya for the first time, Mōri, Special Higher Police Chief, was in charge of the office. Kawasaki told me to come to the Ochanomizu Cultural Academy. When I went there Kawasaki was at the gate waiting for me. She treated me to dinner in the academy's dining room. At that time I was involved in the Sorge affair.

Yamakawa Kikue (1890–1980)

Yamakawa Kikue was not in the Seitōsha circle, but she emerged as a social critic and engaged in a number of debates with those who published articles in the journal Seitō. The Seitōsha circle adhered to a form of romantic self-assertiveness, which to Yamakawa, who was more of a realist and a rationalist, seemed like the sentimental self-indulgence of the petite bourgeoisie. She remained a cool-headed realist and a rational advocate of socialism throughout her long career. She was a supporter of the Sekirankai, but she did not participate in the political activities of the group.

Yamakawa was born into a family with samurai roots. Her mother, Aoyama Chise, was the daughter of a Confucian scholar retained by the Mito Han, one of the collateral houses of the Tokugawa shogunate. As the heir of the family, she remained a strong-willed and active member of it. Kikue's father had married into the Aoyama family and apparently did not play a dominant role in the lives of his children. Chise, on the other hand, was well educated, had firm ideas, and held high expectations for her children. Perhaps because of her mother's influence, Kikue had a lively intellect and read widely in both Japanese and Western works. In 1908 she enrolled in the English-language academy run by Tsuda Umeko. The academy's goal was to prepare women to become professionals, and yet Tsuda was politically very conservative. As Yamakawa notes in her memoirs below, Tsuda forbade her students to read Tolstoy.

Yamakawa's thinking regarding the status of women was influenced profoundly by August Bebel's *Women and Socialism*. She became convinced that the only way that Japanese women could achieve freedom and equality was through socialism. Her interest in the movement was strengthened further when she came in contact with the Heiminsha circle. She met Yamakawa Hitoshi at one of the Heimin meetings, and they were married in 1916.

Yamakawa Hitoshi was born in Okayama prefecture in 1880. In 1896 he went to Kyoto to attend the preparatory school of Dōshisha, a Christian college, and became a convert to Christianity. But he dropped out of school, traveling to Tokyo to start a small journal. In 1900 he was sent to prison for lèse majesté for three years for publishing an article written by a friend which was critical of the crown prince's marriage. After he left prison, he joined Sakai Toshihiko's and Ōsugi Sakae's circle of socialists. This led to further imprisonments. He then returned to his hometown of Kurashiki for awhile and worked in his family's pharmaceutical business. This is when Kutsumi Fusako met him. When the suppression of socialists was relaxed somewhat at the beginning of the Taishō era, he returned to Tokyo.[47]

Soon after she married, Kikue contracted tuberculosis, like so many of her compatriots, and she had to take time out from her involvement in politics. By 1918, however, she was well enough to take on both Hiratsuka Raichō and Yosano Akiko in their debate about whether or not the government should provide special aid to mothers. Kikue's response was that the only path to freedom and independence for women was through socialism. She worked for the cause through her support of the Sekirankai and the publication of the *Zen'ei* (Vanguard) with her husband in 1922.

In 1919 Hiratsuka Raichō, Ichikawa Fusae, and others organized the Shin Fujinkyōkai (New Women's Association) in order to gain political rights for women. Yamakawa Kikue criticized the Shin Fujinkyōkai as a product of bourgeois sentimentalism. "The only way to save the working women is the overthrow of capitalism," she argued. The women's organization destined to carry on the work of the revolution was, she asserted, the Sekirankai.[48] But the Sekirankai did not live up to her high expectations and soon dissolved.

In 1922 Sakai Toshiko, Yamakawa Hitoshi, and others organized the Communist party. Kikue supported her husband in his work. When a proletarian party was organized following the passage of the universal-male-suffrage act of 1925, Kikue succeeded in getting the party to adopt a program that called for equal rights for women, overcoming the initial negative reaction of the male members.

By this time the Yamakawas were turning away from the Bolsheviks who wanted to take their direction from Moscow. After the first Communist party was crushed by the government, Yamakawa Hitoshi favored dissolving the party. He also got into a debate with Fukumoto Kazuo about the latter's insistence on ideological purity. When his position on dissolving the party was condemned by Moscow, he and Sakai cut their links to Moscow and formed their own party, the Labor Farmer party.

In 1928 Kikue got involved in a debate with Takamure Itsue (1894–1964) about her contention that marriages in a capitalist society turned women into "legally recognized prostitutes." Only after a Marxist revolution would the wife be completely equal with her husband, for then she would no longer be economically dependent on her husband.[49]

In the 1930s the government's persecution of left-wing groups intensified. The Yamakawas retired to the countryside in Kanagawa prefecture and raised quails to support themselves. Hitoshi was arrested again in 1937 and was sent to prison for two more years. During World War II the Yamakawas continued to raise quails and produce their own food. After the war they both joined the Socialist party, and Kikue served as head of the bureau on women and minors in the Ministry of Labor for four years. Hitoshi died in 1958, and Kikue continued as a social commentator until her death in 1980.

Excerpts from her memoirs, *Onna Nidai no Ki* (Records of Two Generations of Women), provide glimpses into the atmosphere and mode of thinking of the Taishō era.[50]

Yamakawa Kikue's Memoirs

When I was in fourth grade, we had a class debate. Someone suggested that the class should debate the question Who is superior, Napoleon or Genghis Khan? Everybody wanted to take Napoleon's side; no one favored Genghis Khan. I wanted to argue in favor of Genghis Khan, using some ideas Father had brought back from his trip abroad. But I could not get much information on him, and I was really not very enthusiastic about taking his side. So I was about to give up the idea of arguing on his behalf. Then one of my classmates said, "The whole class is in favor of Napoleon, a Westerner, and no one favors Genghis Khan, who is an Asian. It's outrageous. Let's you and I back Genghis Khan." So we decided to support his cause, but there was hardly any information on him. We asked our history teacher, but he couldn't come up with anything. Several years back a children's magazine, *Shōnen Sekai* (Young Boy's World), had an article on Genghis Khan, so we used this as our source of information and argued his case. After the debate our history teacher praised us for knowing more about Genghis Khan than he did. But our only source was *Shōnen Sekai*.

According to Father, when he was in France, an old woman, who was a young girl when Napoleon was alive, told him, "Napoleon is no hero. He was an outrageous man. People of France suffered terribly because of him. The women of France must not produce another person like him."

Right after summer vacation that year [1905], on September 5, riots broke out in protest against the Portsmouth treaty. . . .[51] During the Russo-Japanese War, the Anglo-Japanese alliance was made much of. In school, the English national anthem was sung, together with the Japanese national anthem. When the Japanese flag was displayed, the Union Jack was flown with it. When rallies were held before the imperial palace and banzais were shouted, the same thing was done in front of the English embassy. There was constant talk of Japan becoming the England of the East. . . .

As the war progressed we became increasingly aware of the great dan-

ger that faced the nation. . . . The story of the total annihilation of the
Ninth Division of Kanazawa is well known. The military reserve unit led
by my aunt's husband, Colonel Mori Yasunori, was also in this division. . . . When his unit was caught in the cross fire of enemy guns, he was
ordered by his superior officer to lead his troops and charge into the enemy
line. The order made no military sense whatsoever, since it could only result in the complete annihilation of his troops. So the colonel twice asked
his superior offier to reconsider his order. The commanding officer exploded at him for questioning his decision. Since the colonel could have
been executed if he refused to obey, he led his troops into enemy fire.
When the general on the division's general staff found out about the order,
he tried to have it rescinded, but it was too late. The colonel's son later
remarked to me that in the military mind his father was not an individual
human being but merely a statistic. . . .

[During 1908–12 Yamakawa attended the English-language academy
run by a pioneer of female education in Japan, Tsuda Umeko.]

Mistress Tsuda could not abide the policies of the Gakushūin [school
for children of the royal family and aristocrats], which focused on educating "little princesses." Moreover, she did not get along with the director of
the school, Shimoda Utako, so she left the Gakushūin in 1900 and started
her own academy at her home with a few students. Her goal was to establish an institution that would enable her to implement her own educational philosophy. Unlike other educators of this period, she ignored the
Ministry of Education's policy that girls should become "good wives and
wise mothers." She was a pioneer in educating women to become professionals. She rejected the slave morality and spineless submissiveness
that characterized schools like Tokyo Women's College. She herself was
independent-minded and forceful and was a natural-born teacher. . . .

Professor Yasui Tetsuko taught ethics and psychology briefly at our
school.[52] We had read in Higuchi Ichiyō's diary that Professor Yasui had
studied under her as a young student.[53] So a couple of my friends and I
visited her at her home to talk about Higuchi Ichiyō. The professor
poured some tea for us and talked about her experiences. Among her comments were these: "Ichiyō was beautiful and strong and talented. But I feel
that she wasted her talents writing mostly about lower-class people. She
had dealings with upper-class people. If she wanted to, she could have
written about more refined matters. It's a shame, since she was such a talented writer." We didn't know what to say and just looked at each other.

Just prior to this, we had heard an older person who had studied under
Higuchi Ichiyō say that Ichiyō often spoke highly of Professor Yasui's
character. We had been impressed by this.

Professors Tsuda, Yasui, and Kawai were all pure idealists. They were
like angels and saints frolicking about in heaven. They were naive and
innocent, totally cut off from the real world. They were completely unaware of what the students were thinking about and what they were
searching for. After all, Professor Tsuda once told our class that Tolstoy
was an apostate and a harborer of dangerous thoughts, so she did not want
students in her school to read his writings. The institution was as strict as a
convent. Even letters from family members were opened and inspected,
and the school authorities intervened in a host of other personal affairs. . . . Since it was a language school, it was only natural that they concentrated primarily on language instruction, but I was not satisfied with
this and felt frustrated. . . . So I looked into the requirements of Tokyo
University. They stipulated that qualified students would be admitted.
Nowhere did it say that admission was restricted to male students only. So
I asked our teacher of psychology, Sugawa Kyōzō, to help me get permission to audit some courses at the university. The university authorities responded that the term "student" signifies male students. Females do not
fall into this category. . . .

At the end of 1908 I went to the headquarters of the Salvation Army in
Kanda to do volunteer work. I helped them distribute Christmas presents
and Salvation Army pamphlets among the slum dwellers. I was not a
Christian, but I admired the dedicated missionary work the Salvation
Army performed and their efforts to help inmates of brothels gain their
freedom. I had read and been enlightened by Mr. Yamamuro's writings on
public brothels. So I went to them more or less as an outside observer.

Early on Christmas morning, I joined Mr. Yamamuro, Kawai Michiko,
and others to visit a textile factory. . . . At that time the factory was running twenty-four hours a day. A few of the girls who had worked for
twelve hours through the night began to show up in the lecture hall after
breakfast. . . . They looked to be twelve to fifteen years of age, but they
lacked the vitality of the young. They looked pale and tired as if they were
sick. Eventually, fifty to sixty girls came to the lecture hall and sat on the
straw mats that were placed on the cold wooden floor. The only heat in
the room came from the charcoal brazier that had been provided for the
speaker on the platform. The sky was grey, and it seemed as if it would

start snowing any moment. The cold penetrated deeply into our bones. Directed by the lecturer and accompanied by an organ, the girls sang a Christmas carol that was written out on the blackboard. Then Mr. Yamamuro got up to speak.

He told the girls that Our Lord, Jesus Christ, was a laborer just like them. Labor is sacred. "You too must become good workers, just like Our Lord Jesus. You must be grateful that you are able to work every day in good health. Then God will answer your prayers."

Mr. Yamamuro was followed by Kawai Michiko, and she also spoke of the sacred nature of work and in a highly emotional voice intoned a lengthy prayer. The meeting closed with a psalm. All during the ceremony I was seated on the platform but hated being there. I was filled with shame and anger. The girls had worked all night beside roaring machines. They were pale and bloodless. How could they be told that the life they led was due to God's blessings and that they should view this kind of slave labor as sacred and holy?

I had hoped that we would be permitted to see the work area, dormitory, and dining hall and be given a chance to question the girls about their work, but we were not allowed to do so. It seemed that the company authorities did not look favorably on this kind of Christian missionary work. None of the company officials came to the meeting. Only those girls who wanted to come were there. After the meeting Mr. Yamamuro and his group left. I felt that I could never join them in their activities again.

After the ceremony the girls either slept or did their washing and other various things. Then they would have to work through the night again. This routine would be followed all week long. They would lose weight during a week of night work and fail to regain it in the following week when they went back on the day shift. Then, back to night shift the week after. Repeating this schedule caused the textile workers to develop tuberculosis at a rate three times that of other women, and to suffer an extremely high death rate.

Several years later, when we heard Fujii Tei speak on the legal status of women, he loaned us the *Shokkō Jijō* (Condition of the Factory Workers),[54] which was stamped "confidential." At that time, he was drafting a labor law for the Ministry of Agriculture and Commerce. He was an ardent national socialist, upheld the emperor system, favored building up the military forces and acquiring foreign territories, and, at home, adopting social welfare measures. He contended that Japanese socialists were thoughtless and impractical. If Kōtoku Shūsui had not attempted to do such a stupid thing [the Great Treason incident], there would be at least one or two socialist parties in Japan by now. What in the world are the socialists doing? They have not formulated a single draft for labor legislation. They leave it up to bureaucrats like him, so that every time the draft is passed on to the higher-ranking officials it is gutted of meaningful provisions. . . .

In 1916 a labor act was finally passed, but only after it had been tampered with in a hundred different ways and had been emasculated. At that time Yamakawa Hitoshi criticized the law as a public endorsement of the fourteen-hour workday. Fujii got his dander up at this. "Socialists can't see that this law makes a big difference for the women factory workers. If they had any criticism, why didn't they speak up sooner? If they had spoken up and stirred up public support, our draft legislation would not have been cut to bits this way. The labor legislation was not such a tepid proposal when it was being drafted."

The *Shokkō Jijō* would have been the best instrument to arouse public opinion in favor of labor legislation, but it did not see the light of day for about a half a century. Only in 1947, after imperial Japan had been destroyed, did it appear in print publicly. . . .

[In 1912, the Seitōsha sponsored a lecture on women's rights.]

Concerning the discussion on birth control and abortion, Miyajima Reiko wrote, "Harada [Kōgetsu] supported abortions, Itō Noe supported birth control but opposed abortions, Hiratsuka Raichō approved of both measures, while Yamada Waka opposed both." Yamada also opposed the marriage of young people who were not yet ready to have and rear children. Everyone, except Raichō, held poverty and difficulties in maintaining a living as grounds for abortion and birth control. Raichō argued that aside from poverty, intellectual and psychological grounds existed to justify these practices. She argued that "traditional-minded Japanese women who have no awareness of their individuality, and have not had the opportunity to live their own lives [may oppose these practices]. Likewise for lower-class, working women who have no education and who have no leeway in thinking about anything but staying alive. But it puzzles me to find people like you not fighting for these causes."

Needless to say, under current social conditions, it is impossible for women to devote all their energies to becoming totally free, autonomous personalities. Does Raichō believe that those who are frustrated by this dilemma are only those women who are self-aware and cultured, engaged in mental and spiritual work; that they are distinct from lower-class, working women who are ignorant and have to devote their efforts to eating and staying alive? Does she believe that lower-class, working women deliberately give their lives over to the single task of finding enough food to stay alive? That they live like animals out of choice? Such questions about Raichō's contention were harbored by us too.

Ōsugi Sakae praised Baba Kochō's speech at the same meeting.[55] In the audience was Baba's younger sister. She stopped by at Baba's house that evening, waited for him to come home, and castigated him for speaking "such fine words publicly" and behaving like a tyrant at home. Ikuta Chōkō [a literary critic, 1882–1936] also was a supporter of the Seitō-sha and was sympathetic to socialism, but a decade later he made a one-hundred-eighty-degree turn and wrote, "Compared with men, women are closer to savages and animals. If it is permissible to maintain a hierarchy of superior and inferior between adults and children, then it must also be permissible to maintain a hierarchy of superior-inferior between men and women."

Iwanō Hōmei, who also spoke at the meeting, soon abandoned his wife, Kiyoko, and his child and moved on to his third wife.[56]

At just about this time my older sister wrote me: "There are many men who appear to be allies of women and speak on women's issues and argue for equal rights and equal status for women. But you must not be taken in facilely. Many of them, when they leave their homes, become allies and friends of women, but take a look at their households to see how they behave at home. They turn into tyrannical princes and treat their wives and daughters as slaves. Their credo regarding women is 'Let them be dependent; keep them ignorant' [the feudal ruling class's policy toward the masses]. They are like tombstones painted in white."

Again, "Before we criticize others or blame society, we mothers must change our ways and stop rearing our sons differently from our daughters. If we carelessly continue to allow our precious daughters to be reared by an educational policy and system that are designed to produce future mothers who believe in treating boys and girls differently, it would be akin to exposing ourselves to a deadly sword. . . ."

In 1913 the Saionji cabinet fell because it clashed with the army, which was demanding an addition of two divisions to the forces in Korea. General Katsura, who had retired earlier, came back as prime minister. The entire nation fell into a state of turmoil as he continued to persuade the emperor to issue decrees to ram through his policies, while the press took the initiative in opposing him.

One evening I went with my older brother to the Young Men's Hall to listen to political lectures. Article 5 of the Police Security Regulations prohibited women from listening to political speeches. But because there was a crowd we managed to get inside and sit at the back of the second floor.

The first person to appear on the platform was Tanaka Shōzō.[57] He was a short, stocky man. He spoke in a booming voice that shook the rafters, attacking the Furukawa Mining Company and the pollution it had caused. The next speaker was Shimada Saburō [1872–1920], a member of the lower house of the Diet. He was known as a great orator, a Christian advocate for the abolition of the public brothels, and a social reformer. But at just about this time he had sold out to the Katsura cabinet and was one of the political party members who were serving as the government's flunkies. So his speech failed to stir us up, and I was thinking about leaving the hall. Just at that moment a policeman confronted me.

"This is a gathering for political talks, so women are not allowed to attend. Please leave." He spoke quietly, apparently trying not to draw the attention of those sitting nearby. But when I was told to leave I did not feel like obeying him docilely.

"My presence here is not bothering anybody, is it? Please let me be."

The young policeman was about to say something more, but the people around us began to get aroused, so my older brother headed for the exit. I followed him out reluctantly. But there was no law against reading political works, so I began to read political commentaries rather carefully. . . .

During the fall of 1918 a few students from Tokyo Women's College began to visit me in my home. . . . The following summer several students from that college and Yamaguchi Koshizu, a fourth-year student at a senior teachers' college, got together and organized a socialist study group. . . . They held their meetings at my home several times and asked Yamakawa Hitoshi to speak to them. They also expressed interest in meeting with women workers and exchanging ideas with them. [Such a meeting was arranged.] Thereupon the police went to Tokyo Women's College to investigate the matter. Professor Yasui Tetsuko was terrified, and the ensuing controversy led to the voluntary withdrawal from college of a couple of students involved in the affair. Several others ceased coming to my home. . . .

In the early 1920s, one of the anarchists' slogans was "Reject the Intellectual Class." This slogan was popular at one time among the working class too. Ōsugi himself was an avid reader of books and was a distinguished intellectual, but he warned against being ruled solely by bookish knowledge. So his ideas were misconstrued among his followers at the lower levels. Also the workers, affected by a touch of inferiority complex, resented young men just out of college taking over the leadership of labor unions. The intellectuals' reaction to this was an inferiority complex of a different sort. While the workers were trying to emulate students, the students wore work clothes and, instead of using words they ordinarily used in college, affected the speech of workers. The more fainthearted they were the more they tried to swagger and act rough and tough like workers. Or else they tried to flatter and fawn upon them.

I felt that it was not my fault that I was not born into the working class. As for intellectual pursuits, I was bothered about my lack of learning, so I could not afford to scoff at learning and knowledge. An intellectual who does not belong to a class independent of the capitalists is not ipso facto a running dog of the capitalists. Intellectuals as intellectuals can contribute to the socialist revolution. I put my ideas on this matter in print once and got a rather unfavorable reception. . . .

[During the Great Earthquake of September 1, 1923, the Yamakawa house was destroyed and the family found a temporary dwelling in a tenement house.]

By the third [of September] the fire had subsided, but rumors persisted that Koreans and socialists could be killed on sight. The whole city took on a murderous air as Koreans and socialists were rounded up. People spoke of Koreans and socialists being arrested, cut down, or being chased around, dripping with blood. . . . A young police officer who was assigned to keep us under surveillance told us that on the evening of the fourth the police were being pressured by the mob to produce Yamakawa or reveal his hiding place. The police had told them that they did not know where we were, but the officer advised us to go into hiding because the mob might locate our temporary residence. . . .

On the morning of the twenty-third, Yoshimoto Tetsuzō, an acquaintance and a newspaper reporter for the *Jiji Shimpō*, came and told us, "Oh, I'm glad that you are safe. How is Mr. Yamakawa? Is he all right? . . . Mr. Ōsugi has been killed. Itō Noe, too. By the gendarmes. There's a rumor that you too had been killed. . . ."

Mr. Ōsugi was kind to children. His younger sister's son, Tachibana Sōichi, was in poor health, so he had gone to bring him home with him in order to take care of the boy during the chaos of the Great Earthquake. On the way home, he stopped at Dr. Okuyama's and had him give the child a shot. When he arrived home, the gendarmes were waiting for him. . . .

The murder of Ōsugi and others was uncovered by the reporter Yoshimoto and exposed in the newspaper *Jiji Shimpō*. The news created a public outburst, and the atrocities ceased. If these murders had not been exposed as quickly as they were by the press, we too could have suffered Ōsugi's fate because we had taken refuge in my parents' home in Kōjimachi, which was right near the gendarme headquarters.

Former army lieutenant Matsushita Yoshio, who had resigned his commission, was active in socialist circles at just about this period. Later, he told Yamakawa that when he attended a reunion of his army academy class, one of his former classmates told him:

During the Great Earthquake I was in charge of guarding the Ōmori area. I intended to do in the Yamakawa couple and looked for them all over, but their house was destroyed by the earthquake and they had taken refuge somewhere. I asked the police and others, but no one seemed to know where they were. Then the news about the Ōsugi affair came out. I was surprised to see Amakasu [the killer of Ōsugi] tried in military court. During that time, we were all under the impression that we would get promoted if we killed some socialists. I almost got myself in trouble.

So the three members of our family survived both the natural and the man-made disasters. . . . We are grateful to our friends and comrades as well as to many strangers who helped us. The police warned us that they were unable to protect us and advised us to go into hiding. The military were searching for us, but the police did not cooperate with them. If they had, we would have been in serious trouble. The police evidently were governed by their conscience and pride. Perhaps they were sensitive about protecting their jurisdiction too. At any rate, we were fortunate that the police were not controlled by the military. . . .

The unlucky ones were the union members of Nankatsu. A group of them had taken refuge from the earthquake together, and a large number of them were brutally murdered en masse. One of the victims, Kawai Yoshitora, was probably barely twenty. He was young and guileless. We looked upon him as a young worker with a great future. The summer before the earthquake he had joined us for supper at our home. Being a playful person, when he picked up the rice bowl and the chopsticks he wailed, "Aah, I wonder if the rice is the usual watery gruel they serve here." We all burst out laughing. I still recall the pitiful face he made. I am sure he was dressed in his shirt without a coat as usual, and died in a shower of bullets and in a pool of blood shouting "Banzai for the revolution!"

Among the others was Adachi Yoshiaki, who had to quit the higher commercial school in Kobe because his father died when he was a student. He was about twenty or so and had experienced all sorts of hardships. The person who used to come and visit us with Adachi was Tsukamoto, a worker of about the same age. He was chased around by a mob in Kotō-ku and finally murdered. Adachi was an expert swimmer, so he jumped into the Sumida River and escaped. . . .

In May or June [of 1924] Muraki Genjirō came to visit us unexpectedly. He had known our son, Shinsaku, since he was born. He was pleased to see him now attending school. He stayed with us for a few days, relaxing. He took Shinsaku out to the beach for walks and to the strawberry field to pick berries. I was not aware that he was paying us a farewell visit. In September he attempted to assassinate General Fukuda Masatarō [martial-law commander during the earthquake] to avenge Ōsugi's murder, but he failed. His friend Wada Kyūtarō committed suicide in prison. Muraki fell critically ill in prison and was released temporarily, but he died soon after. . . .

[On March 15, 1928, the government staged mass arrests of leftists, whose family members were left to shift for themselves.]

How did the families of these people, not just Communists but young fighters, who devoted their time and energy to the cause without holding a fixed job, survive economically? Recently Tadokoro Yaeko and I talked about this.[58] She said:

We didn't have a fixed income. Many barely got by, with the wives taking in miscellaneous work at home. When I think about it, it seems incredible. There was no money even to ride the trolley. Some sold newspapers and magazines to make enough money for transportation. But there was not enough trolley fare for the wives. Once we were completely out of food and money. We were then living behind a Shinto shrine. Tadokoro and I went for a walk in the shrine compounds and found a long *gobō* [burdock] root, which may have been dropped by a vegetable vendor. We picked it up and lived on it for three days. Often comrades from the outlying areas would come and stay with us. But I never thought that the situation was too difficult or unbearable. I was perfectly contented. If we had tried to live by today's "budget planning," none of us would have been able to take part in political activities. Of course, unlike today, we were able to get things on credit and pay at the end of the month. . . .

[Among those arrested in 1928 was Nishi Masao, who was also one of the helpers of the Yamakawas in publishing the *Zen'ei* (Vanguard).]

Soon after his release [late 1932] Nishi visited me at my temporary home. His face was puffy and sallow. He inquired about Mr. Sakai Toshihiko, who was ill. He spoke about the hard times he had experienced, and commented on the fact that the judges treated those with education and those without differently. Even after they are released from prison, college graduates manage to find jobs and sources of income through family ties and friends, but those like him who were not college graduates and had no influential ties found no one to help them and were left in a quandary.

Later, Mr. Nishi managed to find employment with the research division of the South Manchurian Railway and was in China when the war started. He had severed his ties with the Communist party years before, but he was arrested by the military, and he died in prison in Manchuria. . . .

[In December 1937 Yamakawa's husband was again arrested.]

The officer in charge of investigating Yamakawa Hitoshi, Detective Yano, remarked that Yamakawa was at a disadvantage because he had not graduated from college. He had left Dōshisha middle school without graduating. The judges were all college graduates, worshippers of college professors, who were biased toward those with higher education. His remarks confirmed what Mr. Nishi had told me earlier. I heard later that the detective himself had only two years of schooling beyond the compulsory six years of elementary education. As a result, he was constantly being bypassed by young college graduates, who got all the recognition in his department. So he was bitter about the educational bias. It seems that in our country whether one goes to hell or not depends on one's education.

[The Yamakawas eked out a living raising chickens and quails and greeted the end of the war in a village in Hiroshima prefecture.]

SIX

FROM THE FACTORIES AND RICE PADDIES

Tanno Setsu

Most of the women in the Seitōsha and the Sekirankai came from the middle class or the lower middle class, not from the factories or tenant farms. In that respect, if Hiratsuka and others were charged with pursuing essentially bourgeois values, the critics may not have been completely off the mark. But as the labor movement broadened its base of support more and more women workers were drawn into the movement, and some emerged as active labor leaders of the workers. Furthermore, those who did not become leaders did express their aspirations either verbally or by supporting the movement. Some even joined revolutionary movements.

Among the women workers who joined the sociopolitical movement (and who did so fully willing to suffer persecution at the hand of the established authorities) was Tanno Setsu. Unlike many socialist and communist leaders who sought to lead the workers from the outside, Tanno went into the factory as a worker. She insisted that she was a worker, not a theorist, and stayed her course, not because of any intellectual or theoretical convictions but because of her personal experiences.[1]

Tanno was born in 1902 in Fukushima prefecture. Her father, a carpenter, moved to work in the Hitachi mines (as a carpenter) in Ibaraki prefecture, where she joined him and her family when she was ten. As she relates in her memoirs, she went into nurse's training after finishing elementary school. While there, she met several young men who were influenced by socialist and communist thought, Kawai Yoshitora, Kitajima Kichizō, and Sōma Ichirō. Both Kawai and Kitajima were later murdered by the authorities during the Great Earthquake. When these young men left for Tokyo to work in the factories of Nankatsu in the Kameido district of Tokyo, she joined them in 1921. She took a job in a factory and began playing an active role in the Nankatsu labor union. She also joined the Gyōminkai (Enlightened People's Society), a socialist study group organized by Takatsu Seidō, and also became a member of the Sekirankai. Among the leaders of the labor union in Kameido was Watanabe Masanosuke (1899–1928) who, following the mass arrests of the Communist leaders in March 1928, eventually became the general secretary of the Communist party. In 1924 she and Watanabe were married.

Tanno became an active member of the Hyōgikai, the Communist wing of the labor union, and, as was noted in Kutsumi's memoirs, was instrumental in establishing a women's division in the Hyōgikai. Watanabe became more active in the Communist party, and when the controversy over Fukumotoism broke out (see Kutsumi in chapter 5), he initially supported Fukumoto's position. When Moscow called the diverse factions to the Soviet Union to lay down the party line, Yamakawa's faction remained in Japan while Watanabe went with Fukumoto and others. When Watanabe found out that Moscow disapproved of Fukumotoism, he changed his position and embraced the official party line as formulated in the 1927 Thesis.[2] This thesis called for a two-stage revolution in Japan because the objective circumstances that set the stage for a bourgeois democratic revolution were present, and at the same time circumstances also existed for a rapid transition from that revolution to a socialist revolution. Yamakawa's position was condemned for playing down the importance of the party in the revolutionary process, and Fukumotoism was rejected for emphasizing revolutionary theory at the expense of revolutionary mass struggle.[3] After Watanabe took over the party leadership, he went to Shanghai to attend a trade union meeting and on his way back stopped over in Taiwan, where he was discovered by the police and was killed in a shoot-out.

This traumatic experience for Tanno had been preceded by an earlier tragedy. During the Great Earthquake, the authorities had murdered her comrades from Hitachi and Kameido. As she relates in her memoirs, Tanno had managed to hide and escape. Though she had joined the Communist party in 1926, she was not arrested during the mass arrests of March 1928. In October of that year, however, she was arrested and imprisoned. While in prison she heard of Watanabe's death. In November 1929 she was temporarily paroled and left the prison to recover from tuberculosis. She tried to go into hiding but was rearrested and returned to prison, where she remained until September 1938.

After her release she returned to her family in Onahama in Fukushima prefecture. There the family members kept a close watch over her to prevent her from resuming her life as a social activist. The family felt a deep bitterness toward her because her work as a Communist had resulted in social criticism for her family. Her nephews complained because they were being picked on at school; her younger brother beat her, accusing her of causing her parents and brothers unhappiness. Tanno managed to leave home, however, and joined Watanabe's mother for awhile. Then in order to escape surveillance by the special police, she married a man who was employed in China. The marriage did not work out, however, and she returned to Japan after four months. She then got a job as a visiting nurse with the help of Minami Kiichi, a Communist activist who had defected. This perhaps explains why some people have wondered whether or not she did resist the authorities' efforts to get her to defect.[4] She was arrested briefly at the outbreak of the war with the United States but was released the following day. Tanno spent the war years working as a public health nurse. When the war ended and the Communist leaders, who had challenged the government's policies and had been imprisoned, were released, her father remarked to her, "I see, the Communists were right after all. . . . I understand why poor people become Communists. I understand now why you did what you did. I made you suffer too much in poverty in Hitachi."[5] Tanno returned to Nankatsu and established a clinic to provide health care for the workers.

The following is translated from the oral history of Tanno Setsu's life. The interviewers were Makise Kikue, Yamashiro Tomoe, and others. The interviews were conducted in 1966.[6] Because her recollections reach back nearly half a century, they may not be completely accurate, but they do reflect the experiences of a person who struggled for her cause during turbulent decades. The excerpts begin with Tanno's response when she was asked about her life among the miners in Hitachi.

I am not a miner's child. I was born a carpenter's daughter in Onahama in Fukushima prefecture. My father got a job in the mines in Hitachi [in Ibaraki prefecture], so we moved there. I lived in one of the tenement houses of the miners from the time I was in the fifth grade to the upper-level elementary school [two years beyond the compulsory six years of elementary education]. These were the most impressionable years of my life, so living in Hitachi influenced my thinking in a profound way.

When we arrived in Hitachi the Number Two Hydroelectric Plant was being built in the hills beyond Isowara. Father went to Hitachi to work on that project. Those were years of growth for Hitachi. In Hitachi there were the main mines (known as Honzan) and the smelting plants in Daiyūin. Father worked as a carpenter in Daiyūin. . . .

[There were different types of housing, depending on a person's status in the mining company.] We lived in one of the tenement houses for the ordinary miners. We had a single-room unit, eight mats in size, but the room had only four mats on the floor. A two-mat area was unmatted, the kitchen took up another mat space, and the dirt floor consisted of another mat space. There was no sink or running water. We spread straw mats on the unmatted part of the floor, so our living area consisted of six mats. Each tenement building had six of these units and a single toilet. Four houses of twenty-four households shared a common tap. Each unit had a single entrance, and a window with wooden bars was at one end of the room. It was just like a prison cell.

All the children of the mining community—the children of ordinary workers, foremen, section chiefs, staff workers, and administrators—attended the same school. I realized what a vast gulf there was between the lives of the children, depending on their parents' positions. My father was a worker with special skills, a carpenter, and he was fairly old, so he was paid 67 sen a day, which was comparatively good pay. Ordinary workers made about 40 to 42 sen a day. Most workers were young and had two or three children, so they had a hard time. Despite Father's wages, we had a very difficult time, for our family was large.

In those days the Hitachi mine workers were given chits three times a month—every ten days—so they could buy necessities at the company commissary. The amount due each worker was recorded in a company passbook. For example, a worker getting 60 sen a day would have 6 yen credited to his passbook. Our family was large, and we consumed 3 shō [1 shō equals 1.8 litres] of rice each day. One shō of rice cost 18 sen, so we would consume 54 sen worth of rice in one day, and in ten days 5 yen 40 sen worth. Father got paid 6 yen 70 sen every ten days. Because our family had to purchase food, including rice, and other items with this, we had a hard time. Whatever was not available at the commissary had to be purchased in regular stores with cash, so the family was constantly short of money, and Father's passbook account was always in the red.

In those days workers had to work twelve hours a day. They were given three days off during New Year's and one day off during the summer Bon [Buddhist] festival. Later, they were given the first and fifteenth of each month off. In order to get to work by six o'clock, Father had to leave home at five. Mother got up at four every morning. When Mother got up, the baby would start crying, so Mother would wake me up to take care of the baby. My older sister was working as a nurse in a hospital in Kawagoe [in Saitama prefecture], so I was the only one old enough at home to help. Father was a strict disciplinarian, and I would jump right up when I was awakened.

Because our family finances were so strained my parents could not buy me sandals with hemp soles, which cost 10 sen a pair. Instead, I had to wear sandals with soles of bamboo sheath, which cost only 2 sen. For 11 sen one could buy a pair of geta with red straps, but we couldn't afford them. We couldn't even afford to buy geta to wear in the snow, so we had to go to school in the snow with just cloth socks.

[Tanno went two years beyond the six years of elementary education that were required by law and hoped to enter normal school and become a teacher. But her father said he could not afford to send her to normal school, so she enrolled in a nurse's training program in a hospital in Hitachi.]

I was admitted to the nurses' training program in the Honzan hospital. The daily wage at the hospital was eighteen sen. After paying for my meals I was able to save one yen a month.

There were about fifteen or sixteen other trainee nurses. Whenever they went home, they returned with sweets made by their mothers and shared them with the rest of us. I never brought anything back from home, and I was always at the receiving end of these favors. It was so embarrassing I began to buy some yams, have mother bake them, and bring them back to the dormitory with me. I also used to buy something to share with my friends on the way back to the dormitory. After the spring of my sixteenth year I did not receive any help from my family, not even one sen. I had to use my savings of one yen a month to buy my clothes and consequently could not send any money to help them out. This was in 1917. [When Tanno was asked what factors influenced her thinking, she responded]:

I was first influenced by the magazine *Fujin Kōron*. When I became a nursing trainee and began to work on my own, I subscribed to it and read it regularly. My family could not afford to buy me books, so when I could afford my own I was really delighted. In those days *Fujin Kōron,* unlike magazines today, published serious articles. Many of them dealt with issues related to women's political rights. The chief of the hospital called me in and warned me about reading the magazine. He reprimanded me, saying, "You have not even taken the nurse's qualifying examination. You shouldn't be reading a magazine like that."

The hospital authorities began to keep their eyes on me. When I showed Sōma Sada, who was a year ahead of me in the program, a copy of the *Fujin Kōron* she was impressed by the difficult articles.

Sōma Sada was a devout Christian, and on occasion I attended church services with her. I really can't say that I was searching for a "philosophy," but I was beginning to look for something. Sōma's younger brother, Sōma Ichirō, came to the hospital to have a nose operation, and a couple of young men used to come and see him from time to time. They were Kawai Yoshitora and Kitajima Kichizō. The three men seemed to be harboring socialist ideas in a vague sort of way. They evidently had been influenced by Oka Sensei, a teacher at the hospital. At that time I knew nothing about socialism.

I was told that Oka Sensei was a bachelor who lived in the dorm supervisor's quarters. I never met him. On days off I would go with the three men to the seashore along Sukegawa. They would talk to me about what they had learned from Oka Sensei. When I spoke to them about my ideas concerning the political rights of women, they would say, "That is a feminist movement. The liberation of the workers is the more important task facing us now." I did understand what they meant by "workers' liberation." I thought of my father's life in the mines and the poverty-stricken lives that my brothers and sisters led. I realized that I was wrong to have thought that my father was a man without gumption. I began to understand and sympathize with him after I began talking with these three young men.

Sometimes as many as thirty miners suffering from gas poisoning would be brought into the hospital. When I approached them, the smell of gas was overpowering. The family members would be clinging to the victims and wailing. Whenever we gave first aid to victims at the mouth of the mine, family members of miners still trapped in the mine would stand around wailing and crying.

Wives who lost their husbands in these accidents took jobs with the mines as sorters, mine-cart pushers, or menial workers. Patients in the hospital included those who had lost their eyes and legs in mine explosions. There were mine disaster victims who were crippled and unable to walk. I was exposed to these miserable conditions day after day, so that when these men spoke of "workers' liberation" I knew what they were talking about.

My three friends were already reading Ōsugi Sakae's *Rōdō Shimbun* (Labor News). They talked to me about the Kōtoku Shūsui affair. When they described how Shūsui's comrades went after his remains and while gathering his ashes cried, "O Shūsui, O Shūsui," I too cried and my heart raced. They told me that among Shūsui's comrades was a woman named Kanno Sugako. "She was the greatest woman Japan has produced," they said. I heard the word "socialism" for the first time from them.

After we took the nurse's qualifying examination, the other women began to study for their midwife's certificate, but I was no longer interested. My head was full of socialism, and I decided I had to work for the cause. In November 1919 the three young men invited me to a lecture sponsored by the Yūaikai in the Honzan theater.

When we got to the theater, we found the place in turmoil. I had no idea what was going on, but hearing that people were being arrested, I rushed home. The meeting had been called to organize a Yūaikai chapter in Honzan. For this reason, Asō Hisashi, Tanabashi Kotora, Suzuki Bunji, and others had come to speak. As soon as the meeting started, however, the authorities ordered the group to disperse. Later, when I was living in Kameido, I was told by Fujinuma that his wife was then working as a hairdresser in Daiyūin and he was the organizer of the Yūaikai in Hitachi.[7]

Before this incident, my three friends and I had organized a socialist study group. But after the organization meeting of the Yūaikai, we decided that to help the workers it was more important to organize labor unions than to spread socialistic concepts. Labor unions organized by the Yūaikai began to proliferate, but at the same time people active in the labor movement were fired. Kawai was among the first, and he left for Tokyo. Then we heard that when the authorities suppressed the move to organize the Shakaishugi Dōmei (Socialist Alliance), Kawai was among those arrested for "destruction of public buildings." He was sent to prison in Sugamo. This was in September 1920. The following year during New Year's vacation I left the hospital and went to see Kawai in Sugamo.

For a time Sōma, Kitajima, and I met to read Ōsugi Sakae's *Labor News*, which Kawai sent us. Then we decided that there was little we could do for the movement in Hitachi. We had to learn more about labor problems and socialism, so we decided to move to Tokyo. First Sōma went, and then Kitajima and I followed.

I had not completed the three years' service that I owed the hospital for my training, but I left for Tokyo without fulfilling my term of service in order to pursue my study of socialism. Sōma Ichirō's older sister was working as a nurse in Kyōundō Hospital, and I went to see her, to ask if she could not help me find a job. In those days many nurses came to Tokyo to look for work. Another friend was working as a nurse in Juntendō Hospital, and I got a job there.

Since their children were all grown, my parents had left Hitachi and returned to Onahama. After settling in Tokyo, I informed my father that I had quit the hospital in Hitachi and had come out to Tokyo. My parents were surprised, and went to the Honzan Hospital to confer with the authorities. They were advised to bring me back from Tokyo. My older sister's husband arrived from Ushigome and told me, "At least return to Hitachi to bring back your belongings."

I agreed and returned to Onahama. My brother-in-law went to Honzan Hospital and paid a fine of three hundred yen, and I returned to Tokyo.

After I got back, I went to the office of the Gyōminkai in Tozuka Genbei with an introduction from Kawai. I made arrangements to stay there. The Gyōminkai was being managed by Takatsu Seidō. His wife, Tayoko, and their baby, Gyōko, lived there too. Sakai Magara also came there often. Takatsu had just been released after having been arrested in the Gyōmin-Communist incident.[8]

While living at the Gyōminkai I attended meetings of the Sekirankai and also visited Sakai Toshihiko. Sakai said that since I had a nurse's certificate, he would introduce me at the clinic in Shimbashi, which treated patients at cost. That's how I started working there. Shirayanagi Shūko was also associated with the clinic.[9] He would come there from time to time and, showing his concern for me, would ask me, "How are things going? Do you think you'll be able to get by all right?"

The magazine *Tane Maku Hito* (Sowers of Seeds) had just appeared.[10] I decided to attend the Kanda English-language school, in part to introduce the magazine to the students there. It may sound strange today, but I did go to the English-language school to study English. Since childhood, I had a strong desire for education, for learning. I met many people interested in the magazine *Tane Maku Hito*. I realize now that these people were anarchists. We organized a society to study *Tane Maku Hito* and met regularly.

We then decided to start another magazine, one different from *Tane Maku Hito*. I was asked to contribute, so I submitted a poem. A person named Yamaguchi Yosondo had taken the leadership in publishing the magazine. He was charged with lèse majesté for his article and arrested. Perhaps because he had visited me at the clinic I too was taken to the police headquarters and questioned.

I was shocked. I had not expected anything like this to happen. At the time, I was just given a dressing down and released. Yamaguchi Yosondo later wrote to me from prison. When the affair got into the papers, I received a telegram from home, saying, "Mother critically ill. Return immediately." Until then Mother had never been sick, so I was suspicious of the telegram. Then my older brother, who was living in Ōimachi, came and castigated me: "Why are you procrastinating? You've got to go home right away." I was as flustered as a child and returned home to Onahama with him. When we approached the front of our house, I saw the silhouette of my mother's hair, which was put up in Japanese style the way women used to wear their hair in those days, on the paper door. I thought, "Aha, they must have seen the article. They've tricked me into coming home."

At that time, neither my father nor my mother knew anything about socialism. To them, it was only a frightful thing. So they put me under strict surveillance, not allowing me even to step outside. But I was determined to run away. One day when no one was home, I donned Mother's cloak and stepped out into the back alley. My older brother was standing there. He caught me and escorted me back to the house.

The following April, in 1922, a festival in Kamado in honor of the God Osuwa [protector of warriors] was held. A colorful mock procession of a daimyō and his retinue was staged. Grandmother was invited by relatives in Kamado to the festivities. I went along to accompany her and my younger sister, who was not yet in school. After the festival, people headed home, a long line of them strung out along a narrow path. We were surrounded. When I looked back I could see neither my grandmother nor my

younger sister. I decided to seize the moment and run away. I pushed my
way frantically through the crowd and rushed to the railroad station. The
train was just about to pull out. I had set aside three yen for train fare, so I
bought a ticket and hopped on the train. (Afterwards, Grandmother remained bitter about my action and said she would never forgive me.)

When I arrived in Tokyo, I went to Sakai's place. Hirabayashi Taiko
had just arrived from Shinshū [Nagano prefecture] as well.[11] Sakai introduced Hirabayashi to me and said, "She too is a runaway. There are many
runaways nowadays." Once again I began attending the Gyōminkai and
Sekirankai meetings. In those days the word "socialism," even the word
"society," could not be used. The Gyōminkai was raided often, and we
spent many nights in the police station.

The central figures in the Sekirankai were Sakai Magara, Kutsumi
Fusako, Yamakawa Kikue, the writer Kitagawa Chiyo, Orkiu, the wife of
Hashiura, his younger sister, Haruko, Tachibara Okō, and Takatsu Tayoko. Most of them were family members of socialists—wives, daughters,
and sisters. Magara, Tayoko, and others distributed handbills among soldiers and were arrested. This made the Sekirankai famous.

Sano Manabu, who was then a professor at Waseda University, lectured
at the Sekirankai on the *Communist Manifesto*. Takano Minoru and Yamakawa Kikue also came and talked to the group frequently.[12] Inomata
Tsunao used to come with his beautiful Russian wife.[13] She taught us the
Internationale. The Russian poet Yaroshenko also used to attend meetings.[14]

The Gyōminkai and the Sekirankai demonstrated against "legislation
to curb radical socialist activities," sold hand towels with the legend Save
the Starving Russians (May 1922), raised money for hunger relief, opposed
the dispatching of Japanese troops to Siberia by organizing the Alliance Against Intervention in Russia (June 22, 1922), among other things.
The Gyōminkai and Sekirankai worked together and shared a common
outlook.

The Sekirankai and its successor, the Yōkakai, met at Yabe Hatsuko's
place, which was located on the hilltop of Kagurazaka. I am especially
indebted to Yabe. Because I had run away from home I had no place to
stay, so she often let me stay with her. Her mother gave me many kimonos.

At about this time [1922] Watanabe [Masanosuke] and others organized
the Nankatsu Labor Union [in Kameido]. Members of the Nankatsu
union used to come to the Gyōminkai. Among them were my friends from
the Hitachi mine days, Kawai Yoshitora, Kitajima Kichizō, and Sōma

Ichirō. There were a couple of other men who used to come wearing workers' overalls. After I came to Kameido I found out that they were the brothers Yoshimura Mitsuji and Minami Iwao.

Other members of the Gyōminkai were all members of the intelligentsia, and so basically the Gyōminkai was an intellectual organization whose members engaged in intellectual studies. Then, however, a call to "go among the people" arose. I decided to quit nursing and go into the factory, and so I came to Kameido. It was the fall before the Great Earthquake [of 1923]. I decided that it was impossible to stage a revolution through intellectual studies in women's organizations and groups like the Gyōminkai and the Sekirankai. It was perfectly natural for me to go into the factory and make the factory the center of my activities. At just about that time the Nankatsu Labor Union was being formed, so I was fortunate.

When I worked in the Hitachi hospital there had been a student nurse in a class below me by the name of Sakanoue Kiyo. By chance I knew her home, so I used her name and went to work in Seikōsha [watch company]. If I had used my own name, they would not have hired me. The daily wage at Seikōsha was 82 sen. At that time it was good pay for women workers. In the textile factories the pay was 62 to 65 sen a day, and in the Mitazuchi rubber plant it was 72 to 73 sen. The first time I stood before the machine in the plant I felt I would go deaf with the roar of the belts.

Kawai Yoshitora had been arrested when he organized the Socialist Alliance. After his release from Sugamo prison, he went to live with an anarchist, Nakanomio Kōriki, in Ōji Asukayama [north of Tokyo]. Then he came with Kitajima to Kameido, and his mother and younger sister joined him from Hitachi. Sōma Ichirō also came from Hitachi with all his family members and acquired a big house near the Kameido station; he ran a boarding house. So the four of us who had been together in Hitachi were together again in Kameido. The Nankatsu Labor Union used the second floor of the Kawai house, and more and more new members joined the union. There were always six or seven people living on the second floor of the Kawai home.

Kawai spent much of his time hustling around on union business and put very little time in at the factory, and his mother used to complain about that. In those days there were no paid union workers, so one had to earn a living and pay out of one's own pocket all the expenses incurred in union work, like transportation costs. Kitajima used to work at the Hirose bicycle plant where Sugiura was working. Kawai and Sōma also worked in a bicycle plant. Watanabe was working in a nearby soap factory after he was fired from the Nagamine Celluloid Factory for his role in the labor dispute. At about this time a split began to develop between the Bolsheviks and the anarchists. When I first arrived in Kameido, people were singing "Display the Black Flag." I wondered what the song of the black flag was about.[15] At that time the differences between the Bolsheviks and the anarchists were not very acute.

[Regarding her encounter with Watanabe, she related]: Katō Takatoshi, who was killed in the Kameido massacre during the Great Earthquake, had a unit in the same tenement house where Watanabe lived. The Nankatsu group used to meet there and hold study sessions. One cold winter night I saw a man, wearing heavy quilted apparel, standing in front of the blackboard and lecturing passionately on *Das Kapital* in a loud voice. I had never before heard anyone lecture on *Das Kapital*. The study groups I attended examined only the *Communist Manifesto,* and I was amazed to come across a worker who was capable of lecturing on *Das Kapital*. At that time I wondered if I could ever understand the work and also wondered if it was necessary for workers to study it. This guy is incredible, I thought. That person was Watanabe.

Watanabe and I were brought together in a somewhat odd fashion. Kawai and I had been close friends from our days in Hitachi. I had come to Kameido because Kawai was there. When I began going to the Nankatsu Labor Union office in the Kawai house, his mother objected, saying, "I don't want any woman who is active in the movement in my house." One day Kawai brought me over to Watanabe's place and asked him to be my mentor. And he asked me, "Why don't you get acquainted with him?" I had already met Watanabe through our union work but Kawai tried to bring us together this way too.

Kawai may have decided to end his relationship with me, not because of his mother's objections, but because he thought that I would prefer Watanabe to him. Watanabe did not know anything about my relationship with Kawai, and he thought we should become better acquainted. But at that time I wasn't interested. I had just started to work in the factory, and I was also interested in pursuing my studies in socialism. I had no time for anything else.

Each Nankatsu Labor Union member was expected to bring at least one worker from the factory where he or she was working to the office to take part in the study sessions. We had no time to talk about personal matters; we had barely enough time to discuss our study topic because we had to go to work in the factory early the next morning. My personal relationship with Kawai had begun to lapse. I was peeved at him for trying to shunt me off onto someone else just because his mother objected. What kind of love affair was this? Kawai's mother had invited his cousin from Akita to help with the housework, and she had plans to bring the two of them together. So I began to regard Kawai with contempt and no longer cared about our relationship. I'm not a clinging vine. I just drifted away from him.

I used to see Watanabe in our study sessions, but no special relationship developed, though I did think that Watanabe was a more effective leader than Kawai. (It was only later when Watanabe was arrested in the first roundup of Communists and disappeared from the scene that I realized I was in love with him.)

Right about then I was forced to return to Onahama with my older brother. One day, without any advance warning, Watanabe arrived in Onahama to bring me back to Kameido. Members of my family listened to Watanabe, but failed to see his point of view, and he had to return without me. I wanted at least to see him off at the station, but I wasn't allowed to do so, and my older brother saw him off. Later Watanabe told me that he had planned to find out where my home was and then get me to leave with him that night. However, because I came running out when I caught a glimpse of him, he couldn't carry out his plan.

From then on, my family kept close watch over me, and even though I wanted to run away, I couldn't find the right opportunity. Finally, when nobody was home, I managed to get away, but I had to run off without taking anything with me. All I had were the clothes on my back. Counting the first time I left Hitachi, this was the third time that I had run away from home. It was January 1923, and I returned to Kameido.

The Noda Soy Sauce Manufacturer's strike [in Chiba prefecture] took place in March 1923. We from the Nankatsu Labor Union went to support the strikers. . . . The Nankatsu union had not been in existence very long and had no money, not even train fare. So we got up early in the morning and started walking to Noda in our straw sandals. We wore out two pairs of sandals getting there. It was noon when we arrived in Noda. As we walked along the bank of the Edo River approaching the town of Noda, we sang revolutionary songs, waving the Red Flag. We had traveled on foot because we were broke, but it was also partly done to stage a demonstration march. The strikers were waiting for us. We had kept in touch through people running back and forth, so they knew when to expect us. I still remember the delicious rice-balls flavored with soy sauce they served us.

The roof of the factory dormitory was being used as a speaker's platform. I went up there, and for the first time in my life I made a brief speech to the strikers. I can't even remember what I said.

One day Kawai called me out of the union office. I had no idea what he wanted. When I went up to him he spoke in a serious tone of voice. "Do you think there is a Communist party in Japan?" I replied quickly, "I think there is one." Kawai then said, "We are planning to organize a Communist youth league, unite the young people, and fight for the revolution. Would you be willing to join us?" This was the first time I heard that there was actually a Communist party in Japan and that a Communist youth league was about to be formed.

In April 1923 the Communist Youth League was organized and Kawai became the chairman. I joined the league. I recalled the discussions in the Sekirankai by Sano Manabu, Takano Minoru, and others about the *Communist Manifesto*. My heart raced when I thought, "So the leviathan has finally appeared in Japan too." I was delighted, but at the same time I was anxious. I sang to myself, "The revolution is coming. . . . We must be ready, if necessary, to face the dungeon, the scaffold. . . ."

In June of that year [1923], Communist party members were arrested. I was afraid that both Watanabe and Kawai had been arrested, but the two of them returned after about a week. According to Sugiura Buntarō, who was a union member then, they received word that all union members should go into hiding. Watanabe took everyone with no place to hide to Ichikawa Sugano's mother's home and went in hiding with them. Later they got word from Kawai's mother that the police would be satisfied if just one party member from the group turned himself in. The group argued over who it should be. They all said "I'll go! I'll go!" But, in the end, they agreed to let Watanabe, as the leader, have the honor of being arrested. So Watanabe turned himself in. The chief of the Kameido police station came for him in a car. He was then placed in Ichigaya prison to await trial. At that time the Police Security Regulations were in effect and anyone arrested could be incarcerated for up to ten months. So Watanabe must have decided to go to prison for ten months and do some studying

lived like that if we were not dedicated to the ideals of the revolution. Party members today all have their private lives. We didn't have any private life in those days.

When we were short of money, it was really rough. Just before the mass arrests of March 15 [1928], we were in a terrible fix. When Watanabe came back from Kyushu all he had was two sen. At the hideout, Nakano had no money at all. I went to my older sister in Tsurumi and borrowed some money in return for my watch. She gave me five yen. I was so grateful. I never forgot that.

We were always afraid of being arrested. Once I had to go and make change for a hundred-yen bill. One hundred yen was a lot of money in those days. If I went to a money changer he would charge for the service, so I decided to go to Matsuzakaya Department Store and buy something. Then I wouldn't have to pay a service charge. I knew it would be a risky venture, so I took a taxicab to the store. Suddenly, a person who looked like an agent of the Special Higher Police ordered the cab to stop. I was frightened, but when he told me, "Please get out of the cab for a moment," I asked him, "Do you have some business with me?" He then said, "Oh, I'm sorry, I thought you were someone else." Knowing they were on the lookout for me, I told the cab driver to drive farther on and then got out. I was scared. I went round and round trying to lose the lookout. I took off my coat, balled it up, and threw it in a trash bin. I finally managed to get away, but it was really a dreadful experience.

The journal *Akahata* (Red Flag) first appeared on February 1, 1928. . . . I wrote the following article under the name Yamaguchi Haru for the second issue [March 15, 1928].

To the Revolution-Minded Women Comrades

In our society women have no political freedom. Women work as household slaves. In the kitchen and in taking care of children we work from morning to night. We know nothing about what is happening in the world. Not only are we household slaves, we are exploited and enslaved outside the household too. Women workers are forced to labor long hours at low wages in the factories. Farm women work in the heat of the summer in the field, drenched in sweat.

Because women are being exploited ruthlessly by the capitalists and the landlords and are leading a life of extraordinary hardship, they have joined hands with men to fight. Women factory workers are demanding better pay, shorter workdays, and security in the factories. Farm women are demanding lower tenant fees, an end to the practice of driving tenants off the land, and recognition of the right to work the land.

Woman workers! Farm women! We must realize that our living conditions will not improve merely by fighting the capitalists and the landlords. The capitalists and landlords, who are concerned only with ways to exploit the workers and tenants in order to make more money, have the advantage of favorable governmental policies. We women must achieve a real political consciousness and fight the government as well as the capitalists and the landlords. The Diet has been dissolved, and men over twenty-five have been given the right to vote. Universal suffrage will now enable us to send representatives of the workers and peasants to the Diet.

But we women have not been given the right to vote. We do not have the right to choose our representatives. We have only a tiny bit of freedom, the freedom to get on the platform and support those who will represent the workers and the peasants in the Diet. Armed with this small freedom, women throughout the nation are battling in the electoral districts. We must win the right for women to take part in political activities and the freedom to join political parties. In order to participate in this movement, women—women workers and farm women—must stand on the platform and speak out during the election.

We must join the men in the daily fight to eliminate the problems that affect us in the factories and on the farms. We must rally women workers and peasants under our party slogan "Bring down the government of landlords and capitalists—all the evildoers—and create a government of workers and peasants."

After the first election under universal male suffrage, the men who had stood for election in the local districts, and those who had campaigned in the elections from their hideouts, such as Mitamura Shirō, Kawai Etsuzō, and Kasuga Shōjirō, came back to Tokyo.[18] Tokuda Kyūichi was arrested by the authorities on his way back to Tokyo.

When the mass arrests of March 15, 1928, began, I was afraid that I would be killed if I were arrested. But I was ready for that eventuality.

I was sure that if I were caught they would torture me to death or execute me. When the Peace Preservation Law was revised [in 1928], I was alarmed, for the death sentence was made part of the provisions. Before the maximum term had been ten years in prison. Since I was still young, I thought I could survive ten years. But after they introduced the death sentence, I was afraid I would be executed if I were arrested. At that time I said, "I'd rather be executed than be sentenced to life imprisonment." Watanabe admonished me, "Don't be a fool. If you are executed, it's all over. It's better to be sentenced to life imprisonment than to be executed. Even if you are in prison for life, the masses will know that you are there." He also said, "I'll never commit suicide." For this reason I never believed the enemy's claim that Watanabe killed himself.

I escaped the March 15 roundup. I closed down our hideout and with the help of Tanaka Tsugi, who had come from the countryside, managed to rent a house in Nippori. Our comrades were scheduled to gather there, so Tsugi worked hard cooking tempura. At just about the time she finished cooking the others arrived. Five or six of us, together with Ichikawa, were about ready to start eating when the police came. They wanted to check our birth certificates. When I was asked about my family record and where my birth was registered, I hemmed and hawed. I had a forged record that said I was born in Kagoshima prefecture, so I said, "My home record is in Kagoshima." I couldn't recall the precise location, so I made it up. But it turned out that one of the policemen was from Kagoshima, and he began to ask me all sorts of questions. I made up answers as best I could, but when the police left, I realized we were in trouble. We decided to flee as quickly as possible, and we left everything behind.

We managed to rent an upstairs room in Kakikara-chō. We had to step out everyday to carry on our work, and though I was not ill, I told the landlord I was sick and that I had to go to a gynecologist every day. Watanabe told him that he had a job in a brokerage house. However, we decided a single room was not enough. We had to rent a house so that our group would have a place to meet. We found a house in Naniwa-chō, a chic place just in front of a geisha house. After we moved in, we got in touch with our friends, and we also asked Tsugi to join us. Tsugi was an expert seamstress, so she took on the job of retailoring the clothing of our group to make them look like stock brokers. She went to a used-clothing store and bought some summer haori and other Japanese clothes and altered them. In those days, people used to go around in Japanese clothing, so we could rely on Tsugi to take care of all the clothing problems. She was a big help. It would have been too costly for us to pay a professional seamstress.

We made contact with Nozaka Ryō and got in touch with those who had returned from the KUTV [Kommunisticheski Universitat Trudyashchikhaya Vostoka, a Communist college for Asian workers] in Soviet Russia. Hakamada Satomi and Sōma Ichirō had just returned from the university.[19] At that time a large number of other people were returning from Soviet Russia.

Kawai Etsuzō had a hideout, so we sent Tsugi there to contact Sōma. Then Sōma was arrested. Soon after, Kawai and Tsugi were arrested too. We realized that our hideout in Naniwa-chō was in danger, but we could not abandon our equipment and run away. We had a phonograph, which we used to muffle the sound of the mimeograph machine. We had purchased some apple crates, stacked them up, and covered the boxes with patterned cloth wrappers to make it look like a bureau. The mimeo machine was hidden underneath. We couldn't leave all these things behind and run off, so we asked Watanabe's mother to come and move them with a truck to Ichikawa's parents' home. Mother brought along Fujinuma's younger brother to help. This was how the authorities discovered where we were, and Mother and Fujinuma's younger brother were caught. He was thrown in jail and interrogated for a week, but we were not captured.

Again we had no home. Mitamura was living with Morita Kyōko on the second floor of a house near Bansei Bridge. Watanabe and I moved in with them. Then Watanabe had to go to Shanghai. He and Nabeyama left for Shanghai on August 29. They were expected back by October. I knew nothing about the meeting in Shanghai. My main job was to find places for us to hide out and to do the cooking. After Watanabe and Nabeyama left for Shanghai, the responsibility for overseeing things in Japan was taken, I believe, by Mitamura and Kokuryō. So I went to live at Mitamura's place, and Nabeyama's wife went to Kokuryō's hideout. We needed a house rather than a room, so we rented a house in Asakusa, and Mitamura and Morita and I moved in.

On December 2 I returned home after doing some liaison work. It was past ten. Half a dozen people were standing in front of the house. I knew instinctively that something was wrong. When there's trouble I can sense it immediately.

I had no other place to go but to Kokuryō's hideout. But before I left our hideout I asked one of the bystanders, "What happened?" "There was a shooting—with a pistol," he replied. "Oh, is that so? Dangerous business, isn't it?" I said and left. I went to Tawara-chō through unfamiliar, narrow streets. I then picked up a cab in Tawara-chō and went to Kokuryō's place near Edogawa Bridge. I told him of the danger and advised him to run away. He said, "I have no money, so I can't run off right now. Let's wait till tomorrow morning to see what happens." I thought that was really taking a chance, but could do nothing about it. The next morning the papers reported the shooting incident. The headlines said, "Police Shot at Communist Hideout. Shot from Upstairs While Climbing the Stairs. Culprit Jumps from the Building and Escapes." [Mitamura had shot a police officer when they came to arrest him.]

I told Kokuryō that I would go to get some money and asked him to meet me at eight at Shimbashi. I went to Kobayashi Takejirō, the stock broker, to get some money. I then went to Shimbashi, but no one showed up. I was afraid that everybody at Kokuryō's place had been arrested. I waited there, wondering what to do or whom to get in touch with. Finally, I decided to go back to Kokuryō's to see what had happened. When I got there a towel was hanging out the window, a signal that all was well. Thinking that it was safe, I went bounding up the stairs and called out, "Come on. Let's get away as quickly as possible. Why are you shilly-shallying?" As soon as I sat down, the police came charging in. Kokuryō pointed his pistol at them, shouting, "I'll shoot!" But he struck the screen as he pointed it. It got stuck in the screen, which fell down. All the police were armed, so we were helpless.[20] They quickly arrested Kokuryō. Utako Nabeyama tried to escape through the window. I followed her and leaped from the window onto the roof and fled along the rooftop. When I tried to jump from the roof of our house to the next house, I missed and fell to the ground. I got up frantically and ran into the neighbor's house, crying, "They're after me. Can you please hide me?" At first I hid in a toilet in the hedges. Thinking that this wasn't safe, I came out and hid in the hedges. The police arrived at the neighbor's house. I was in my bare socks and had left footmarks all over (though I didn't realize this till later). I heard the police ask the neighbor, "Didn't someone come in here?" The neighbor didn't know what to say and was hemming and hawing. I decided to make a run for it and climbed over the fence. As soon as I got out of the yard I was caught, for the police had the house surrounded. I was like a mouse trapped in a sack. I don't know where Utako was caught, but it was impossible for her to escape by running along the rooftops, and she too was arrested. That was on October 3. I was taken to the nearby Tomizaka police station.

If they had been tailing me from Asakusa, they would have struck that night or before sunrise the next morning. Since they didn't, they must have known beforehand the location of Kokuryō's hideout. That night I had told Kokuryō, "You must run away by yourself. It doesn't matter if we women get caught." I gave him all the money I had, but Oharu said, "We'll be in trouble if only we women are left behind. Wait till tomorrow morning." Well, Kokuryō revealed his weakness by listening to Oharu, who is forceful.

I didn't want to press the matter further because I could not think of any place that he could flee to. Later I heard what Mitamura had done. It was really remarkable. He spent the entire night riding the tram back and forth and thereby eluded the police. It really was extraordinary that he was able to break through the tight police net and board the train. I had been convinced that he could not possibly escape.

The wives of party members then were all extremely involved in political activities, though they were not party members themselves. In that respect they were different from the wives of party members today. Nabeyama Uta, Kokuryō Oharu, and others were all active in the party's women's division. As a result, they knew what was going on. They were all carrying on the struggle as part of the mass movement and were as influential as today's party members.

At any rate, if they had all left the house when I set out to raise some money, they might have escaped arrest. When they didn't, I considered Kokuryō a weakling, but when I saw him later in the courtroom where we were examined, I saw that he was standing his ground and that he really was a courageous person. He didn't look physically weak either, so I was surprised to hear that he died in prison. Ichikawa Shōichi was in poor health. During the mass arrests of March 15 he was in bed with a fever, so I went to help him escape. The three of us—Ichikawa, Watanabe, and I—hid in the basement of Kobayashi Takejirō's house. Ichikawa died in prison on March 15, 1945, and Kokuryō died in prison on March 17, 1943.

Kokuryō and I were arrested when the authorities were tracking down those of us who had escaped in the mass arrests of March 15, 1928. We were among those apprehended between the mass arrests of March 15, 1928, and those of April 16, 1929. These were known as "interim arrests."

I had not been active politically. I had merely helped set up hideouts and done the cooking. Until the arrests of March 15 I had worked with Sano in the Communist party cell in Ishikawajima Shipyards. Members of the cell were arrested on March 15. My name appeared as a member of the cell, so they were bound to come looking for me. In those days, members of the central committee, like Sano, Ichikawa, and Watanabe, were all active in local cells.

I had no idea which police station Uta was sent to, but she was not indicted. The authorities decided that she did not have any ties to the party. She was merely Nabeyama's wife.

I was questioned relentlessly for three days, about Watanabe, at the Tomizaka police station. I was brutally tortured. Yamagata [Tamezō] of the political police claimed recently, "I never tortured anyone." That is a blatant lie. I was severely beaten by him.[21]

A story like this may sound strange for someone like me, but on the night of the sixth when I was sitting in the detention cell with my legs stretched in front of me, a big black butterfly landed on my leg. There was no opening through which the butterfly could have come into the cell. There wasn't even a crack. It startled me, and I pulled up my legs. Then it disappeared. Again, there were no openings through which it could have flown out. There were several prostitutes in the cell with me. Seeing the black butterfly, they said, "That's really eerie. It's like the spirit of some person." That night I had a strange dream. When the first arrest of the Communist party members took place in 1923, I used to go to the prison with Nozaka Ryō to visit the party members. In my dream I had gone on one of these visits with Nozaka. There was Watanabe without his head. "Oh, he has no head!" I exclaimed. Nozaka Ryō also cried out, "That's right!" She then looked in a square box that was nearby and shouted, "Here it is!" Then, when it was time to say goodbye, Watanabe's head was back where it belonged. I woke from the dream and thought, "I wonder if he is dead."

After I was questioned and tortured severely for three days, the questioning suddenly stopped. I thought it was strange but decided that the authorities wanted to take their time with the investigation. A week later an official from the national police headquarters came and escorted me to a room different from the interrogation room. The officials were sitting in the room with some sushi prepared for me. I thought it was odd.

As soon as I sat down one of the officers said, "Tanno-san, you mustn't lose heart." I said, "Watanabe was killed, wasn't he?"

They were taken aback and asked, "How did you know?"

I replied, "I can tell by the way you are treating me."

The political police said, "Take it easy today. Relax and eat."

"I don't feel like eating," I replied.

I didn't cry while I was with them, but as soon as I returned to the detention cell I burst into tears. The guard was baffled and asked, "What's the matter? You're usually tough. You weren't tortured today, were you? Your face isn't even swollen. People cry like that only when their parents die."

It must have been my sixth sense. Once before I had had a similar experience, when Watanabe went to the Soviet Union to attend the meeting in which the 1927 Thesis was adopted. One day when I got off at the Kinshichō station I thought, "I think Watanabe is back in this country." As soon as I got home, Watanabe's mother told me, "Set-chan, Watanabe is back. I just saw him. He asked me to tell you to come to Saigō's statue in Ueno Park."

After October sixth they stopped torturing me completely. I found out later that that was the day that Watanabe had been killed and it was no longer necessary for them to question me about him.[22]

After I spent twenty-nine days in the Tomizaka police station jail, the landlord of the Asakusa hideout insisted that I move our things out of his house. So I asked the police to transfer me from the Tomizaka police station to the Zōgata station. When I arrived in the Zōgata police station and was placed in the detention room at the end of the hallway, I saw Kobayashi come out of his cell, wearing a dark blue, patterned kimono. He looked just like the bronze statue of Saigō. I was taken aback. I can't describe how seeing him shocked me. We had gotten this kind man in trouble. I didn't say a word about Kobayashi, and the police did not even ask me about him. I couldn't let it be known that I knew Kobayashi, so I pretended not to recognize him. I didn't want him to recognize me either, so I kept out of his sight. His wife, Hagino Osada, brought him his meals, and at every mealtime, three times a day, he was brought out from his cell. He was treated better because he was merely a sympathizer. Whenever I saw him go back and forth I felt relieved because he was looking well.

Eventually Kobayashi was released. I was shocked to learn later that because he was arrested as a sympathizer his relatives held a family council and declared him legally incompetent to hold property. He could not endure the poverty that followed, and he committed suicide. Kobayashi had been aiding the party financially by ostensibly employing Tokuda [Kyūichi] as his lawyer. He had also opened a restaurant in Asakusa, which Hagino Osada ran. Party members went there to hide and to get financial help. After the pistol incident, I went to Hagino's place to get some money.

When I was taken from the Zōgata station to the house in Asakusa and saw the landlord, I wept. I didn't think there were so many tears in me. They kept pouring out while I talked to him.

I cleared things out of the house, took care of Morita Kyōko's clothing, and sent some of her things to the prison. I was kept in the Zōgata police station jail for twenty-nine days and then was sent to the Ichigaya prison to await my trial. I was arrested on October 3 and spent twenty-nine days in two police stations, so it was early December when I arrived at Ichigaya.

The year 1928 sped by, and now it was January 1929. One day Watanabe's mother came to see me. She began to cry the moment she saw me. "Set-chan, Masa was killed. . . ," she told me in tears. I told her, "It can't be helped. We all knew that we could be killed at any moment." But when Mother left and I returned to my cell, I burst out crying. I cried and cried and cried. When the guard brought me my supper, I looked out. It was snowing. I thought Mother must be having a difficult time going home in the snow. I had been crying from the time she left till suppertime. I regained my composure and thought that people who lose their minds must do so in times like these. I told myself I must be strong.

The other day (in the fall of 1966) I received a copy of the letter that I sent Mother Watanabe. It is a Xerox copy of the original in the possession of Karl G. Yoneda, who is living in the United States.[23] The legend "KGK Society for the Relief of the Victims of the Liberation Movement" is written on it. KGK are the initials of Kaihō-undō Giseisha Kyūenkai. This letter was carried to the United States by a seaman, Nishiuji Tsunejirō, because he believed that it would be dangerous for it to remain in Japan. That's how Yoneda got it.

[From Tanno Setsu in Ichigaya Prison to Watanabe Chō, January 30, 1929]: Mother, after your visit, I left the visiting room and walked through the long corridor back to my cell. The moment the cell door was locked I broke down and cried. When I recovered my senses it was already snowing. My supper was delivered to me. Usually I can hardly wait for supper, but today I could not eat. I've spent many days here, and you have visited me four times. Then on the fourth visit, on January 28, what I had feared for a long time finally came to pass. I can't describe how I felt when I saw you break down and cry in the visitors' room. When I try to write about that visit now I find myself crying. I can't write about it. But I know that you understand how I feel, since you must feel the same way. But here, I am in prison. You are at least on the outside and can talk to others about your feelings. And there must be other ways in which you can take your mind off the tragic news. But I have no way of doing that here.

Mother, when you come to visit me, please don't cry. Please resign yourself to accepting what has happened. And wait for me to come home. Now, I'm crying again, and I find it hard to write. So, Mother, let's not cry anymore. We knew what to expect from the very beginning. And this is not the first case of government persecution. You haven't forgotten what happened during the Great Earthquake, have you? So you are not the only one in your situation. You haven't forgotten how it must have been for the many mothers and brothers and sisters then, have you? Even now many people are undergoing the same thing. Think of Nakao's mother and Minami's father. They are all suffering as you are. All of us will undergo the same fate sooner or later. As long as we live in this kind of society we are bound to experience the same miserable tragedy. We are not watching a movie or a play. We are facing the real world, our own world. But things will get better after we have endured all this pain and sorrow. You mustn't let your sorrow ruin your health. Don't think about the past. Let's think about the future. Then you will understand that this is not the time to be crying.

There is much work to be done. There are many things that you can do, Mother. Go visit your friends and comfort each other. And try to think of others and not just about your own troubles. Please carry on by being courageous and patient. Mother, you must not give up or fall into despair. We must be careful not to follow in the footsteps of Kawai's mother or Sada. Think carefully. We mustn't dishonor what Masanosuke has accomplished so far. You mustn't do anything that will cause people to scoff at Masa's mother. I promise you that I will not behave in any way to dishonor him. Now that Masa is gone we must be even more careful not to become the object of criticism by others.

Mother, please stay well. When I come out I will tell you all that Masa told me. Now that Masanosuke is gone I have two tasks before me. I can't do anything about them while I am in prison. But I must not worry about this and ruin my health before I get out. So I don't think about these things. I believe that Masa is here with me and that when I leave this prison I will be able to see him again. You too must believe this, Mother.

I am reading day and night the books that you got me from the Kanda bookstore. I plan to read books, think about things, and come out with many new ideas. So, Mother, I hope you too will keep well and work hard.

From today they have started to give me milk. Next month be sure to let me see your cheerful face. I'll be waiting. The only pleasures I have are visitors. So come and see me; and please don't cry. Please be well. I shall be waiting.

On the third please go to Satō's and get a good rest, and regain your energy. When I think of how you were the other day I feel sad. Please be well and come and see me as soon as you can.

Tenant Disputes in Kisaki Village, 1922

Factory work tends to produce activists who are capable of expressing themselves verbally, and workers who later recount their experiences on paper. However, women tenant farmers tend not to be quite so verbal. Perhaps this is because factory women live in an urban setting and are subject to greater stimuli from their environment. They are more likely to be exposed to radical ideas. But given an opportunity to express their views and recount their experiences, rural women too are willing to do so.

In the Taishō years (1912–26) tenant disputes began to increase also. One of the most bitterly fought tenant disputes took place in Kisaki village in Niigata prefecture. In 1922 a tenant union was organized in that village, and the tenants asked for a 20 percent reduction in rent. Many of the landlords agreed, but one of the major landlords, Majima Keijirō, refused to comply and brought the police in to drive out the tenants. The dispute went through the courts and dragged on for eight years. During the course of the dispute, the union members took their children out of the public school, because Majima was the chairman of the local board of education, and started their own school. In the end, the tenants lost the battle.[24] Their story is recounted below by some of the farm wives who were involved in the struggle. The interviews were conducted in 1968.[25]

Takizawa Mii's Recollections

I was born in 1898 in Yoshimura village near Kisaki (in Niigata prefecture). When I was a child, my father owned about five or six chō of land;[26] he was a small landowner. He served as acting village head for awhile. When I was growing up we had a relatively easy time of it. But as our family fortune slowly worsened, I began to see social injustices.

The family I married into had two chō five tan [about six acres] in all, including both rice paddies and upland. In other words, they were not very well off. The family was frugal. I guess you could say they were economy-minded; they were careful about little things. Because I had been raised in a family that was better off, I had a hard time. I didn't know what I was getting into when I married into my husband's family.

My mother-in-law had a child who was only a year apart from my son, so there were some problems. Unlike my parents' family, my husband's family was frugal about rice, so they cooked what was known as "kate-meshi," which was a mixture of broken rice and daikon. I used to stay up late into the night chopping daikon to feed the eleven family members. I had to do this with my baby on my back. It was really tough.

After our third son was born, that is, after I became the mother of three children, my husband got actively involved in the peasant movement. The second son was devoted to his father and kept following him around, saying, "Daddy, Daddy." So my husband used to attend peasant-association meetings with this child on his back. The boy died while his father was in prison. My younger brother was active in the peasant movement too.

While my husband was active in the peasant movement all his relatives would gang up on him and criticize him. "You're a fool. Since you go around supporting the movement, you're bound to waste away the family property." They even used to abuse the children, saying, "If we let children of a man who is ruining the family property stay alive, the family will go broke. We've got to kill them. We'll kill them." And they would chase them around. As a result, our oldest son seldom stayed at home. He went to my parents' home and ate with them until he was about ten.

During rice-planting time, my husband would be out working for the movement. "Where in the world did that beast go?" my mother-in-law and her mother would yell at me. I didn't know where he had gone, because he always went out without telling me where he was going. He'd stay away for days. Once I discovered that my good kimono had disappeared from the chest of drawers. He had sold it to attend a meeting of the Kantō Alliance of Peasants. He then went on to attend the second meeting of the Kobe Peasant Association. Young wives were really mistreated in those days. As a result, I had a nervous breakdown. In those days, they didn't send us to the hospital when we got sick, so I went back to my parents' home to rest and be taken care of.

Many people used to come to our home and talk about the movement. Kamimura Susumu and Asanuma Inejirō were among those who came.[27] Inamura Junzō used to say, "There's no hope for agrarian women if they don't change their ways."[28] If it weren't for these discussions I probably would have remained ignorant about agrarian problems. I learned from them that there was no hope for us unless we changed our ways. That our suffering was all due to our ignorance became clear to me. Kisaki was about three ri [about 7.35 miles] from my home but I used to go there [to attend meetings] with our third son on my back. At that time there was already a woman's division in the movement, and everybody was united. . . .

In those days they used to arrest people over minor infractions. Once my husband became active in the peasant movement, the police tailed him constantly. The private police employed by the landlords used to circle around our house to see what the union organizers were up to. When my husband was released by the police, many supporters went to greet him, waving red flags. They paraded around the landlord's house and around the village. When he was arrested in the mass arrests of March 15, 1928, a council was held among the relatives. I asked my mother to attend it. She told me that everybody kept saying, "He's a fool. There's no bigger fool than he."

When the police came I always told them, "I'm not going to answer any of your questions," and refused to talk to them. The police who were sent to our house used to be unhappy about that assignment.

When the peasant school was opened, I went to the opening with the third son on my back. A large number of people from our village attended the opening ceremonies. Yamada Yoshiko from our neighborhood was head of the women's division and was scheduled to read a statement commemorating the event, but she was too shy to make the speech, so my younger sister and I read it for her. I had on a kimono with splashed patterns, and my red underskirt was showing, but I got up and read the statement anyway. The meeting was crowded, and representatives from all over the country read congratulatory messages. Kagawa Toyohiko came too. I shall never forget that day.

It was dark when I set out for home. I came across a number of police cars heading for Kisaki. That's when the clashes at Kyūhei Bridge took place. My husband was arrested and sent to prison in Shinhatsuda. I went to visit him in prison with our baby. The chief guard yelled at me: "You can't come in here with a baby on your back!" But I ignored him and visited my husband anyway. Then he was sent to prison in Niigata in the mass arrests of March 15, 1928. I used to go and visit him often with Satō Satōji's wife.[29] I would say to her, "Your whole family is united on this question, so it must be easy for you to come to these visits." In my case, the whole family abused me for visiting my husband. My mother-in-law was a strong-minded person, and I had a hard time.

After my husband's arrest and imprisonment, no one was able to hold the villagers together, and the movement became fragmented. Then the war started and everybody was absorbed in the war effort. The whole village agreed that the war had to be won. When the airmen came to the village everybody got busy making rice cakes and dumplings to entertain them. I didn't favor such activities, so I only helped out a little. But two of my sons went off to war. I wrote them at the war front, "Don't worry about being promoted. Just come back safely."

Now none of the women have retained the feelings that motivated us then. I've kept on friendly terms with only Yamada Yoshiko. After the postwar land reforms were put in effect, the villagers also began to take on the airs of landowners. The old tenants became landowners. If they cooperate with us [Communists], they won't be able to get rich.[30] The villagers are willing to support the movement when they can get something out of it, but otherwise they are useless. Now, all our family members understand what we were trying to accomplish and tell me, "Old woman, you had a hard time didn't you?" I laugh and tell them, "No one can survive in this family unless she's a fool or is very wise." Thanks to my husband's influence, I managed to get by all these years, but if it hadn't been for him, I don't know what would have become of me. Now I realize how fortunate I was.

Ikeda Seki's Experience

I was born in 1895. In those days, elementary school was limited to four years. But I hardly went. Few people did around here, because everybody was so poor. When I heard that tenant disputes had finally broken out, I didn't know what to say. I had worked hard until then, convinced that no matter what happened we had to continue farming. There were my husband's parents as well as our four small children, so I kept working. People used to comment about my husband: "All he does is go around causing trouble." Since he was on the road all the time, I had to make up my mind to stick it out or I wouldn't have been able to keep going. In those days all we did was work. And all we had was spades and sickles, so farming was hard work. If we had had machines like those of today, one person could have done all the work. During the dispute, when my husband left home in the morning I had no idea when he would be back. He did what other people were not willing to do and was criticized for it. It was really rough. . . .

I was raised in a poor family and had practically no schooling, so I didn't know what was going on. It was hard. I thought that as long as it was going to help the poor it must be good, so I decided to endure all the hardships that came our way and I kept on working. If everybody held this kind of attitude today, it would be a snap to win. However, today not many people want to carry on the struggle. During the disputes even someone like me who didn't know anything would feel, "That's right," when we heard people explain the issues. So we became seriously involved in the movement. During the disputes, a person by the name of Ogura Sadako came from Tokyo and stayed at our house, as well as at my parents' place. When I heard her talk, even though I didn't know anything, I thought "Is that the way it is?" and began to understand the issues in the dispute.

Once the confrontation started, the village split in half, and adults and children all began to quarrel. Since our family was involved in union activities, even if we wanted to ask our fellow villagers to help us with our farm work, we felt we couldn't. And some people refused to come and help us even when they were not working and had free time. Those opposed to us criticized us in all sorts of ways. When we ran into them on the road, they would look the other way and wouldn't even say hello. I really can't describe how terrible I felt.

In our hamlet, we rented space in the Buddhist temple on Hayatōri and started a peasants' school. Our oldest daughter went there for about a year. Each hamlet rented space in temples and other places and started its own school for peasants. At the Hayatōri school, Takeuchi Gorō came from Tokyo and became the teacher. His wife also came, and she stayed with us for awhile. When the construction of the [new] school was completed, my husband and his friends got together some dumplings and rice cakes and brought them to the school on a big cart with the school children. The new school was so far from our house that our children couldn't go there. We talked it over and decided to let them attend the public school. However, teachers and students came from Tokyo and gave many talks, and I used to take my children to them.

When the war started, the tenant movement had to be discontinued because of public pressure. Everybody concentrated on the war, so the villagers got together again, but I wonder how people really felt. They established neighborhood associations to support the war effort, but I didn't feel like cooperating with them. Our oldest and second sons went off to war. But the army soon found out that they had come from Kisaki. The military police discriminated against them and viewed them with distrust. The military police kept their eyes on even the sons of families that had nothing to do with the disputes. They kept a close watch over them if they were known to have come from Kisaki. Our younger son did not come back for a long time after the end of the war. We heard that he was sent from Manchuria to Soviet Russia. The following year we got a letter from him. He wrote, "Since childhood my parents taught me that Russia was the land of peasants and workers. I am now working in this land of peasants and workers, and have everything that I need, so please don't worry." I guess he understood the situation there right away because of his parents' views about Russia. There were some who couldn't understand this point of view and were not allowed to return and were crying in Russia. This son was only a small child during the disputes and did not even attend the peasant school, but I guess even though he was only a small child he somehow understood what his parents were trying to accomplish.

The peasant school was built with the help of many people, but there's no trace of it now. Already forty years have passed. I guess it's in the blood. My sons and grandchildren all work hard. When we tell them about union activities of the old days our grandchildren listen to us avidly.

Satō Tsugi's Story (Satō Satōji's wife)

I was born in this village, four houses from here, in 1907. My husband's family was poor, so from the age of nineteen to twenty-four he worked in the Yūbari mines in Hokkaido. Just before he came back he met Inamura Ryūichi and began to study [social issues].[31] After he came home he became active in the peasant movement. I came here as his wife in 1925, during the Buddhist Bon festival. May fifth of the following year was a farm holiday.[32] My husband left the house early. Then someone came and told me, "Your husband has been arrested." I left the house immediately to look for him, but they had taken him away in a car. That was the first day that the landlord stopped us from entering the fields. The police sprayed red ink on people they suspected and arrested them. Some of those arrested were tied to trees. The ruckus was terrible. I heard that my husband had been taken to the Katsuzuka station. I went there, but they refused to let me see him.

I can't describe the hard time I had after his arrest. Our family couldn't survive if I just worked a normal amount, so I got up early and worked on the uplands before breakfast. Then I went to work on the rice paddies at 6:00 A.M. Still, though, I couldn't get the work done, so during rice-planting time members of the union came to help me. Ikeda helped me a lot. During the disputes, a women's division was established in our village, and we women gathered at Ikeda's place and listened to people who talked about the issues.

I had just come to my husband's family as a young bride and had to work in the field with the old folks, so I was very busy and had a real hard time. Though my parents sympathized with my situation, my relatives castigated me and I had a hard time. During the Kisaki disputes many people helped us, so it was all right, but we had a lot of trouble afterward.

Our first daughter was born after my husband was released following his arrest over the Kisaki disputes. This was in 1927. Then the next year he was arrested in the mass arrests of March 15. After that, the villagers became wary of associating with us, and nobody would come near our house. If they were friendly with us, they too would be stigmatized as "that kind of person." Only Ikeda and Grandma Ikeda's home family, that is, the Kazama family, helped us. So we had a terrible time after my husband's arrest. Before he ended up in the Niigata prison, I didn't know which prison he was in. Some people thought he was in the Mizuhara police station, and I went there, but they refused to tell me where he was being held. Someone told me that he was in the Numatare police station, and I went there next, but they too insisted that they didn't know where he was being held. I finally found out that he was being held at the Shinhatsuda station. I went there to try to see him, but they refused.

My husband was sent to the Ichigaya prison in Tokyo. They had yelled at me in Niigata, so I was prepared to be hollered at more fiercely in Tokyo. However, they were so gentle I couldn't believe it. When they called out my name, I was so flustered I didn't know what to do. They then escorted me to the visitors' room and even said, "Thank you for coming from such a long distance." Such polite talk really flabbergasted me.

Since I was farming, I used farm business as an excuse to go and visit him. That way I got to see him twice as often. When I visited him, I could talk to him openly only about farming. I couldn't say what I really wanted to tell him. Occasionally, when the guards were not keeping a close watch, I was able to tell him quickly, "So-and-so got arrested." But that was about it. When my father died, the prison authorities escorted my husband to the funeral. My parents' family prepared a bath for him, and my younger sister's husband helped to bathe him. Seeing my husband's back blood-red from the torture, my brother-in-law said he couldn't help but weep.

My husband was not given enough food in prison, so he asked me to throw some rice-balls to him over the prison wall. To make sure that the rice-balls wouldn't fall apart, I wrapped them up in paper. He told me where he would be working on a given day, and I went to the prison wall on the designated day. I first threw a rock over the stone wall. The rock made a rattling sound as if it had landed on a tin roof. I was afraid that this might have alerted the guards, so I ran away. But I returned and threw the rice-balls over. I believe he got them.

On another occasion someone else threw some rice-balls over the wall for him. Unfortunately, the chief guard or some other high officer happened to be there. The next time I went to visit my husband the officers warned me, "We're not going to let you see him any longer." I protested vigorously that it wasn't I who had thrown the rice-balls over the wall, but they refused to believe me. They took me to see the chief guard, who bawled me out.

Eventually my husband was released, but he was arrested again in 1931 and again in 1941. The last arrest had to do with his activities with the medical-care alliance. During the war, whenever there was the slightest disturbance in the village, he was the first person arrested. If posters were posted in the village the day before some recruits departed for the army, he and his younger brother, Watōji, were arrested the following morning. When they were arrested in connection with the medical-care alliance, his younger brother fell ill. We were told that he had only a month to live, so we borrowed some money by mortgaging one tan of our land and posted bail to get him out of prison. However, he died soon after [in 1942].

The police searched our house constantly. Sometimes they would descend upon us when we were asleep. In those days we used to have what was called a "rag mattress" under the regular bedding. We hid all the important papers in the rag mattress. They say that when the higher political police came to search Mrs. Inamura's house she would defy them by telling them, "If you are so eager to search the house, why don't you look in the charcoal brazier too?" and dump the ashes on the police. She would also spray the contents of the children's urine pot on them.

Whenever anyone came to our house, we made sure we knew who they were before we even said hello. Even when the village policeman dropped by and asked for a cup of tea, we would tell him, "We don't have any tea to serve you," and turn him away. He came around to snoop, and we feared that he would use whatever we said against us. We had to be rude. When the incident over the Zen'nō Zenkai-ha (All Japan Peasants' Conference) occurred in 1931,[33] many people were arrested, but my husband went into hiding. The police came often to look for him, but of course he wasn't at home. However, they finally caught him. The higher political police escorted him home to let him change his soiled clothes. One of the officers waited for him outside the house, and the other one stayed close to him. My husband whispered to me to help him escape. I told him, "Since you were arrested right after you woke up, you must wash your face and feet and eat before they take you away." Then I told the political policeman who was keeping watch over him, "Please have some tea," and served him some. My husband went into the other room to change his clothes, but did not return to the sitting room. He had fled the back room and run into the rice field. The rice plants were full grown, and he managed to hide in the field.

On that occasion, Ikeda was arrested and was questioned by the police, but my husband hid at his comrades' home during the day and wandered from place to place at night. Whenever I found out where he was, I pretended to go out to take care of some chores and went to see him. He managed to escape arrest much longer than the others. Finally, he was caught and sent to the Shinhatsuda police station.

During this period, I suffered many difficulties. The Protective Observer's Office kept urging me to persuade my husband to renounce the cause. As if this weren't enough, the police and relatives all urged me to get him to desert the cause. Since I was urged by many people to "convert" my husband, I went to my father to consult him. "There are some things you can't do anything about. A husband is not likely to mind what his wife tells him. It's pointless to argue about these things with people who are pestering you. Just don't listen to them," he told me. So I decided to ignore them. Our daughter also seems to have been subjected to lots of criticism at school but she never said a word about it at home. She just endured it. Fortunately, there was one teacher who was understanding and sympathetic to us.

In those days I had just about forgotten how to laugh. And I didn't sing any war songs. I used to think of myself as "the canary that forgot how to sing," as the song went. After the war, my husband was tried by the military court over food [rationing] problems. When I add it up, it turns out that he spent half his life in jail or in prison.

SEVEN

THE WORLD OF THE STARS
Yamashiro Tomoe

Yamashiro Tomoe was among the last of the prewar women in the left-wing movement to go to prison. Her life as a Communist started after the heyday of Taishō democracy, for she did not join the movement till the early 1930s.

Yamashiro was born in a village in Hiroshima prefecture in 1912. Her family was fairly affluent, and she attended the prefectural girls' school. In 1919 she entered what is now the Tokyo University of Arts. When some bad business investment forced her father into bankruptcy, she was forced to leave college and made a living as a commercial artist. While she was in college she had become involved in left-wing circles, and in 1931 she joined the Communist party.

Recalling her activities in the early 1930s, Yamashiro commented that the Communist party leaders of the thirties did not have the pragmatic determination of the activists in the 1920s, like the Nankatsu labor group. In 1932 workers in the Harada Aluminum Factory went out on strike, demanding higher wages. The Communist party members, Yamashiro included, went to the aid of the strikers. Initially they stuck with the specific demands of the workers, but soon they turned to broad, general issues that had nothing to do with the strike. Among other things, they called for aid to tenant farmers, opposition to the Manchurian war, release of their comrades in prison, and opposition to the dismissal of city transit workers. While this convinced them that they were at the vanguard of the revolutionary movement, it proved in fact to be futile sloganeering.

Yamashiro recalls, "I believed that I was at the forefront of the revolutionary movement, and I obeyed the directives of the leaders faithfully. I would attend meetings that had nothing to do with the party and mouth slogans calling for the destruction of the emperor system, support for the 1932 Thesis.[1] I worked for the cause with naive fanaticism." The Communist party was dissolved by 1935 after further factional disputes and a scandal involving the lynching in 1934 of a member who was suspected of being a government spy. After that, Yamashiro remarks, "We began to grope in the dark."[2]

Yamashiro went to work in the Asahi Glass Company and eventually met Yamashiro Yoshimune, who had begun his career as a political activist fighting for the interests of the miners in the Iwaki coal mines in Fukushima prefecture. This work had led to his arrest in the mass roundup of socialists and communists on April 16, 1929. After his release, he found work in a factory in the Tokyo-Yokohama region. He and Tomoe were married in April 1937. Their life together is related in Yamashiro Tomoe's memoirs below, though she does not use their own names in the account.[3]

In May 1940 the two were arrested. Yoshimune was charged with planning to revive the Communist party, and Tomoe was accused of aiding this effort. At the trial, the judge told her that even if she had not taken an active part in the endeavor, her failure to report the plan made her an accomplice. He sentenced her to prison, and she remained there until the end of the war.[4] Her husband died in prison in early 1945. In February 1943 Yamashiro was transferred from the prison in Miyoshi in Hiroshima prefecture to a prison in Wakayama prefecture where Kutsumi was also incarcerated for her role in the Sorge spy affair.

After Yamashiro Tomoe left prison, she began to work in the agrarian movement in her hometown, and she also played an active role in the anti-nuclear movement. She began writing about her experiences in a form very close to folktales. Her first major work, Fuki no To (Bog Rhubarb Shoots), was published in 1948.[5]

The story Yamashiro Tomoe tells of her prison life is a remarkable testimony to the human spirit.[6] Her husband, in another prison, writes to her about atomic physics, and she studies mathematics. It is reminiscent of Kanno Sugako, who studied English on her own almost to the very day she was executed.

Bog Rhubarb Shoots

YAMASHIRO TOMOE

The snow outside was deep. The high wall near the prison was hardly visible. The isolation cells were located in a single building standing in a 120-square-yard compound surrounded by the wall. The building looked like a small temple. It had two isolation cells with latticed doors in the north and the south. The arsonist sang her song in the western cell, and Mitsuko listened to her in the eastern cell. The latticed doors were constructed with sturdy five-by-five-inch wooden rods. The shiny black lock and metal fixtures were as formidable-looking as the doors. The entire setting was so old-fashioned that an official with a samurai hairdo would not have looked out of place.

Mitsuko was in her cell working on the project she had been laboring on for over a hundred days before she heard the song from the next cell. Every morning and night, a prison official would appear before the latticed door with the logbook and bark out, "Your number, number 1 cell." Mitsuko had become accustomed to replying "Number 25" and kneeling properly on the floor. She would bend down with her two arms stretched out low so that her head and body touched the floor. Initially, she had been unable to bend down low enough to pass inspection.

Mitsuko had been sent to Miyoshi prison in wartime. After a twenty-hour train ride she had arrived at the Tōkaichi train depot and had been escorted on foot through the streets to the Miyoshi prison by three guards. She had been completely exhausted by the time she had been locked in the cell. Then she had heard the shrill word "Inspection!" barked out near the western entrance to the prison. Three guards had approached her cell, and one had rattled the lock. Mitsuko had thought they were going to open her cell door. But, instead, the three guards had lined up in front of her cell. The chief guard had stood in the middle. She had held a big, hardcover logbook. The guard on the right had said, "Number 25, kneel properly. The chief guard is before you. When I say 'Cell number 1, of the isolation cabin,' you must respond 'Number 25' in a loud voice and kneel down with your hands on the floor." Then the guard had barked out, "Cell number 1, of the isolation cabin." Mitsuko had answered "Number 25" and had knelt down with her hands on the floor. The chief guard had

yelled out, "Your head is too high! Try again." The guard on the right of
the chief guard had then barked out in yet a louder voice, "Cell number 1."
Mitsuko had again answered "Number 25" and had bowed down lower
than before. The chief had commanded, "Once more!" So the process had
been repeated until Mitsuko had managed to get her face and body flat on
the floor. The guard on the left of the chief had finally said, "Everything is
in order in cell number 1."

The guard who had barked out the order had moved toward the exit to
the east. The chief guard had shut the logbook and had started to leave but
then stopped and had said to the guards, "Number 25's identification
number on her lapel is too low. Have it raised two or three inches more."
The two guards had replied simultaneously, "Yes, ma'am," then had left
from the eastern exit, gone around to the back of the building, and left the
compound.

Mitsuko had gotten up and had looked into the small mirror on the
wooden wall. She had seen a woman with a pale face, dressed in red-brick-
colored kimono. A white cloth about 0.7 of an inch in width and 1.5 inches
long with the number 25 on it was sewn on her lapel. She had found it
hard to believe that the woman in the mirror was herself. She had not
thought that the day would ever come when she would be insensitive to
the kind of humiliation she had just experienced.

Every morning the squeaky heavy door of the cell opened and three
guards would call out, "General inspection!" and come into the cell. A
prisoner must then undo her hair and be prepared to quickly take off her
red sash, red undergarment, and everything else and stand before the
guards. The guards would take the prisoner out into the corridor where
the light was better, and inspect all her clothing and hair. Even when it
was freezing, the prisoner, shivering in the nude, was inspected by the
guards. Then they searched the entire cell. If they found one more than the
four sheets of tissue paper that were allocated to them each day or a morsel
of leftover food, they questioned the prisoner about it.

All day long while the prisoner in the solitary cell worked on her task,
the guards took turns making the rounds to check on the prisoners. They
affixed their seal on the sheet tacked on the pillar in the corridor when they
came by to check on Mitsuko. In the evening the guards checked the
amount of work the prisoner had finished, and recorded it in the log. If the
work fell below the norm, they questioned the prisoner about it. Before
the evening roll call all the tools and equipment used in the prisoner's

work—needles, scissors, rulers, and so on—were collected by the guards in all the workrooms. If anything was missing, especially scissors, the entire area was gone over with a fine-tooth comb until the missing item was found. No one was allowed to go to sleep until the missing instrument was accounted for.

After about a hundred days, Mitsuko was no longer upset by such procedures. Also, during the first hundred days, the other cell in the isolation cabin remained empty, and she had never heard the door of that cell open.

Whenever Mitsuko thought of her parents she thought of her village, Yamasaka, with its sandy soil and shiny white granite. The hillside was covered with pine and brushwood. The rice paddies and dry fields climbed halfway up the hillside, and terraced plots with stone embankments covered the steep valley as if they were shelves to display dolls. No one has ever claimed that the soil or the topography was suited for farming. All the farm families worked from early in the morning till late at night as if they were racing to see who could work the hardest. A cluster of seven to eight houses were situated along the swift Mizo River, while half a dozen houses were perched on the hillside facing south on small plots carved from the mountain slope and shored up with stone embankments. The houses were crowded so closely together that an outsider could not tell which shed belonged to which house. However, all the families boasted about their family lineage and family standing. Unless the families' backgrounds were checked out, no marriages could be arranged.

Mitsuko's father would defend his family against all outsiders and against anything that was new. He seldom left the village, and he took meticulous care of his farm plots, which came to less than one chō [2.45 acres]. He spent practically his entire life, day after day, in the rice paddies and dryland plots.

In the depression, the small silk filature that was operated by an old family in the village went bankrupt. Though he had practically forgotten it, Mitsuko's father had placed his seal on a document making him a guarantor of the plant, so his farm plots were confiscated and were auctioned off by the bailiff.

Right after her family went bankrupt, Mitsuko and her sister left for Tokyo to find work. She could see the room where she and her sister nursed their sick younger brother. The room was in the attic of a small copper-and-iron plant near the sea. Along the wooden walls, there were twelve boxlike beds, about two feet wide, attached to the walls in three tiers. There were two small windows near the top of the walls, but they had no view of the sky, and the sun did not shine directly into the room. The room was semidark, like the hold of a ship. There was hardly enough room on the bed to sit on. They could hear the racket from the factory below, and the smell from the chemical used in welding came through and permeated the entire room and the bedding. Even during the day, when people were walking around in the room, bedbugs could be seen crawling on the beds.

Mitsuko used to place a pan full of water by the bed and wet a towel to cool her brother's feverish head. The owner of the factory insisted that her brother be sent home because he had beriberi, which had afflicted his heart. Mitsuko's parents had now been reduced to tenant farming and needed the money sent home by their children working in the factory. Mitsuko had hardly any savings and could not think of any way to send her brother home or to put him in a rest home. Worry and fear filled Mitsuko, who was then twenty, with anxiety.

One evening after Mitsuko had gone to bed, the guard on duty, wearing a black cloak sparkling with snow flakes, silently peered through the bars and dropped in a folded newspaper. Mitsuko picked the paper up without a word. The paper reported that on February 3, some 220,000 crack troops of Nazi Germany had surrendered at Stalingrad. If the prison authorities found out that Mitsuko had the paper, she would be punished severely, and the guard would be fired for certain. The guard had taken a big chance in delivering the paper to Mitsuko.

Earlier, while she was being transported to this prison, Mitsuko had caught a glimpse of an item in the newspaper which reported the penetration of the Nazi troops into Stalingrad and the imminent fall of the city. That was well over one hundred days ago. Mitsuko had no idea of the violent struggles that had taken place between the armies of the world fighting for freedom and liberation and the forces of aggression. The only changes that she was aware of since her arrival at the prison and the receipt of the newspaper were those in her immediate environment.

Mitsuko had never told the guard that she was eager to get some news of the outside world. She had never spoken to her about her beliefs, as she had with number 72. Mitsuko knew that the guard was sympathetic to her, because she tried to make it possible for her to write even one extra word to her husband, Tsuneo, and ensure that the letters would pass inspection and be sent on. She even permitted Mitsuko to secretly read letters from Tsuneo that had been held up by the censors.

The guard was not sympathetic to Mitsuko, because she was a harborer of dangerous thought. Evidently, she felt sorry for the couple because they had both been arrested, and she was touched by the letters the two exchanged. She seemed to want to make sure that their letters would get through. As Mitsuko thought about the guard's goodwill, her background, and the chance she had taken tonight, she felt the impact of a powerful force she had been unaware of until then.

Mitsuko tried to remain calm as she reflected on the changes that were taking place around her. She tried to grasp from the newspaper the turmoil that was being triggered by the war. She thought about the army that had defeated the supposedly invincible Nazi army. The people's army fighting the Nazis in the front lines must have been large and supported by the masses. Two hundred thousand Nazis had surrendered on the snow-covered banks of the frozen Volga River.

The falling snow near the isolation cabin sounded like the quiet footsteps of hundreds of millions of people, but it also sounded like a powerful, massive army marching through the snow.

The inmates had to get permission from the prison authorities to send letters out of the prison. Also, unless the authorities permitted it, no letter from the outside would reach the inmates. Letters between inmates of different prisons could be exchanged as long as the authorities gave their permission, but such permission was granted only if the letters were being sent between parent and child or husband and wife. Moreover, the letters had to be inspected and approved by two groups of censors. That is, officials assigned to the forwarding and the receiving end had to read and put their seals of approval on the letters before they could be sent out or passed on to the inmates. If the incoming letter was judged to be unacceptable, the censor would note this in the log and paste a note on the letter, stating, "There are questionable statements in this letter. To be handed over upon release of the prisoner." Then the envelope would be marked with a stamp stating, "To be handed over upon release," and locked in a cabinet for safekeeping. If the inmate should die in prison, he or she would never see the letters locked up in the cabinet.

The number of letters an inmate was permitted to write each month was fixed. Prisoners ineligible for parole were allowed only one letter a month. Mitsuko had been convicted of dangerous thoughts and was ineligible for parole, so she could write only one letter of postcard length each month. Even though the frequency and length of the letters were limited, they still had to be checked over by four persons: the guard, the chief guard, the chaplain, and the supervisor of the guards. Under these circumstances, one hundred words had to do the job of ten thousand in the letters that Mitsuko and her husband exchanged. If a letter written under such restricted conditions failed to pass the censors and was stamped "To be handed over upon release," the letter itself would probably shed tears.

It was May 1940 when Mitsuko and her husband were taken from their home. The fields near the banks of the Tama River were covered with a mosaic of colors—green, yellow, white. They were at their most beautiful. The tulips were in full bloom in the spacious fields, and the dark leaves of the cabbages blanketed the cabbage patch. White and yellow butterflies flitted about.

It was two in the morning when the police came after them. They were put in separate cars. When the two cars began to drive apart, Tsuneo smiled faintly as he silently bade farewell to his wife. From then until September of 1942—when Mitsuko was sent to Miyoshi—the two were not permitted to exchange letters. Then, from the fall of 1942 to the spring of 1943—when the judge pronounced his verdict on Tsuneo—the two exchanged letters between the Tokyo detention center and Miyoshi penitentiary. Among the things that were left behind by her husband, now dead, were the letters that Mitsuko sent to him from Miyoshi to the Tokyo prison. Among them were letters that had not been passed on to him.

Mitsuko filed away in her mind all the letters Tsuneo sent her. She felt that everything he wrote had profound significance, even the most ordinary words. In the first letter that she wrote to Tsuneo after her conviction Mitsuko said:

November 3, a holiday [Emperor Meiji's birthday].

Are you well? I have so many things that I want to write to you about. But I had to wait till today to write. It was unbearable. I want to tell you about what happened after we parted until I came here. But I shall not write about that. They say that when two people's minds are in perfect harmony, their thoughts are transmitted to each other, so I feel that we both understand how we feel even if we don't put our thoughts down in writing. I am sure you can fathom my thoughts and feelings from that day until today.

When I was sent here from Tokyo, I boarded the Fukuen railroad which runs north–south through Bingo. They say that the scenery north of Fuchū city is like the scenery along the railroad that runs through the Kiso forests. En route we passed through the desolate areas of San'in where the soil is poor. Buckwheat fields and cabbage patches run along the tracks. Farmers climb the steep mountainous trails, clawing their way up on their toes to transport drinking water, night soil, and firewood on their backs. They have to creep along cautiously up and down the steep pathways. Such scenes are so familiar to me that I see them in my dreams. My friends and relations live along these mountainous trails. Memories of the days I lived there are etched in my mind. But now I was looking out the train window as a traveler passing by the landscape so familiar to me. Along the river, which burst into white foam as it hit the huge stones, I saw lumberjacks at work. The bright autumn sun glittered above the workers transporting the timber. As I stared out at the landscape, tears came to my eyes, but I told myself, "Don't cry!" And so I arrived at Miyoshi.

When I arrived at the prison and took a bath, the stars were out. The vegetable plots of the prison stretched out into the evening mist. From the window of the bathhouse I could see the purple flowers of the eggplants. I felt as if I had come home. My pent-up feelings exploded and I felt like crying out, "Mother!" I realized then that, despite my experiences since I left home, I was still a farmer's daughter. The flowers that bloom in my heart are not from flower gardens but from eggplant and cucumber fields.

The fog is very deep here. When the weather is good, the morning fog gets very heavy. The area around the cell is enveloped in grey, and neither the sky nor the sun appears until eleven o'clock. The temperature drops rapidly from about the tenth of October. Since the beginning of October I have been working with frost-bitten hands. It snows a lot, too. I am told it snows steadily for one whole month. You may think then that there is nothing good about this place, but it is not so. There is a large vegetable garden in the prison, and so we have plenty of vegetables to eat, even though the bulk of the produce is sent to the market. I planted peas and horse-beans in the plot that I tilled by the prison cell during my exercise period. They have sprouted and are getting taller. If I were Father I would probably compose a haiku poem saying something like "Green peas and horsebeans are in the ground. Now let us hibernate for the winter." The nickname for green peas is "snow-breaker." On cold, snowy days they will probably give this weakling moral support.

When you took me in, I remember your calling me a wilted marigold. At that time, you said that the marigold is a hardy flower and that at the jails of Akita it blooms in the snow. I feel that even a wilted marigold in the snow will become revitalized if it is planted in the soil of its native land.

As for my own work, in September I was able to produce 73 percent of the norm, and by October I was able to produce 100 percent. I have not yet been permitted even to see the book list of the prison library, so I have nothing to report on my education. I hope that by the time I am allowed to return home with you I will be able to report on some achievements that will please you.

Whenever I get sick I worry that we will never see each other again. During the three years that I was with you, I was unable to perform any normal wifely duties. I find it unbearable to think that you will have to endure the cold winters without my help for God knows how many years. But I am looking ahead to the future. I hope that in some future years we will be able to rebuild our lives together even if it is in an isolated hut in the mountains, cut off from everything. I look forward to that day. I am determined to work hard, endure whatever hardship that comes my way so that I can make a warm comfortable home for us.

I have no idea if the springtime will come when we reach fifty or sixty, but I am convinced that it will be a spring when even the weeds can be made into cakes, because we will be getting ready for spring no matter how many cold winters we have to endure and because we have faith in each other.

Please take care of yourself. Don't catch cold. Don't hesitate to ask my mother for warm clothing. Keep yourself as warm as possible. It has been three years since we parted, so I have much more to say, but farewell for now.

Mitsuko filled the entire page with tiny letters. But they also had to be spaced properly so that they could be read. She also had to be careful about what she wrote, so that the officials would not black out any sentences. But despite her efforts, some letters failed to pass inspection.

One night she received four postcards with labels stating "Contains unacceptable statements. To be held until recipient is released from prison." The labels were marked "Instruction" and had the seal-mark "Matsuda" on them. The cards said:

October 10. My dear Mitsuko-san:

It is now the peak of fall. My mother used to say, "If one must die, the middle of October, about the tenth, would be the ideal time." It is now the best time of the year, isn't it? I hope you are working diligently at the task of self-improvement. When the autumn sun beats down, I think of the picnic we held on the Tama River bank, and when I look up at the autumn sky, I think of *The World of the Stars*. The other day your father sent me two haiku poems on autumn, so I too tried my hand at composing one.

The fleeting autumn,
    remembrances of
        the pristine stream of Tama.

Recently I read one of the publications of Shinchōsha, the miniature People's Library. It was volume two of a book called *What Have Human Beings Accomplished?* I was astounded by the magnificence of human beings who endeavor to fathom, step by step, the profound mysteries of the universe by probing into the inner depths of the universe, the source of human life, the ultimate structure of matter, etc. Have you ever read *Our Bodies* in the same series? If you haven't, I urge you to do so. Farewell for today. Take care of yourself. Goodbye.

October 20. Dear Mitsuko-san:

Now that it is late fall the autumn air is getting chilly. Are you well? Of course I do not expect you to reply.

I recall a story in the newspaper about Mr. Longlegs [*Daddy-Long-Legs*] by America's Mrs. [Jean] Webster. (It was a story about an orphan girl who writes to her patron, Mr. Longlegs, but she never receives any letter from him.) I am reminded of that right now. It is discouraging to write letters for which you know there will be no response.

I am passing my days in good health, so please do not worry about me. I do not have a map on hand, so I am not certain, but am I right in thinking that Miyoshi is a small city in the northern part of the prefecture en route to the San'in region? I don't know if it is in a basin or a valley, but though it is in the Sanyō region, it is on the Chūgoku Range and must be very cold. As late fall arrives, we know that winter is near at hand. This will be your first winter in prison, so please take good care of yourself. Don't do anything strenuous. After all, for people in our situation winter is the worst time. Goodbye.

November 4. My dear Mitsuko-san:

Are you well? The other day I received a note from our sick friend Tsuda who is in Fukushima prefecture (he is currently resting in Yotsugura). He was concerned about your health. I too am worried. I am well as usual, so please do not worry about me.

Recently I read a book by Faraday called *The Science of Candles*. Once before I read this book, sitting by one of the machines in the Fuji Electric Company. It consists of lectures that the physicist Faraday gave on the combustion of candles to a group of young boys and girls in England. It is elementary physics, but it was worth rereading.

Your father once compared your mother to a candle. I think it is a profound, astute analogy. In concluding his lecture, Faraday told the pupils, "I hope your lives will last as long as the candle, and that you become bright lights that illuminate the world, and that your actions will be as beautiful as the flame of the candle. I hope that you will dedicate your lives to the well-being of humanity, and work toward the fulfillment of this responsibility." Farewell for now.

November 11. My Dear Wife:

Yesterday I received the letter you wrote on Emperor Meiji's birthday. Thank you so much. Well, General Winter is almost here. I was worried about your situation but having received your letter I am relieved. I was pleased to read about your native land, impressions of your trip, and the landscape of that area.

Despite the wartime food shortage, it seems that you have enough to eat. I am relieved. But I am sorry to hear that you have nothing to read. Since you have arrived at the prison only recently, there must be many inconveniences, but the absence of books, food for the mind, must be the most distressing. You need not write to me directly. Since the number of letters you are permitted to write is limited, I do not expect to hear from you often. Your mother has been very kind. Kinder than one can expect one's own mother to be. I am truly grateful. I am not strong physically, but I am trying to build up my resistance against the cold by massaging myself with cold water. So I am staying healthy. I send you my warmest handshake. Goodbye.

On the day that Mitsuko received these cards, the guard in charge of the solitary cell simply put her check mark on the sheet on the post and did not say a word to her all day until she handed the letters to her. In the afternoon, number 13, on cleaning duty, told Mitsuko that she was especially busy that day because two prisoners were to be released the next day, and a new prisoner was expected to arrive.

The day before a prisoner is released, she is put in a single cell. She is given her belongings, which have been kept in the prison storeroom, and she readies herself to leave the prison. The prison chaplain delivers a private sermon, and then the prisoner is sent to pay her respects to the warden.

When a new prisoner arrives, she is first placed in a solitary cell. There she puts together her belongings that are to be put in storage. Then the prison chaplain gives her moral instruction. All these activities are time-consuming for the guard in charge of the solitary cells.

When Mitsuko was in prison, the Miyoshi prison could house eighty inmates, but there were only six single cells. In addition, there were two cells used for solitary confinement, and the two cells in the isolation cabin where Mitsuko was housed. So, all together, only ten prisoners could be detained in single cells.

At about dinnertime Mitsuko heard an inmate in solitary confinement yell out, "Kill me, kill me! You stupid fools, you fools! Kill me!" Mitsuko guessed that all the solitary cells were occupied except for the cell next to hers. The guard did not come by Mitsuko's cell between inspection and lights out. Then the guard arrived, calling out "Bedtime!" When she came by Mitsuko's cell, she said, "Quick, read these," and handed her four post-

cards [the ones mentioned above]. Mitsuko was taken aback, but took
them in her hands. This was the first time she had received letters that had
not passed censorship, and these were the first letters that she had received
from Tsuneo.

Because the guard whispered nervously to her to read the cards quickly
and waited by the cell door apprehensively, Mitsuko raced through the
four letters from Tsuneo the way a thirsty person gulps down water without catching her breath. As soon as she finished reading them, she returned them to the guard and whispered, "What parts of these letters do
you think were objectionable?"

The guard replied, "I don't understand why they were withheld either.
I'll read them over and think about it. Then I'll let you know." She then
put the cards in the sleeves of her uniform and left.

The head guard on duty did not make her late-night inspection rounds
for a long time. From time to time, loud laughter could be heard from the
guard office, which was located on the other side of the high walls that
surrounded the isolation cabin. The isolation cabin, the guard office, and
the solitary cell buildings were all close together. Mitsuko had learned that
when the head guard heard a younger guard speaking in the isolation cabin,
she warned her not to speak to the inmate convicted of harboring dangerous thoughts. Mitsuko wondered if the guard who had Tsuneo's cards
with her had managed to pass the guard office without being caught.

A little later, the head guard on duty stood before cell number 1 of the
isolation cabin. Mitsuko pretended to be sound asleep.

The chief guard called, "Number 25, number 25."

Mitsuko didn't respond.

"Number 25, get up," the guard yelled. Mitsuko opened her eyes and
faced the cell door.

The chief guard said, "You must sleep with your chin outside the bedding," and peered into the cell.

Mitsuko removed the bedding from her chin. She didn't know how
long the guard stood there glaring at her. Soon she heard the east door
open and footsteps fading out behind the cabin. She listened intently to the
receding footsteps. Then she heard the new prisoner in the solitary cell
scream, "Kill me, please kill me! How can I sleep with my hands cuffed
behind me. Chief guard, take the handcuffs off me. Help! Kill me! Hey,
chief guard!"

Mitsuko wanted to mull over Tsuneo's letters quietly. But it was a noisy night. Her mind was crammed with Tsuneo's words. Soon the guard for whom she was waiting came. To attract Mitsuko's attention, the guard thumped lightly on the cell door and squatted awkwardly. She pushed her face against the lattice at eye level with Mitsuko, and smiled like a little girl. Mitsuko felt relieved when she saw the guard. She felt as if she had been waiting for this moment for a long time.

"I still don't understand. The chaplain doesn't think like ordinary people like us, so it's hard to understand what she found objectionable. Maybe she finds life as a whole unpleasant. The only reasons I can think of, farfetched as they may be, are the use of terms of endearment like 'Dear Mitsuko' and the casual use of quotations from people of enemy nations. Also, none of the letters refer to the great debt we owe the imperial family. Prisoners are expected to write that they are grateful to be allowed to stay alive, thanks to the emperor's grace. Since the letters are so unconcerned with such sentiments, the chaplain probably found them distasteful." The guard remained silent for a moment and then continued, "But I am happy that you were able to read the letters. You go to sleep now, number 25. I have to go off duty."

Her smiling face left the cell door, and her footsteps faded away. But Mitsuko kept thinking about Tsuneo's remarks about the picnic along the Tama River. About *The World of the Stars,* the pure waters of the Tama River, the approaching winter, serving humanity. All these were related to their activities that brought them to where they were now—in prison.

When Tsuneo and Mitsuko were on the outside living together, they were surrounded by hardworking young boys and girls. Their smiles and their aspirations were closely linked with Tsuneo's daily life. Unless one is familiar with his life story, one cannot understand why Tsuneo wrote "When the autumn sun beats down, I think of the picnic we held on the Tama River bank."

Tsuneo was born in 1900 in the area where the Jōban coal mines [in Fukushima prefecture] are located. About the time he was old enough to understand what was going on, there was a major disaster in one of the mines. A mine operator discovered that gas was seeping into the mines, and, in an effort to minimize the amount of coal that would be consumed by a fire, he sealed the entrance to the mines. The miners who were trapped in the mines and sacrificed by the owner to save the coal must have suffered horribly before they died. Their dead bodies were found piled on top of one another at the entrance to the mine. Some evidently had suffocated while trying to dig their way out with their bare hands, which were now bloody pulps.

The police prevented people from taking photographs of the dead, and mounted officers drove away those who came to search for the remains of their parents, brothers, husbands, and wives. The newspaper headlined the news that the imperial court was donating money to help the families of the victims. When it was allocated, it came to about ten yen per family. The company's condolence fee came to about ten yen per person too. The owner of the mines, Asano,[7] was near the peak of his economic ascendancy, and soon after, he came to be seen as one of the nation's super-capitalists. Tsuneo observed all this from the shacks of the mining community.

Tsuneo was a studious boy, especially fond of mathematics and physics. People would say that his temperament suited him for a life in a laboratory, working with test tubes. Perhaps they were right. But he wanted to use his learning to help the miners, to improve the life of all people in the society. So, when he graduated from college, he returned to the mines. There was a saying, "Deep shaft mining, three thousand feet. Once you go down, you are in hell." But Tsuneo joined the miners, going down early each morning with a miner's lamp in his hands to wield a pickax and haul the coal out.

When the miners decided to go out on strike, Tsuneo was chosen as their leader. Then he was picked to run for the prefectural assembly as a candidate of the Farm Labor party. On April 16, 1929, he and a large number of his comrades were arrested under the Peace Preservation Law. In 1931 those who had been arrested in the spring of 1929, including Tsuneo, were indicted and tried as Communists. The trial was held in the Tokyo District Court, which encompased five judicial districts.

The miners, as well as others, traveled a great distance to attend the trial. They sang the song of the Red Flag to support the defendants, and this led to fights between them and the police.

The defendants all contended that they represented the will of the workers, peasants, and general public of their districts. They were merely fighting for the well-being of these people, and they argued that that was not a crime. The audience applauded the defendants. Among them was Tsuneo's aged mother. The trial ended in a tumultuous uproar when Tsuneo and those who represented the Communists of the five districts were convicted of violation of the Peace Preservation Law.

Tsuneo remained in prison till 1936. Once he regained his freedom, he began working in the factories of the Tokyo-Yokohama area. Until he lost his freedom again in May 1940, he and Mitsuko lived together.

When he was free, Tsuneo spent his days in the polluted air of mining towns and the factory districts of the Tokyo-Yokohama district. He believed that the cities covered with black smoke were the mineral veins of young Japan; they were the cradles of the people who would shoulder the burdens of Japan's future. He loved living in the industrial cities. More than that, however, he loved fresh, pure air and the picnic trips he took with the young factory workers who clustered around him.

When they were living in the factory district of the Tokyo-Yokohama area, both Tsuneo and Mitsuko were factory workers. In those days, huge factories stretched in a seemingly endless line one after the other. The working hours also stretched out without limit. The glass factory where Mitsuko worked was straining to meet the needs of the military for high-grade plate glass, which could no longer be imported from abroad. A large number of women workers had been hired to replace the male workers who had been conscripted to fight in the China incident.[8] The women had to be quickly trained for the complex, demanding, and dangerous work. In order to meet the massive orders being submitted by the military, the factories had to operate continuously. No time was taken even to repair them, and they were deteriorating rapidly.

Mitsuko had a dual role as a factory worker and as a housewife. After returning home late from work, she had to prepare dinner. When she cut her hand at the factory and had to prepare dinner without any help from Tsuneo, Mitsuko yelled hysterically at him as he sat working at his writing while waiting for dinner. In the mornings, she wished she could sleep longer, even a minute longer. But she could not be late for work, so she forced herself to get up. There was barely time to clean the room and walk to work. During the long walk from Kawasaki to Suehiro-chō in Tsurumi, she often felt like crying, especially when she had to wade quickly through the muddy streets in Kansei-chō. Days like this followed one after another.

One evening after working overtime, Mitsuko joined a group heading for home. Primroses were blooming on the sandy mound along the landfill. Overhead, the sky was dotted with stars. As Mitsuko walked with the young women one of them looked back toward the factory and exclaimed as she caught sight of the stars, "Look at that bright star. I wonder which one it is?" None of the young women could say, and when Mitsuko got home she asked Tsuneo if he knew the name. He looked it up in one of his books.

The next day when Mitsuko went to the factory, she told the girls the star's name. One of the girls, a cute seventeen-year-old named Nogawa Chiyo, said, "I wonder why stars have names? I wonder who names the stars and why?" Mitsuko couldn't answer her. When she returned home that evening, she asked Tsuneo the same questions. To answer the questions, Tsuneo wrote a simple booklet, *The Story of the Constellations*. He finished it in two or three days. Mitsuko gave the booklet to Nogawa Chiyo. Chiyo was delighted. She placed the booklet on her workstand during the break and read it aloud. About half a dozen girls gathered around her and listened. During the lunch break, she and another seventeen-year-old, Misako, read the book aloud in unison. They sounded like school children reciting stories from fairy tales. They spent the ten-minute break in the afternoon in the same fashion.

When the time came for the regular and the overtime crews to change shifts, the women workers at the eastern end of the factory climbed into three of the now empty carts that were used to move the plate glass from the drying stand. Among the girls that squeezed in the carts were Chiyo and Misako, and they had the booklet Tsuneo had written about the stars. Chiyo remarked, "I'm not good at book learning, and I can't write very well. I certainly wish I could write a book like this. Then I could bring it with me when I get married."

That evening during supper Mitsuko told Tsuneo about all this, and he listened silently. Finally he said, "Even though it's nightfall, it's still hot, isn't it? After all, it's still mid-August. It must have been really hot at the shop today."

"It was really awful," Mitsuko replied.

"I'm sure it was. I wonder why the girls who are crowded together during the change in shifts talk about their hopes when it's so hot?"

Tsuneo spoke slowly and hesitantly. Mitsuko thought about that question for some time. After supper, Tsuneo said, "Mitsuko, you can't answer my question?" as if he were trying to comfort her.

"Well, if you ask for a formal answer, I can't reply right away," Mitsuko said.

"Is that so? But don't you talk about the hot workshop all the time? You talk about what the girls say all the time too. You talk about how you can't open the windows even in the summer, and so you don't get any breeze at all. The plant is full of dust from the glass. It's as bad as the lint in cotton-textile plants. Your workstand is white with glass dust. Your work dress is white with it too. By evening your throat is sore. Because your rest period is too short you have to go to the toilet to catch your breath when you get tired. The accident rate jumps in the afternoon. Your workshop is jerry-built, so that even though it is a big plant, you don't even have a dining hall. You have to eat your lunch by the workstand surrounded by dust from the glass. Isn't all that true?" Tsuneo concluded with a smile on his face.

"Yes, that's right," Mitsuko said and looked at Tsuneo as if she were baffled.

"Your work area has a little over eighty workers, hasn't it? The eighty workers are separated into those who wipe the plates of glass, those who sort them out, inspect them, wrap them in paper, cut them, and transport them. Initially, the women workers only wiped the plates of glass and wrapped them in paper. Now the male workers only work as cutters. The elevators transport the huge plate glass to your work area, right?" Tsuneo repeated in minute detail what Mitsuko had told him casually over many months.

"Misako came from a farm community in Akita, and Haruko and thirty some other girls came from Okinawa, didn't they? Chiyo's father is a worker at the Tsurumi shipyard, and her dead mother used to be a tex-tile-factory worker, right?"

Mitsuko said, "That's right. You remember everything I told you. I'm amazed."

"What I remember is far less than what you know. Mitsuko, you should take a better look at your workshop and the environment around you. You mustn't feel that it is bothersome. If you observe things more carefully, you should be able to understand why the girls crowded together in a hot place talk about their hopes. You will be able to understand it by yourself. I would like to hear your conclusions about this. I'll be waiting for your reply," Tsuneo said.

That night while she repaired her mittens Mitsuko kept thinking about what Chiyo and Tsuneo had said. Tsuneo's remark that he would be wait-ing for her reply made her feel as though a burden of responsibility had been placed on her shoulders. Sitting beside her, Tsuneo began writing *The World of the Stars,* which he planned to give to Chiyo. He wrote in a simple style. He wrote the letters neatly, as if they were printed, and used simple words, as he always did when he wrote his books. He added *kana* [phonetic] symbols beside the *kanji* [Chinese characters] to make it easier to read, and he cut out pictures from a science magazine and pasted them in. Here and there he inserted his own sketches. Thus *The World of the Stars* was completed.

This then was why Tsuneo wrote *The World of the Stars*. What was Tsuneo's daily life like when he was working on the book? He got up at four in the morning, scrubbed his body with cold water, and did calisthenics. He repeated this routine every day without fail. Then, until breakfast, he read Marx's *Das Kapital*. After he completed the morning's reading, he jotted down the year, month, date, and time beside the last line he read. After breakfast, he read two or three newspapers and marked the articles that he wanted Mitsuko to cut out. It was Mitsuko's job to cut out the articles and paste them in scrapbooks.

After Tsuneo finished with the newspapers, he donned his work clothes and cap and rushed off to the factory. In his pocket, he might have a copy of Faraday's treatise on the science of candles or Fabre's study of insects or H. G. Wells's children's world history.

When he returned from the factory in the evening, young factory workers often followed him home and spent an hour or so with him. After they left, he began his reading, usually some selected works. He used to urge Mitsuko to read them too. He often cited passages to her, such as the comment by someone called Lenin that "Karl Kautsky kisses the shoes of the capitalists." He read until bedtime, then he would open the window, take a deep, deep breath, and then go to bed. He followed his daily routine meticulously and regularly like clockwork.

Even when an unexpected visitor came or when he had to go out unexpectedly, Tsuneo did not waste any time. Even if the business involved important matters about his comrades, he seldom stayed away overnight—not because he was conscientious about family matters, but because he did not like disrupting his daily routine.

When they lived in the workers' housing in Kawasaki, Tsuneo was friendly with the children in the alley. The children used to chase after him when he walked home from work, and he would tease them by pinching their noses. They considered him an expert top-spinner, and they would come and ask him to join them in spinning tops. Mitsuko used to think that there was an interesting analogy between the top that he spun expertly and smoothly and his daily life, which functioned so regularly. She told him, "You're just like a top. If the time ever comes when you can't follow the daily routine that you have worked out, you might just topple over like a top when it stops spinning."

It was just a casual observation, but her words were prophetic. Tsuneo got sick at 8:00 A.M. on January 14, 1945, and died at 8:45. The cause of death was unknown. That was the report that his family got from the prison authorities. Four days before his death in prison he had written Mitsuko a long letter, full of zest for life. He had written, "It will soon be spring. Wait for its arrival. Stay healthy and vigorous. Farewell."

Writing the simple book, *The World of the Stars,* had become part of Tsuneo's daily routine. During the period when he was writing the book he and Mitsuko were invited to Nogawa Chiyo's home in Shioda-chō. The six-mat room in Chiyo's house was crowded with Chiyo and her two sisters' friends. Numerous comments were directed at Tsuneo.

"Mister, it won't do us any good to learn only about stars."

"It does us no good to want to study. We can't go to school, and we don't have time to study."

"Still, we like to learn about things like the world of the stars."

"Yes, despite everything, we want to study."

"People who study are smart, aren't they? We too can become smart if we study, can't we? But girls like us who come from poor families, some without mothers, can't study, because if we go to school instead of working, our families will suffer."

"I wonder why we have to stay poor. We are all working, my mother, my older sister, my younger sister, and I, but. . . ."

They bombarded Tsuneo with questions and remarks like these. He simply smiled as he listened to them.

Near the river that is on the way to Kawasaki from Shioda, there was a plot of land owned by the Tokyo Shibaura Plant, which was overgrown with weeds. While they were walking home from Chiyo's place that night, Tsuneo, for the first time since they had been married, asked her to go for a walk with him in the field. Tsuneo talked about his life as a young man living in a tenement house in the mining town and how he used to be bombarded with questions by a gathering of miners, much like that evening. He had struggled in trying to answer them, but it was a new experience to have questions directed at him by young women working in a modern industrial plant. The wind rushed past them as they walked in the grass. Tsuneo walked as if he were floating; at times he seemed oblivious of his wife walking beside him.

He repeated what one of the girls said: "Still, we like to learn about things like the world of the stars." Suddenly he stopped and looked up to the sky and exclaimed, "Look, that star is so bright. I wonder what it's called." Then he asked his wife, who was much younger than he and who was unfamiliar with theoretical matters, "Have you ever thought about such remarks as 'Even so,' 'In spite of that, I had to do it,' 'In spite of that, the outcome was like this'?

"Louis Pasteur, a biologist who is now looked upon as a benefactor of mankind, said that once a person gets used to doing his best, he cannot live unless he does his best. Because of his efforts and his courage he was able to discover the existence of bacteria, in spite of the limitations of time and circumstances that hampered him. Edison is called a genius as an inventor. You must know that he invented the electric light bulb. He said that his success depended on 1 percent inspiration, 99 percent perspiration. An amazing amount of hard work. China is called a semicolony today. Imagine the terrible conditions under which the workers and peasants are living in that country. In spite of that, the anti-Japanese people's resistance movement is making great progress. Let's imagine that the workers of Japan are trapped by oppressive forces, like mice caught in a sack. We might then conclude that they are in a hopeless situation. That is, if we forget the one important condition, 'In spite of this,' we would have to say that the situation is hopeless. But as long as the workers continue their struggle with 1 percent inspiration and 99 percent hard work, they will succeed in breaking down a section of the wall of oppression that surrounds them. In the end, they will be able to turn the tables on the oppressors and turn them into mice trapped in a sack and destroy them. I am firmly convinced of this. No matter what sort of difficulties surrounds us, we must not give up hope. Human beings always have that one condition, 'In spite of this,' on their side. That is what makes life so interesting."

During this period some of his old friends were beginning to say that fascism is a progressive theory. And there were people who, though intellectually opposed to war, went along with the tide of war, desperately trying to protect their personal security. Some were scared out of their wits and denounced people like Tsuneo who had refused to defect [from communism] and who were special targets of surveillance by the police and security officers. It was a time when he could not even drop his guard with the few remaining friends he had. In spite óf this, Tsuneo could not stop working for peace and the end of the war. These were the days when he seemed to cling to the words of the girls who kept saying "In spite of that. . . ."

Tsuneo and Mitsuko's life was strenuous even before Tsuneo started to work for the advancement of the aspirations of people like Chiyo. As the factory work became more demanding Mitsuko could barely keep up with her work at the plant and at home. Once Tsuneo started writing *The World of the Stars* life became more difficult for Mitsuko. Time became more precious than anything else for Tsuneo. He cut back on the time that he worked in the factory and worked on *The World of the Stars*. Consequently, the meager income that the two earned became even smaller. With this reduced income, Tsuneo purchased reference books and went to study with specialists to get their help. As a result, there was not enough money to pay the household expenses. Mitsuko decided that she would have to take on extra work, something that she could do at home. Because of the shortages caused by the war, people were shopping around desperately for clothing, and hoarding was becoming more widespread. The price of clothing continued to rise steeply, and winter was now near at hand. Mitsuko began to mutter, "What a fix, what a fix."

One night, with winter approaching, Mitsuko was mending Tsuneo's old overcoat. She exclaimed, "What shall we do?" A few minutes later, when she was going through the wicker basket, she muttered, "What a fix, what a fix!" She blurted these words out almost casually. She was worried that there would not be enough cloth to mend the overcoat and no yarn to mend the sweater. They had no money to buy any yarn. How was she going to get the winter clothing ready?

Tsuneo, as was his wont, was busy writing at his desk by the window, muttering to himself from time to time. It didn't even appear that he was aware of the presence of his wife in the room. But suddenly he turned around and said, "You keep saying 'What a fix.' I don't feel that I'm in any trouble. And even if I am in a fix, I don't moan about it."

Mitsuko was taken aback and asked, "Why not?"

"Hardship and difficulties are like that flame," he said, and pointed out the window to the flame that could be seen coming out of the smelter in the steel mill. It looked as if a fire were burning close by.

"That flame is tempering ordinary iron into steel. You too have started to work to help the workers fulfill their hopes. Consequently, everything has gotten more difficult than before. The difficulties that you are undergoing may be having a revolutionary effect on you, like that flame. Unless you rise above the difficulties, you will be unable to fulfill your hopes. Isn't that so? Don't you agree? If so, aren't your difficulties the starting point for the fulfillment of your aspirations? I believe this to be so. That's why I am working hard at my task."

He then stretched his arms out toward the autumn sky glowing in the flame, inhaled the fresh air, quietly closed the window, and resumed working.

What had he written that night? The notes that he scribbled down on paper that night were undoubtedly recopied by Chiyo and others who got together at night for that purpose. Chiyo and her friends waited for Tsuneo to finish a given chapter and then made copies of it. The copies that they made were then recopied by some young men whom Tsuneo did not know at a place he did not know. While composing his thoughts, Tsuneo would mutter to himself as if he were talking to the unknown copiers.

Chiyo and her friends continued the task of copying Tsuneo's writings. And they kept saying they wished they could write the way Tsuneo did, so that when they got married they could bring their writings with them to their new homes. Circumstances would prevent them from fulfilling their dreams. But they continued to come to Tsuneo to talk about their aspirations. And he had to respond to them. He told them the only way to change the conditions that quash their aspirations was to struggle against those conditions. That struggle would lead to unity among the workers.

He knew that if the answers he was providing the girls got to the ears of the Special Higher Police he would lose his freedom again. As long as the Peace Preservation Law remained in effect this would be so. Nevertheless, Tsuneo tried to answer the girls' questions forthrightly and courageously. He felt that in order for them to understand what he was saying and to gain courage from his answers he not only had to be accurate in what he was saying but also had to express his ideas in a clear, simple fashion. In addition, he had to be creative if they were to build up their courage. So the circle of people who came together because of *The World of the Stars* made Tsuneo strive to be as creative and imaginative as possible. The circle went through several phases, but at the end of two years it became a movement that demanded of Tsuneo even more courage and effort.

Undoubtedly, Mitsuko thought, Tsuneo was thinking of the days with the circle of his followers as he looked up at the autumn sky from the cell of his jail. "As late fall arrives we know that winter is near at hand," he had written in his letter to Mitsuko. This made Mitsuko think of the fall of 1939. One day she and Tsuneo walked from the station of the Nambu Electric Tram Line toward the Fuji Electric Company. Along the way they passed by a young men's school where the teacher was lecturing on algebra. He was explaining the formula $(a + b)^2 = a^2 + 2ab + b^2$.

Mitsuko observed, "It looks like a sleepy class. Most of the students seem to be dozing." Tsuneo continued to observe the class proceedings without saying a word. Two days later he came home with two of the young men who were in the algebra class. Immediately, he began to work with them on their algebra homework. He repeatedly wrote and erased diagrams on the slate and spoke to them in a low, deliberate tone. From time to time the two young men burst into laughter. Before they left, they told Mitsuko, "Mrs., we will be coming to get help from the Mister for an hour on Tuesday and Friday. We want to thank you." They then bade Tsuneo a cheerful farewell and left. So Tsuneo took on more work. In order to help Tsuneo with his work, Kashima Yoshimi introduced him to the young men's math teacher.[9] It was arranged to have Tsuneo meet the young men in one of the classrooms rather than at home. His tutoring was to be conducted in a more serious fashion.

One day late in the fall, in order to get better acquainted with the young math students, Tsuneo and Mitsuko went hiking along the Tama River with the math teacher and the students. After the walk, Tsuneo and Mitsuko walked home by following the path along the bank of the river. It was almost sunset. As they were walking along the grassy path, bathed in the late afternoon sun, they approached a wooded area. Tsuneo said, "Let's rest here for a while. It's been a special day." He sat down on the grass, which had turned yellow. Even the hardier weeds had been wilted by the frost.

After Mitsuko sat down Tsuneo said, "Our circle had its beginning in a sleepy classroom. It's as if we are mocking the popular saying 'It can't be helped.' This shows that urgent matters that are confronting us now must and can be taken on."

"What, for example?" Mitsuko asked.

"I've been saying this for some time, but the Peace Preservation Law and the Special Higher Police are rigorously suppressing all movements working for autonomy and democracy. They make it dangerous to carry on any group activity, with various levels of self-awareness, that we see around us. Even natural and commonplace gatherings are threatened. The authorities can crush them at will. So these groups must be organized in a well-structured fashion. We must protect these organizations from repression. That's the most urgent task facing us today."

After pausing for a moment, Tsuneo continued, "We are about to be engulfed by the growing desires of the young workers. If we had ignored the first signs of their budding aspirations, we would not be in this position today. But we were moved by their desire 'to write something like this myself.' After that we got involved deeper and deeper. Was it a mistake? I don't think so. Of course a circle can be created by anybody at any place. But if the circle does not have a sustaining leadership, it will disappear like a bubble. The five or six circles that we are now involved in cannot be led by one individual. You must be aware of this too. We need well-structured organizations to provide the leadership for these groups. We urgently need to create a leadership organ that can survive whatever repressive force is brought to bear against it and fight back courageously. We need an organizational structure that we can depend on. Without it, all the work that we have poured into these groups will end up having no more significance than a form of self-gratification. That's what I think. So there is our urgent task. Can you understand that? I don't want to force you into this."

The two of them remained silent for a while. Then Mitsuko asked, "Are you going with Mr. Kashima to join a new group of comrades that I know nothing about?"

"Yes, I'm going there," is all Tsuneo said.

"Aren't you going there to discuss ways of organizing a group that can carry on the struggle?"

"Maybe so," he said, and remained silent.

The air began to get cooler and the wind began to stir.

"What's the matter? What are you thinking of? Are you going to cry?" Tsuneo said sharply.

"That's not so. When the circle of *The World of the Stars* was being formed you asked me why the girls crowded together in a stifling hot place and talked about their hopes. And you said you would wait for my answer. Don't you remember? I haven't forgotten. I don't want the girls to abandon their hopes and aspirations. To support the spirit that is behind their aspiration I am willing to make any sacrifice at all that is necessary. Chiyo's aspirations will not appear selfish or unreasonable to anyone. People with such aspirations are all around us. They were there even in the classroom where half of the students were dozing off. I was thinking how amazing they all are. Anyone who has seen such hopes come to the surface will not want to see their aspirations wither away.

"Isn't it true that this important, urgent task is to be undertaken, not because you have extraordinary courage or leadership capacity, but because you want to be faithful to the workers' hopes? That being the case, even a woman like me, who has no leadership ability and no self-confidence, can join you in undertaking the urgent task that you speak of."

The air was turning colder and the sky was getting darker. The late fall wind felt bitterly cold on Mitsuko's cheeks. Tsuneo placed his rough hands on hers and grasped them firmly. 'Mitsuko, you understand what I mean because you have inner strength. I am really pleased. I am neither strong nor heroic. I'm an ordinary person. I don't think I can accomplish very much by myself. But I have faith in the strength of the working class. Why? Because it is a reality that you and I have seen. That's why. All I want to do is to work for the happiness of the workers and fulfill my responsibility to the workers who possess self-respect."

Tsuneo continued to grasp Mitsuko's hand firmly. "The cold wind is getting stronger, isn't it? Winter is near. No, it is already winter. I remember a poem that goes: 'Blow wind, blow! After the storm the blue sky will appear, and the trees will grow big and strong.' I still believe in what the poem says. I hope you embrace this poem too."

"As late fall arrives we know that winter is near at hand," Tsuneo had written in his letter. When Mitsuko came across this passage as she was glancing hastily over his letters, she thought of this poem about the storm. He had also quoted Faraday's remarks to his students: "I hope that you will dedicate your lives to the well-being of humanity and work toward the fulfillment of this responsibility." Mitsuko had first heard Tsuneo express this sentiment to a gathering of a small group of women workers of the glass company. He had come to the gathering to speak to the young women, who were there to be exposed to the most elementary level of scientific knowledge.

In the beginning, they merely chatted aimlessly. Then they began to talk about how dangerous it would be if someone were to throw a bomb in the factory. Then they talked about how scared they were when they first had to work by the opening through which cartloads of faulty glass were thrown down to the underground workshop. There they could see a mound of broken plate glass with sharp edges glistening ominously. The noise of hundreds of pieces of defective plate glass being thrown on top of the pile of broken glass grated on their nerves. Even to think of it made them feel nervous and edgy. By now, they should have gotten used to that noise, but it still jarred. It was strange. What accounted for this? The more scientific advances are made, the more people have to suffer, it seems. Why doesn't science help people end wars? they began to ask.

Tsuneo listened to the discussion without saying a word. Then he talked to them about science at a very elementary level. Then he talked about Faraday. He concluded by saying, "It is only natural that you hate wars. I hate wars of aggression. The forces that oppose war depend on gentle people like you. I hope that you, as Faraday says, will dedicate your entire lives to the advancement of human well-being. To that end I hope you will devote all your energies to abolishing wars and bringing about peace. That is what science wants."

In early January, Chaplain Matsuda came to cell number 1 and with a cheerful look said, "Number 25, are you cold? Have you gotten used to your job? Today is a lucky day for you, you've got a letter." She handed her a letter from Tsuneo, a sealed postal card. It read:

> November 18. I think I ended the last letter to you rather abruptly so I shall continue where I left off. First, as to my reading, since arriving here I have been trying to read primarily books on history, economics, and science. (Then four lines were blacked out.) That was my intention (one line blacked out). After I am released I plan to read books on the ancient classics and religion (six lines blacked out). I have read the official versions of Tokutomi Sohō's history of Japan from the beginning to the Ansei persecution [mid-nineteenth century], the five volumes of Shirayanagi Shūko's *People's History of Japan,* and *History of World Economic Struggles*. They are all informative. (Twelve lines deleted.) Take care of yourself. Goodbye.

Two days later the guard on duty handed Mitsuko another letter from Tsuneo.

> December 5. Dear Wife:
>   Are you well? The end of the year is here. Has your city of fogs turned into a city of snow? At the end of last month I received a

letter from your father. I received the message you sent me through him. (Twelve lines blacked out.) For the first time in a long while I got hold of *Scientific Knowledge,* the November issue. It was a special issue dealing with precision measurements and instruments used for this purpose. Topics dealing with measures, time, light, magnetism, cosmic rays were discussed by nine professors. Professor of physics, Dr. Mutō, has an article that deals with the law of nature that governs the microscopic world. It has to do with the nucleus of the atom (whose size is about one billionth of a centimeter). The nucleus is at the core of the atom. The atom (whose size ranges from one hundred millionth to one billionth of a centimeter) consists of the nucleus and electrons that revolve around the nucleus. (Nine lines blacked out.) Thus far neutrons have been detected only in cosmic rays; they have not been isolated from the nucleus of the atom yet. The author speculates that the laws that govern the world of atomic particles is likely to bring about a revolution greater than the one caused by the theory of relativity or the quantum theory. I would like to write about this in greater detail, but I am running out of space. There is also an article on the Mendelian theory. I think you too will find the November issue of *Scientific Knowledge* interesting. Be well and wait for my next letter. Goodbye.

A week later the guard on duty told Mitsuko, "Number 25, there are two letters for you," and handed her two sealed postcards. They had been posted on December 18 and 27. Mitsuko scrutinized the minute writing (of what remained after the censor had made the deletions) and tried to read between the lines about Tsuneo's true feelings and to fathom what his daily life was really like.

In the letter of December 18, Tsuneo wrote that his explanation of the atomic world in his last letter was written simply and in haste, so it was no doubt difficult for Mitsuko to understand. The letter was evidently written to explain the atomic theory clearly and carefully, but Mitsuko could not understand what he was driving at [because of the deletions].

Tsuneo started his letter of December 27, "It is getting colder, but I hope you are well. I too am well so please do not worry." He then concluded by saying that he hoped Mitsuko would greet the New Year in good health. Mitsuko surmised that the portions that had been blacked out must have dealt with comments about the end of the year. She wondered why Tsuneo was using up the precious space in his letters discussing scientific matters. Perhaps he was trying to write about matters that would not be deleted by the censor so that Mitsuko would at least be able to read his letters in their entirety. Mitsuko got up to the cell door where there was more light to try to make out the parts that were blacked out.

Observing her do this, the guard said, "I too tried to read the blacked-out part under a bright light. I managed to make out just one part. Toward the end, after the word 'it' the blacked-out line contains the word 'Einstein.' So it reads 'Einstein expanded it further.' But with the deletion it reads '. . . expanded it,' so it makes no sense. I couldn't make out the other parts, but the deletions in other parts indicate that they were blacked out to make the sentences unintelligible."

Mitsuko continued to lean up against the latticed cell door and tried to read the blacked-out portions by the light in the corridor.

The guard continued, "What I told you must make you, number 25, feel bitter toward the chaplain. But let me tell you something so that you won't feel quite so bitter." She turned her face away from Mitsuko and, leaning against the cell door, continued, "Consider a situation when, under the order of the warden, I have to put handcuffs on a prisoner and guard her when I believe she is innocent. As a human being I find it hard to do so. But the responsibility for the action rests with the warden and the order that he gives. As a guard, the only thing that I can do is obey his command. Likewise, the chaplain has to censor stringently the letters of people accused of harboring dangerous thoughts. The higher authorities order her to do so. Perhaps she is incapable of following her order except by censoring the letters the way she does. Maybe she is too conscientious. In both our cases, the responsibility lies with the higher-ups who give the orders. But I am a human being too. So I have been agonizing over the problem of being a jailer as well as a human being. As an outlet for my dilemma I have been composing poems. Even if I have to break the rules that must not be broken by jailers, I wanted to find a way to satisfy the humanistic outflow of love that exists between you and your husband. That's how I am. The chaplain too must experience mental anguish. But she can cling to the faith that convinces her that as long as she calls out the name of the Buddha, she will be saved. So she manages to stay cheerful even when she has to black out what people have written. That is the only difference between the chaplain and me."

The guard spoke as if she were talking to herself. She had her back toward Mitsuko and seemed to be looking up at the sky.

Mitsuko kept waiting for letters from Tsuneo even though they were mutilated with deletions. One day toward the end of January, number 13 was ordered, early in the morning, to clean the area around the isolation cabin carefully. Number 15, who took number 7's place as the cleaning woman, went around to the single cells right after breakfast to give the inmates a shave. Number 25 was told to change into a new red garment.

After lunch, more than ten important-looking gentlemen led by the warden came to inspect the prison. Soon after, Mitsuko was taken to the neat room which served as the warden's office as well as the reception room. The aged warden came in and sent the guard out of the room. Then he spoke to Mitsuko in a quiet voice. "The men who came to visit the prison today were the director of the Hiroshima penal system, the chief judge of the Hiroshima court of appeals, the chief of the protective custodial agency of Chūgoku and Shikoku, and representatives of the prosecutor's office. They are all prominent people. All of these men are concerned about your welfare. Have you changed your mind about things? If you wish to make a statement about yourself or about your thoughts to the government, you should take advantage of the opportunity present today and meet and speak with these important officials. How do you feel about this?"

Mitsuko thought for a while and said, "I truly appreciate your kindness. But I can talk to my parents and my husband about personal matters and about my thoughts. I do not have any special matter that I feel I must speak to the honorable officials about. If I do have anything particular that I must tell the government, I believe it would be best to speak to you about it directly. Even though these are important people, they are total strangers to me. I would not have anything to say to them even if I were to see them. I wish to thank you for your kind thoughts, but I do not wish to see them."

The warden gave no indication that he was offended and said, "All right. I understand. I shall arrange it so that you will not have to meet them. Since there are many important visitors here today, I must cut this meeting short. I would like to speak with you in a more leisurely fashion, perhaps tomorrow." He then summoned the guard to escort Mitsuko out of his office.

On the following day, Mitsuko had another conference with the warden. He told Mitsuko that the head of the protective custodial agency of Chūgoku and Shikoku had asked to meet with Mitsuko because he saw it as his responsibility to do so. The warden said that as the head of the penitentiary he could not refuse his request and asked Mitsuko to see the official. The chief of the custodial agency was then led into the office. He spoke cordially to the warden and Mitsuko. He told her, "Here, here. Sit down here."

He then explained at length his duties as head of the custodial agency. He said he not only had to oversee the welfare of the convicts' families, but he had to watch over the convicts' interests after their release, including their means of livelihood. That was the assignment given him by the state. He repeatedly told her that he would assist in any way he could to obtain books for her while she was in prison because books are food for the spirit. Then after a moment's silence he continued, "Your husband's trial will soon end. May I ask if you still have no intention of dissolving your marriage with him, even at this stage?"

When Mitsuko indicated that she had no intention of terminating her marriage, the official said, "Well then, I think my subordinates will be visiting this prison again. If you have anything that you want to have taken care of, like sending messages to your family, please speak up without hesitation. The custodial agency will do the best it can." He then left the room.

Because the chaplain happened to be away at that time, Mitsuko spoke to the warden about obtaining some reading material. She told him that she wanted to continue studying mathematics, a subject that she had begun to study during her incarceration in Tokyo. He granted her permission to obtain the necessary books.

She couldn't wait to write to her husband and was anxious for the advent of February. It was very cold on February first. That night she wrote her husband:

Thank you so much for your many letters. I appreciate hearing about what you are reading and learning about new scientific knowledge involving the structure of atomic particles. I would like to learn a great deal more about this subject, but now that your trial is starting I fear I will be unable to receive your interesting letters for awhile. In the letter I wrote in November, I mentioned that I was unable to do much reading, but recently I received permission to continue my studies in mathematics which I had started in the Tokyo jail. So I have finally started studying trigonometry. I plan to start on differential calculus and integral calculus soon. Isn't it ironical that I am beginning to study mathematics, something that you have been urging me to do, only after entering prison. Well, enough about my studies. Now I shall report on my efforts to stay healthy. First of all, in order to avoid catching cold I have been massaging my body with cold water every day since the beginning of winter. When the temperature is about 10 below zero (centigrade) the wet towel freezes the moment I stop massaging my body with it. When I try to squeeze it dry, it turns into a little ball. But every day at the end of the day, I feel great happiness in having survived one more day. Next, I do physical exercises three times a day: once right after the cold-water massage, once during the exercise hour, and once before I go to bed. Ordinarily, I am unable to stick to a single project very long, but here I have to continue exercising because it is cold. Since the advent of winter I have been exercising even more vigorously. Today is February first, so the cold weather will not last much longer. But a popular song mentions seven snowfalls after the vernal equinox, so I cannot let up on my physical fitness program. I have had my baptism in frost bites, snow bites, and chapped hands, but otherwise I have been in good health. I have said enough about my physical fitness program.

Next I shall report a little on the ferocity of General Winter, and its beauty, things that I had not experienced before I came to Miyoshi. They tell me the snowfall is lighter than usual, but it is still quite heavy. When the first snowfall came, I thought the upper half of my body would freeze when I was seated on the floor doing my work. On those occasions, my old toothache would start to bother me, and I felt like giving up in despair. I dread the cold, but between snowfalls when the thick morning mist drifts by, the trees bloom with flowers of ice. As the sun mounts high into the sky and sparkles on the beautiful crystals of ice, they suddenly vanish. Between the branches of the big cherry tree in the compound, one can see Mount Takatani, as well as the roofs of the prison buildings enveloped in the mist, and the hazy horizon in the distance. All this is framed by the light-blue sky. It is like a painting on canvas. The glass partitions in the corridor sparkle in the sunlight and the air shimmers and glistens. Perhaps the nerves in our body fall asleep from time to time, because on these occasions my toothache subsides and I feel extraordinarily serene. This noon I had rice cooked with soy beans and barley and a small portion of pickled greens. The pickles, which I was able to chew because my toothache had ceased, were incredibly delicious. This has been one of the delightful moments for me this winter. Mount Takatani to the south is the highest and the most distant of the mountains that surround the prison. The fields that appear between the trees climb to about seven-tenths of the way to the summit of the mountain. The fields cannot be seen very clearly right now because of the snow, but when spring comes, I am sure the wheat fields will become visible. The fields located between the trees and the gently sloping outline of the mountain remind me of many things. Near our cabin are peas and beans that we planted last fall. They seem to be straining to push their way though the snow. It's hard to believe that before long they will be bearing beautiful blossoms. I hope that I too will continue to grow bit by bit during the winter and become the bearer of delicate flowers.

By the time this letter arrives at your prison, you may have been released. You must regret having had to give up the robe my mother sent you. I hope you can keep warm during the cold nights by dreaming of Mount Takatani, the peas, and me.

I want to mention before ending this letter that in my father's letter to me he mentioned your coming trial. He also said that the first time Mother smiled this winter was when you wrote that the robe she sent you was keeping you warm. My parents apparently are waiting till spring to visit you and me. Today is the coldest day of the winter yet. Please stay well. Goodbye.

Mitsuko had written a long letter, but she had no wish to mention the fact that she had been asked if she wouldn't consider dissolving her marriage to him. Soon another letter arrived from Tsuneo. He wrote,

February 12. Dear Wife:

I was delighted to receive your letter of February 1. I am fully aware of how you really feel, so you need not take the trouble to write to me when you are severely handicapped. I am satisfied to have your father pass on messages from you to me. Well, my trial started on the second. (Seven lines blacked out.) It should be over by the beginning of March. When March comes it will be warm enough that, even without the robe, I will no longer be cold. Compared with where you are, the winter here is fairly comfortable. It has been a good year. It didn't even snow. (Fourteen lines deleted.) So you are now studying trigonometry, the beginning of higher mathematics. (Thirteen lines deleted.) The fact that I did not suffer much from the cold weather is all due to your mother's kindness and the robe she sent me. Well, so much for today. Take care of yourself. Keep up your studies and your work. Goodbye.

This was the last letter Mitsuko received from Tsuneo while he was in prison in Tokyo.

According to the convicts in Miyoshi, February is the coldest and most difficult month. But they consoled themselves by saying, "February flees, and March marches off." All sorts of things happened to Mitsuko during February. That was the month when an official from the Chūgoku-Shikoku custodial agency appeared with a message from her parents. It was toward the end of the month, which seemed to be flying by so quickly, that Mitsuko walked past the little gate in front of the cabin to see the official. The remains of the winter snow had turned into chunks of ice along the steps. Dirt had covered it, so the edge of the walk had turned into a strip of blackish, grey ice.

When Mitsuko entered the warden's office, the official was already seated by the brazier and was warming his hands. His name card on the table read: Custodial Agent of the Chūgoku-Shikoku Region, Maruoka Noboru.

When Mitsuko stood before him, the bald-headed old official stood up, bracing himself against the brazier. He then placed his two hands by his knees and bowed deeply. "I am pleased to meet you. This is who I am. I hope we have good relations in the future," and he handed Mitsuko his name card. Mitsuko was at a loss about the proper way to respond to his courteous greeting. The official continued, "Please sit down by the brazier. The charcoal is burning well. Don't hesitate. I'm sure it is difficult to be in a cold place like this day after day. I sympathize with you. Miyoshi is known as the Hokkaido of Hiroshima, and it is really cold. When I was a youngster, I was a friend of the heir to the Asano family, the former feudal lord of Hiroshima, so I am quite familiar with Miyoshi, which has strong ties to the Asano family. Now, don't stand on ceremony. Please sit down on this chair. I have a lot of things to discuss with you today, so please be seated." He then moved the chair toward Mitsuko. When Mitsuko sat down, the official moved closer to her as if they were close friends.

"Now, I attended your husband's trial and on the way back I stopped by to see how your father was doing. I have some messages from him to you. I stopped by here after I left your father's home."

According to the official, Mitsuko's father had a stroke when he heard of Tsuneo's arrest and was now paralyzed on one side of his body. Because of his advanced age his condition had worsened and he had been bedridden ever since the stroke. When Mr. Maruoka told him that he would convey to Mitsuko any message he wanted to send her, her father was reported to have said, "Even though she is my child, as long as the state makes its decision about her guilt or innocence and fixes the punishment it deems to be just, I am willing to accept the official decision whether it be freedom or death. But when it comes to the question of human feelings, it is another matter. As their father I have been well treated and received many kind favors from Tsuneo and his wife. I put my hands together in prayer and worship them. I never go to bed by pointing my feet in their direction. Three times a day I make food offerings to them at the Buddhist altar in my home and pray for their well-being. Please tell Mitsuko this."

After telling Mitsuko this, Maruoka continued, "I am familiar with what transpired at your husband's trial. His sentence is to be handed down when the trial ends, but I feel that it will be a long-term prison sentence. I don't know if he will ever come out of prison alive. What do you expect to do with such a husband?"

When Mitsuko did not respond, the official moved closer to her and continued, "Your father is getting old. On top of that, he has had a stroke and is very worried about this trial. I have the impression that he will not live much longer. What do you plan to do for your father? I understand you have two younger brothers. They are both set to enter the army soon. They probably do not expect to come back alive. And no doubt their chances of coming back alive are just about nonexistent. Then your family line will come to an end. What do you plan to do about that?" he asked.

Mitsuko had no way of responding. She remained silent, trying to think of some sort of reply.

The official continued, "I feel sorry for your older sister. I hear she has four children, but she is about to be divorced. It seems that her husband's family has decided that unless they cut their ties with a family that has produced a member who is willing to shoot an arrow at the emperor, it will be impossible for their sons to get ahead in life, and their daughters will not be able to marry. I agree with their decision. A prominent family like that must take the position they are taking. That is only common sense. How do you feel about this? How can you ever face your sister?"

Maruoka continued, "Your mother is having a difficult time too, isn't she? The two of you are in prison. And to be frank, I don't believe your husband will be able to come out of prison alive. In fact, lots of people feel that it would be better if he does not come out of prison. Your father has been ill for quite some time and requires a lot of care. Your mother's two sons will be going in the army soon so she can't count on their help. Then your older sister is going to be divorced. It doesn't look like your mother has any source of income. She surely must be having a difficult time, though she probably can't talk to anybody about her troubles. She looks gaunt and careworn. I feel sorry for her."

The official stirred up the charcoal in the brazier and went on, "Come closer and warm yourself. It's really cold, isn't it? You seem to have a bad case of frostbite on your hands. Don't hesitate. Warm yourself. Your father is a man of integrity. Unusual for a farmer. He also seems to be an expert haiku composer. I wonder how someone like you who was brought up by a father like him can endure the hardships of a place like this. I don't mean to be rude, but are you determined not to divorce your husband even if you have to live apart from him for the rest of your life? From the way it looks, it's not likely that you'll ever be able to live together as husband and wife again. Four years from now when you get back into society, the world will have changed beyond your imagination. What do you plan to do when that time comes?" Maruoka looked at Mitsuko as if they were good friends.

Mitsuko felt like asking him what he hoped to accomplish by telling her, a person locked behind high walls and deprived of her freedom, about the difficulties of the close members of her family who were her constant source of worry. He would probably respond, "What do you plan to do about it?" And how was she to answer his query "What do you plan to do after you leave the prison?" when he told her that the world would be changed beyond recognition. Mitsuko felt that the old official kept posing questions that could not be answered. Before Mitsuko could say anything, the old man pulled up his knees and began rubbing his hands.

"I'm truly sorry. I was told that you were devoted to your family and your brothers and sisters and that you would make sacrifices for your family. I came expecting you to give me a favorable answer. Now, it appears that I have to return without getting any reply from you. I feel as if I have lost face. But think matters over carefully, and while you are doing so, if what I said today turns out to be of some help to you, I shall be satisfied. I will not give up; I shall come back again soon. When I come back, I hope you will give me a favorable answer. Miyoshi is a very cold place, so take good care of yourself while you perform your duties." He then concluded the meeting, bowed his bald head several times politely, and left the room.

That night in bed Mitsuko kept seeing the grey-haired, emaciated image of her father. No matter how hard she tried, she could not get his image out of her mind. Even though half of his body was paralyzed, he had been writing to her every day. He gave no indication to Mitsuko in prison that he was sick. In the letter she had received from him only two or three days ago he had written, "There is an old saying that sages seek out a life of solitude which gives them peace of mind. As this saying indicates, things of this world do not bend to one's wishes. Even an ordinary person like me envies those who can lead a life of solitary existence. You two are literally leading a life of solitary seclusion. Like the ancient sages, you must spend your days reading as many books as you can." At the end of the letter he added two haiku poems written in an old-fashioned style.

Pampas grass, standing too tall, they are broken in two by the wind.
Pampas grass, standing tall, they force the wind to retreat.

Mitsuko's father had never left his mountain home. He had lived his entire life convinced that the thoughts of Confucius and Mencius were the most precious concepts in the world. He also paid strict heed to the teachings of the Buddha. This old man named Michiyuki [follower of the way] told the official on his way to Miyoshi to perform his duty as an agent of the government, a government which had imprisoned his daughter and her husband, a government that may execute them or free them. "I put my hands together in prayer and worship them. I never go to bed by pointing my feet in their direction. . . . I pray for their well-being." As Mitsuko thought about how he must have felt when he said this, she couldn't stop crying. The image of her aged father, who must have gritted his teeth when he said this, could not be erased from her mind.

As March approached, the weather became very unpredictable. In the middle of the night, a strong wind-storm broke out. The windows in the corridor began to rattle violently, and outside the wind raged and roared fiercely. The poles and beams of the prison creaked and groaned. Snowflakes mixed with dirt came swirling into the room through the cracks in the floor. Mitsuko listened intently to what was probably the last of the winter's north wind roaring violently across the landscape of the Miyoshi basin. She could feel the force of the wind, which seemed intent upon destroying before winter lapsed the few weeds and shrubs that had survived the winter wind and blizzard until then. She thought there must be a few stalks of lonely pampas grass being whipped about in the storm. The image of the pampas grass began to turn into that of her emaciated father. Mitsuko cried violently for a long time. She kept repeating the haiku poem, "Blow, blow, blow as much as you wish. After the storm the sky will clear."

Soon dawn arrived and the storm subsided, leaving behind windswept layers of snow. But the blue sky did not appear; the whole day was enveloped in dreary grey. At midnight it began to rain. The rain melted the snow on the roof; chunks of snow began to hit the ground with resounding thuds. The following day was clear and warm. The calendar showed that February had left and the long-awaited month of March had arrived.

It snowed again in March, but the snow melted almost as soon as it hit the ground. Every noon Mitsuko was allowed to go out in the yard for her exercise. Near the high wall where the southwest sun warms the ground, she came across bright yellow blossoms of the wood-sorrel plant amidst clusters of maroon leaves. She almost exclaimed, "What a surprise!" Near the stone by the little ditch on the south side, tiny white flowers of chickweed were in bloom too. Underneath the green leaves of the chickweed, she saw a strange-looking greyish substance. Mitsuko wondered what it was and poked at it with a twig. It looked like a dead lizard. One warm evening it must have thought it was spring and come out to frolic. Then the temperature must have dropped suddenly. It must have started to go back to its hole but froze to death before it made it to its home. Mitsuko burst out laughing. With a smile on her face she walked about breathing deeply. She pretended she was playing jump rope and pranced around. "Spring is here, spring is here," she told herself.

Mitsuko could hear the convicts, the young ones as well as the old ones, shouting "Aye, Yaa!" They were performing the noon-hour bamboo-spear exercises in the area in front of the chapel. Mitsuko was not allowed to join them, but the guard assigned to watch over her while she was in the yard behind the isolation cabin let her peer at their activities. From the entrance in the high wall, Mitsuko could see straw figures roped onto the big cherry trees standing on both sides of the chapel. The straw figures had drawings of Roosevelt and Churchill attached as their faces. The convicts took turns charging the straw figures with their bamboo spears. Mitsuko could see number 72 and number 13 among the convicts. She also saw on the stone steps by the chapel entrance Chaplain Matsuda in her black robe, and the old warden with a long sword by his side. The convicts were divided into three groups: red, green, and dark blue. They were dressed in kimono and drawers. They wore headbands of white toweling and straw sandals. Each held a green bamboo spear in her hand. The chief guard and the other guards, dressed in the official blue-serge upper garments and Japanese skirts, were standing alongside. Their long sleeves were tucked in with white sashes.

The area where Mitsuko was standing was a thin strip of ground sandwiched in between the isolation cabin and the high wall and was cut off from sunlight. The snow that had fallen from the roof stood high on the ground. When Mitsuko glanced at the foot of the snow pile, she saw a single bog-rhubarb shoot poking its head through the ground. Mitsuko exclaimed, "Oh, a bog-rhubarb shoot!" and rushed toward it. There she found not just one shoot but several pushing their way through the ground. Mitsuko said, "Spring is here. Tsuneo's verdict should be handed down soon, perhaps today. But I won't worry about it. Look how well I am." She talked to the shoots as if she were talking to number 72.[10]

NOTES

Chapter 1

1. Hiratsuka Raichō, *Hiratsuka Raichō Jiden* (Hiratsuka Raichō's Autobiography), Kobayashi Tomie, ed., 4 vols. (Tokyo: Daigetsu Shoten, 1971–72), I: 328.

2. Murasaki Shikibu, *The Tale of Genji,* trans. Arthur Waley (New York: Random House, 1960), p. 666.

3. Inoue Kiyoshi, *Nihon Joseishi* (History of Japanese Women) (Tokyo: Sanichi Shobō, 1967), pp. 99–102.

4. Monzaemon Chikamatsu, *The Major Plays of Chikamatsu,* trans. Donald Keene (New York: Columbia University Press, 1961), p. 76.

5. Basil Chamberlain, *Things Japanese* (London: Routledge and Kegan Paul, 1939), pp. 503–7.

6. Ienaga Saburō, *Nihon Dōtokushisō-shi* (History of Japanese Moral Thought) (Tokyo: Iwanami Shoten), pp. 143–46.

7. Inoue Kiyoshi, *Nihon Joseishi,* pp. 143–49.

8. George Sansom, *A History of Japan 1615–1867* (Stanford: Stanford University Press, 1963), p. 99.

9. Inazo Nitobe, *Bushido, the Soul of Japan* (New York: Putnam, 1905), p. 135.

10. Fukuzawa Yukichi Chosaku Hensankai, ed., *Fukuzawa Yukichi Senshū* (Selected Works of Fukuzawa Yukichi), 8 vols. (Tokyo: Iwanami Shoten, 1951–52), I: 151; II: 66; V: 320; VI: 30–32.

11. William Braisted, trans., *Meiroku Zasshi, Journal of Japanese Enlightenment* (Tokyo: University of Tokyo Press, 1976), pp. 105, 189.

12. Tanaka Sumiko, *Josei Kaihō no Shisō to Kōdō, Senzen-hen* (Thought and Behavior in Women's Liberation, Prewar Years) (Tokyo: Jiji Tsūshinsha, 1975), pp. 53–61.

13. Nagabata Michiko, *No no Onna* (Women of the Plains) (Tokyo: Shinhyōron, 1980), pp. 206–7, 210–11.

14. Tanaka, *Josei Kaihō no Shisō to Kōdō,* pp. 107–8.

15. *Ibid.,* p. 112.

16. Fukuji Shigetaka, *Kindai Nihon Joseishi* (History of Modern Japanese Women) (Tokyo: Sekkasha, 1963), p. 60.

17. Mikiso Hane, *Peasants, Rebels, and Outcastes* (New York: Pantheon Books, 1982), p. 210.

18. Inoue, *Nihon Joseishi*, p. 234.

19. The opponents of the system won a small measure of success when an American missionary, U. G. Murphy, argued that the civil code of 1898 provided for the right of brothel inmates to leave of their own free will, because an article in the code held that laws that are injurious to public order and undermine morality are invalid. This interpretation was pushed by Yamamuro to get a law enacted in 1921 to allow the inmates to leave the brothels if they wished to do so. But because the inmates were heavily in debt to the brothel keepers, this was not feasible for most of them. Nagabata Michiko, *Honoho no Onna* (Women in Flame) (Tokyo: Shinhyōron, 1981), p. 76, and Yamakawa Kikue, *Nihon Fujin Undō-shōshi* (Short History of the Japanese Women's Movement) (Tokyo: Yamato Shobō, 1979), p. 143.

20. Tsurumi Shunsuke et al., eds., *Nihon no Hyakunen* (Hundred Years of Japan), 10 vols. (Tokyo: Chikuma Shobō, 1961–64), IV: 34.

21. Tanaka, *Josei Kaihō no Shisō to Kōdō*, p. 296. Also see Hane, *Peasants, Rebels, and Outcastes*, pp. 207–25.

22. *Fukuzawa Yukichi Senshū*, V: 291.

23. Fukuji, *Kindai Nihon Joseishi*, pp. 33–34.

24. *Ibid.*, p. 35.

25. Inoue, *Nihon Joseishi*, p. 224.

26. Tanaka, *Josei Kaihō no Shisō to Kōdō*, p. 137.

27. Ai Hoshino, "The Education of Women," in Inazo Nitobe et al., *Western Influence in Modern Japan* (Chicago: University of Chicago Press, 1931), p. 224.

28. Tanaka, *Josei Kaihō no Shisō to Kōdō*, p. 136.

29. *Ibid.*, p. 138.

30. Kaigo Tokiomi, ed., *Nihon no Kyōkasho Taikei, Kindai-hen* (Comprehensive Collection of Japanese Textbooks, The Modern Age), 27 vols. (Tokyo: Kōdansha, 1961–67), II: 650–51.

31. Shidzue Ishimoto, *Facing Two Ways: The Story of My Life* (New York: Farrar & Rinehart, 1935), p. 78.

32. Tanaka, *Josei Kaihō no Shisō to Kōdō*, p. 130.

33. Nagabata, *Honoho no Onna*, pp. 270–71.

34. Tsurumi et al., *Nihon no Hyakunen*, VIII: 307–11. Also see Hane, *Peasants, Rebels, and Outcastes*, pp. 173–204.

35. Tanaka Sumiko and Hidaka Rokurō, *Fujin Seisaku–Fujin Undō* (Women's Policy–Women's Movement) (Tokyo: Aki Shobō, 1969), pp. 147–48.

36. Yamamoto Shigeru, *Aa, Nomugi Tōge* (Oh, Nomugi Pass) (Tokyo: Kadokawa Shoten, 1977), p. 329.

37. *Ibid.*, p. 328.

38. Nagabata, *Honoho no Onna*, p. 254.

39. Tsurumi et al., *Nihon no Hyakunen*, V: 163.

40. Yamakawa, *Nihon Fujin Undō-shōshi*, p. 90.

41. Lois Dilatush, "Women in the Professions," in Joyce Lebra et al., eds., *Women in Changing Japan* (Boulder, Colo.: Westview Press, 1976), p. 191.

42. Hoshino, "The Education of Women," p. 227; Tsurumi et al., *Nihon no Hyakunen*, V: 164.

43. Tanaka, *Josei Kaihō no Shisō to Kōdō*, p. 52. Also see Sharon L. Sievers, *Flowers in Salt* (Stanford: Stanford University Press, 1983), pp. 29-30.

44. Tanaka, *Josei Kaihō no Shisō to Kōdō*, p. 52.

45. *Ibid.*, p. 47.

46. Yamakawa, *Nihon Fujin Undō-shōshi*, p. 64.

47. Nagabata, *No no Onna*, p. 198.

48. Sumiya Mikio, *Dai-Nihon Teikoku no Shiren* (The Crucible of the Japanese Empire) (Tokyo: Chūō-Kōronsha, 1966), p. 298.

49. Nagabata, *Honoho no Onna*, p. 11.

50. *Ibid.*, p. 21.

51. *Hiratsuka Raichō Jiden*, I: 296.

52. *Ibid.*, p. 328.

53. *Ibid.*, II: 426-27.

54. Nagabata, *Honoho no Onna*, pp. 15, 107.

55. *Itō Noe Zenshū* (Collected Works of Itō Noe), 2 vols. (Tokyo: Gakugei Shorin, 1970), II: 19.

56. *Ibid.*, pp. 74-75.

57. *Ibid.*, pp. 334 ff.

58. Imai Seiichi, *Taishō Demokurashii* (Taishō Democracy) (Tokyo: Chūō-Kōronsha, 1966), pp. 174-82.

59. Mikiso Hane, *Japan: A Historical Survey* (New York: Charles Scribner's Sons, 1972), p. 412.

60. Yamakawa, *Nihon Fujin Undō-shōshi*, p. 144.

61. George M. Beckmann and Okubo Genji, *The Japanese Communist Party, 1922-1945* (Stanford: Stanford University Press, 1969), p. 49.

62. Robert A. Scalapino, *The Japanese Communist Movement, 1920-1966* (Berkeley and Los Angeles: University of California Press, 1966), pp. 29-30.

63. Beckmann, *The Japanese Communist Party*, p. 122.

64. *Ibid.*, p. 250.

65. Yamakawa, *Nihon Fujin Undō-shōshi*, p. 147.

66. Susan J. Pharr, *Political Women in Japan* (Berkeley and Los Angeles: University of California Press, 1981), p. 34.

Chapter 2

1. *Warawa no Hanseigai*, in *Nihonjin no Jiden* (Autobiographies of Japanese), 25 vols. (Tokyo: Heibonsha, 1980), VI: 5-7, 17, 22-27, 29-31, 36, 38-39, 40-43, 45-47. Written in 1904.

2. Inoue Kiyoshi, *Nihon Joseishi* (History of Japanese Women) (Tokyo: Sanichi Shobō, 1967), p. 245. For an article on Fukuda's life, see Sharlie C.

Ushioda, "Fukuda Hideko and the Woman's World of Meiji Japan," in Hilary Conroy et al., eds., *Japan in Transition* (Rutherford, N.J.: Fairleigh Dickinson University Press, 1984), pp. 276 ff.

3. Marukawa Kaseko, "Fukuda Hideko," in Setouchi Harumi, ed., *Onna no Isshō, Jimbutsu Kindai Joseishi, Hangyaku no Onna no Roman* (A Woman's Lifetime, Personalities in Modern Women's History, The Romance of Rebellious Women), 8 vols. (Tokyo: Kōdansha, 1980), VI: 60.

4. *Ibid.,* p. 62.

5. She also attended an English-language school run by Yajima Kajiko, a Christian reformer who fought to end the system of public brothels. Yamakawa Kikue, *Nihon Fujin Undō-Shōshi* (Short History of the Japanese Women's Movement) (Tokyo: Yamato Shobō, 1979), p. 69.

6. In the 1880s a power struggle developed in Korea between the conservative and progressive factions. Japan favored the advocates of modernization in order to counteract the conservative faction, which was linked to China. In late 1884 a military skirmish broke out between Chinese and Japanese troops, and the Japanese minister to Korea was forced to leave that country. In order to prevent a major confrontation the two countries concluded a treaty providing for the withdrawal of their troops from Korea and including an agreement not to dispatch troops there in the future without notifying each other. Ōi and his cohorts regarded this as a national humiliation and decided to create an international crisis by going to Korea and assassinating the leaders of the conservatives then in control of the government. This, they believed, would not only further the cause of reform in Korea but also force the Japanese government to make concessions to the reformers in Japan in order to unify the people and enable them to cope with the international crisis. Murata Shizuko, *Fukuda Hideko* (Tokyo: Iwanami Shoten, 1959), pp. 40–41.

7. Nagabata Michiko, *No no Onna* (Women of the Plains) (Tokyo: Shinhyōron, 1980), p. 232.

8. Marukawa, "Fukuda Hideko," p. 91.

9. Sumiya Mikio, *Dai-Nihon Teikoku no Shiren* (The Crucible of the Japanese Empire) (Tokyo: Chūō-Kōronsha, 1966), pp. 80–85.

10. For a discussion of Fukuda's activities during this period, see Sharon L. Sievers, *Flowers in Salt* (Stanford: Stanford University Press, 1983), pp. 114 ff.

11. Setouchi Harumi, *Bi wa Ranchō ni Ari* (Beauty in Discord) (Tokyo: Kadokawa Shoten, 1969), p. 153.

12. Kamichika Ichiko, *Waga Ai, Waga Tatakai* (My Love, My Battles) (Tokyo: Kōdansha, 1972), p. 138.

13. Marukawa, "Fukuda Hideko," p. 100.

14. *Abstracts from the Eighteen Histories* (*Shih-pa Shih-Lüeh*) was written by a Chinese historian of the Mongol period, Tseng Hsien-chih. The *Unofficial History of Japan* (*Nihon Gaishi*) was written by Rai Sanyō (1780–1832), a Confucian scholar employed by the lord of Aki-han (Hiroshima).

15. Fukuda uses the name Haishi for Kobayashi, Omoi for Ōi Kentarō, and Furui for Arai Shingo in this account.

16. In the early Meiji years political activists usually came from the former samurai class or wealthy peasant families, so they tended to be accorded better treatment than common criminals, who tended to be from the lower classes.

17. Nakae Chōmin (1847–1901) was a liberal advocate of popular rights and an admirer of Rousseau. Kurihara Ryōichi (1855–1911) was a newspaperman who was a supporter of Itagaki Taisuke.

Chapter 3

1. Setouchi Harumi, *Tōi Koe* (Distant Voice) (Tokyo: Shinchōsha, 1975), p. 76.

2. Kondō Tomie, "Kanno Suga," in Setouchi Harumi, ed., *Onna no Isshō, Jimbutsu Kindai Joseishi, Hangyaku no Onna no Roman* (A Woman's Lifetime, Personalities in Modern Women's History, The Romance of Rebellious Women), 8 vols. (Tokyo: Kōdansha, 1980), 6: 30–31.

3. *Ibid.*

4. Hosoda Junichirō, *Meiji no Onna* (Meiji Women), vol. IX of *Meiji no Gunzō* (Meiji Configurations) (Tokyo: Sanichi Shobō, 1969), pp. 214–15.

5. Kondō Tomie, "Kanno Suga," p. 44.

6. For Kōtoku's experiences in the United States, see F. G. Notehelfer, *Kotoku Shusui: Portrait of a Japanese Radical* (Cambridge: Cambridge University Press, 1971), pp. 120–32.

7. Setouchi, *Tōi Koe*, p. 161.

8. Kondō Tomie, "Kanno Suga," p. 47.

9. Setouchi, *Tōi Koe*, p. 224.

10. *Ibid.*, pp. 100–1.

11. *Ibid.*, p. 288.

12. Shioda Shōbei, ed., *Gendai Nihon Kiroku Zenshū, Kakumei ka no Gunzō* (Collection of Contemporary Japanese Records, Configuration of Revolutionaries), 24 vols. (Tokyo: Chikuma Shobō, 1969), XI: 16.

13. *Ibid.*, p. 17.

14. Hosoda, *Meiji no Gunzō*, IX: 224–25.

15. Itoya Sumio, *Kanno Suga* (Tokyo: Iwanami Shoten, 1970), pp. 197–98.

16. Kondō Tomie, "Kanno Suga," p. 51.

17. Nagabata Michiko, *Honoho no Onna* (Tokyo: Shinhyōron, 1981), pp. 9–10.

18. *Ibid.*, p. 10.

19. *Ibid.*, p. 21. For a more detailed analysis of Kanno's life, see Sharon L. Sievers, *Flowers in Salt* (Stanford: Stanford University Press, 1983), pp. 139 ff.

20. Kanno Sugako, *Shide no Michigusa* (Reflections on the Way to the Gallows), ed. Kanzaki Kiyoshi, in *Meiji Kiroku Bungakushū* (Literary Collection of Meiji Records) (Tokyo: Chikuma Shobō, 1967), pp. 326–46.

21. This article provided for the death penalty for anyone who harmed or plotted to harm members of the imperial family.

22. On Sakai Mā-bō (Magara), see chapter 5. Kanno also refers to her as Mā-san. Hori Yasuko was Ōsugi Sakae's wife, and Yoshikawa was a socialist and Kanno's friend.

23. *Tan'ishō* was written by Shinran, a thirteenth-century Buddhist monk and founder of the True Pure Land Sect.

24. Kanno Masao, who was living in Los Angeles at that time.

25. He was adopted into the Kōtoko family to carry on the family line.

26. Sakai started a business providing writing services in order to earn a living after he was released from prison following the Red Flag incident.

27. Yoshikawa spent a year and a half in jail for having demonstrated against an increase in trolley fare.

28. Former follower of Kōtoku who later joined the Salvation Army.

29. Kanno broke down and cried, because Hori Yasuko and she were close friends. After Kanno was released from prison following the Red Flag incident, she had no place to go, so Hori took her in and let her stay with her for half a year. Setouchi Harumi, *Kaichō wa Itsuwari Nari* (There Is No Harmony), 2 vols. (Tokyo: Bungei Shunjū, 1984), I: 81–82.

30. Kanno had been in prison since May 18, before the plot against the emperor was uncovered, charged with the violation of the press laws for her work in Kōtoku's magazine, *Jiyū Shisō* (Free Thought).

31. Koizumi was Kōtoku's friend and supporter; Katō Tokijirō was a doctor who was a supporter of the socialists. When Sakai Toshihiko was imprisoned he had Katō take care of Magara. See chapter 5. Watanabe Yayoko was Watanabe Masatarō's wife. Masatarō was a socialist who turned to anarchism. In her note to Okano she wrote, "I believe I'll be all right another ten days or a half a month, so please let me know of any interesting news." She was hanged three days later.

32. Kanno took care of her younger sister, Hideko, until she died of tuberculosis.

33. But her friends had her buried in Seishunji temple where her sister was buried.

34. He was the most aggressive of the prosecutors. He succeeded in getting convictions for defendants with the least bit of connection with the conspirators. He later became a Diet member representing the Minseitō.

35. The transcript by the prosecutor, Taketomi, has not been found.

36. It is said that Taketomi went around boasting that he made Kanno spill her guts by flattering her and thus succeeded in building an iron-clad case against her.

37. Aizu-han was a feudal domain in the north that opposed the imperial faction during the Meiji Restoration.

38. Koizumi was a politician and Kōtoku's friend. Minami was a union organizer among miners, Kayama Sukeo was a merchant and a socialist, and Tomiyama was a socialist newspaperman.

39. *Suikodō-Kensō* (*Tsui-ku-t'ang Chien-sao* in Chinese) is a collection of say-

ings and maxims culled from a variety of sources extending from antiquity to the Ming period. Lu Shao-heng compiled this ca. 1624 for readers to contemplate and reflect upon.

Chapter 4

1. Mikiso Hane, *Peasants, Rebels, and Outcastes* (New York: Pantheon Books, 1982), pp. 236–42.

2. Imai Seiichi, *Taishō Demokurashii* (Taishō Democracy) (Tokyo: Chūō-Kōronsha, 1966), pp. 203–11.

3. *Ibid.*, pp. 328–91.

4. Morosawa Yōko, ed., *Dokyumento Onna no Hyakunen, Onna to Kenryoku* (Documents on One Hundred Years of Women's History, Women and Power) (Tokyo: Heibonsha, 1978), V: 288–90.

5. Kaneko Fumiko, *Nani ga Watakushi o Kō Saseta ka?* (What Made Me Do What I Did), in *Nihonjin no Jiden* (Autobiographies of Japanese), 25 vols. (Tokyo: Heibonsha, 1980), VI: 110–11. Kaneko wrote this in prison, 1926–27.

6. *Ibid.*, p. 117.

7. *Ibid.*, p. 127.

8. *Ibid.*, pp. 180–81.

9. *Ibid.*, p. 148.

10. Kaneko, *Nani ga Watakushi o Kō Saseta ka*, VI: 248–51, 255–58, 281–85, 287–94, 296–98, 300–34.

11. Sawaji Hisae, *Tsuma-tachi no 2.26 Jiken* (2/26 Incident and the Wives) (Tokyo: Chūō-Kōronsha, 1980), pp. 160–61.

12. Tsurumi Shunsuke, ed., *Gendai Nihon Kiroku Zenshū, Seikatsu no Kiroku* (Collection of Contemporary Japanese Records, Records of Living), 24 vols. (Tokyo: Chikuma Shobō, 1970), XIV: 14–15.

13. Kaneko seems to have been driven by a death wish. Or perhaps she was behaving in a fashion typical of the rebels in Japan—they had to die for their cause. "Modern Japanese hero-worship still bears the traces of this. People admire rebels and fanatical non-conformists (the more fanatical the better). But in the end, these heroes must destroy themselves." Ian Buruma, *Behind the Mask* (New York: Pantheon Books, 1984), p. 168.

14. Tsurumi, *Gendai Nihon Kiroku Zenshū*, XIV: 18. For Takamure Itsue, see E. Patricia Tsurumi, "Feminism and Anarchism in Japan: Takamure Itsue, 1894–1964," in *Bulletin of Concerned Asian Scholars*, XVII, no. 2 (1985): 2 ff.

15. Takao Heibei was a leftist activist who got into a hassle with Yonemura Kaichirō, leader of an anticommunist, rightist gang. In the course of the physical struggle Takao was shot in the back by Yonemura. Setouchi Harumi, *Kaichō wa Itsuwari Nari* (There Is No Harmony), 2 vols. (Tokyo: Bungei Shunjū, 1984), II: 141–44.

16. (Reconstruction), a magazine that dealt with current social, political, and economic issues.

17. Probably refers to the Gyōminkai (see chapter 6).

18. Kunō is Kutsumi Fusako (see chapter 5).

19. Mikimoto is Mitamura Shirō (see chapter 5).

20. Peter A. Kropotkin (1842–1921), a Russian anarchist.

21. Tokyo District Court Interrogation Records for November 22, 1923.

22. Setouchi Harumi, ed., *Onna no Isshō, Jimbutsu Kindai Joseishi, Hangyaku no Onna no Roman,* 8 vols. (Tokyo: Kōdansha, 1980), VI: 168–69.

Chapter 5

1. Esashi Akiko, *Sameyo Onna-tachi* (Women, Wake Up!) (Tokyo: Daigetsu Shoten, 1980), pp. 20–22. Additional familial connections between the women and male socialists in this group are these: Takatsu Tayoko was Takatsu Seidō's wife, Hori Yasuko was Ōsugi Sakae's spouse, Sakai Tameko was married to Sakai Toshihiko, Hashiura Tameko to Hashiura Tokio, Nakasone Sadayo to Nakasone Genwa, and Akizuki Shizue was with Nakanomio Kōriki, and several others were wives of members of the watchmakers' union in Kameido. Watanabe Etsuji, *Tatakai ni Ikita Onna-tachi* (Women Who Lived for the Struggle) (Tokyo: Domesu Shuppan, 1980), pp. 33–38.

2. Esashi, *Sameyo Onna-tachi,* pp. 23–24.

3. Named for the eighth day of March 1923 when the first International Women's Day was held in Tokyo.

4. Among these was Nakanomio Kōriki, who beat up his opponents and demanded money from banks and business firms. Esashi, *Sameyo Onna-tachi,* pp. 235–41.

5. A business set up to help people write letters, draft documents and statements, translate foreign writings, etc.

6. *Jiyū Shisō,* April 1960 issue, pp. 32 ff.

7. For a biographical sketch of Takase, see George M. Beckmann and Okubo Genji, *The Japanese Communist Party, 1922–1945* (Stanford: Stanford University Press, 1969), p. 384.

8. Esashi, *Sameyo Onna-tachi,* p. 49.

9. *Ibid.,* p. 75.

10. Makise Kikue, *Kikigaki: Hitamuki no Onna-tachi* (Interviews: Zealous Women) (Tokyo: Asahi Shimbun, 1976), p. 28.

11. *Ibid.,* pp. 10–15, 17–24.

12. This religion was founded in 1882 by Kurozumi Munetada, a Shinto priest from Okayama prefecture. He taught his followers to adhere to the teachings of the Sun Goddess, Amaterasu, follow the way of the gods, and achieve unity with the gods.

13. Earlier Tokio got into trouble with the authorities when he was a student at Waseda University. He wrote a letter to his hometown newspaper during the Kōtoku Great Treason incident. He criticized the trial, arguing that socialism was the rational current of thought suitable to the social conditions of his time. If

Kōtoku were executed it would turn public opinion against the authorities. The officials thereupon arrested him for violating the press laws. When they searched his room they found a diary in which he criticized the practice of surrounding the emperor with security guards whenever he left the palace. Tokio also compared the emperor's face to the carving of a dragon's face on the wall of his hometown. This thought occurred to him because the emperor's face was customarily referred to as *ryūgan* (dragon face) in line with the Chinese practice of relating the dragon to the imperial throne. Esashi, *Sameyo Onna-tachi,* pp. 81–82.

14. Mushanokōji said that the New Village would be a communal society where people could freely develop their natural talents and would help each other like brothers and sisters.

15. Arishima was a prominent novelist (1878–1923). He was sympathetic to socialism, and in line with his beliefs, he turned over his Hokkaido farmland to his tenants. In 1923 he committed double suicide with a female magazine reporter. He believed that there were three phases to human life: habitual, intellectual, and instinctive. True freedom, he believed, is to be found in the instinctive or impulsive phase.

16. A religious cult founded as an offshoot of Shinto at the end of the Tokugawa period in 1855. Initially it rejected all superstitious beliefs and practices, but later it incorporated astrological beliefs and came to be regarded as a religion that helps a person become financially successful.

17. Excerpted from Makise Kikue, ed., *Kutsumi Fusako no Koyomi* (Kutsumi Fusako's Calendar) (Tokyo: Shisō-no-Kagakusha, 1975), pp. 9–10, 12–19, 25–26, 28–29, 33–35, 43–44, 50–51, 67–71, 77–85, 97–99. The interviews were conducted in the early 1970s.

18. Esashi, *Sameyo Onna-tachi,* p. 167.

19. *Ibid.,* pp. 177–79.

20. Richard Sorge, a German journalist in Japan, maintained close ties with the German embassy and used that as a cover for his espionage activities on behalf of Soviet Russia. He had the cooperation of Ozaki Hotsumi, who was in the inner circle of the Japanese ruling class. See Chalmers Johnson, *An Instance of Treason* (Stanford: Stanford University Press, 1964), and Gordon W. Prange, *Target Tokyo* (New York: McGraw-Hill, 1984). On Kutsumi, see pp. 127–30 and p. 425 in Prange, referred to as Kuzumi.

21. Karl G. Yoneda, *Ganbatte* (Los Angeles: Asian American Studies Center, University of California, 1983), pp. 21–22, and Johnson, *An Instance of Treason,* pp. 90ff.

22. Esashi, *Sameyo Onna-tachi,* p. 189.

23. Setouchi Harumi, *Onna no Isshō, Jimbutsu Kindai Joseishi, Hangyaku no Onna no Roman,* 8 vols. (Tokyo: Kōdansha, 1980), VI: 211.

24. Esashi, *Sameyo Onna-tachi,* p. 191.

25. When a family has no male heir, the oldest daughter takes a husband who joins her household and adopts his wife's family name.

26. A class of people who had been classified as outcastes in the pre-Meiji era.

Even though they were given legal equality after 1871, they continued to be discriminated against. In the family register they were identified as "new commoners."

27. Nishida Tenkō (1872–1968) was a religious-cult leader and an admirer of Tolstoy.

28. Ryōkan (1758–1831) spent most of his life as a monk, wandering about the country, living like a "nature boy."

29. See Prange, *Target Tokyo,* p. 129, on Taguchi.

30. Asanuma Inejirō (1898–1960) was a prominent socialist leader active in the prewar and postwar years. He was assassinated by a fanatical right-wing youth in 1960. Asō Hisashi (1891–1940) was a socialist leader who, in the 1930s, cooperated with the ruling elite.

31. Matsuoka Komakichi (1888–1958) was a leader of the right-wing of the Sōdōmei. He organized moderate socialist parties like the Social Democratic party and the Social Masses party.

32. Minami Kiichi (1904–70) was active in the labor and socialist movements. He was arrested on March 15, 1928, and defected. Later he became a successful businessman. Yamabe Kentarō (1905–77) was active in the labor movement but later turned to historical writing.

33. Yamamoto Senji (1889–1929) was a member of the Diet and a supporter of the labor movement. He was assassinated by a right-wing radical.

34. Ichikawa Shōichi (1892–1945) was a Communist party leader, who was arrested in 1929 and died in prison just before the end of the war. See Beckmann, *The Japanese Communist Party,* pp. 365–66, for a biographical sketch.

35. Tokuda Kyūichi (1894–1953) was a Communist party leader who was arrested in March 1928 and spent eighteen years in prison. He played a key role in rebuilding the party in the postwar years. See Beckmann, pp. 385–86.

36. Kawabata Yoneko (1908–55) was active in the women's movement in Hokkaido.

37. Kamei Katsuichirō (1890–1966) agreed to abandon his political activities after his arrest and turned to literary, cultural, and intellectual pursuits.

38. Yamamoto Senji was then a Diet member from the Labor Farmer party. He denounced in the Diet the brual measures being taken by the authorities in suppressing the socialists and communists. He reported that Kutsumi's daughter was abused by the police before Kutsumi's eyes and that Kutsumi's blood-stained garments had been destroyed by the police. Setouchi, *Jimbutsu Kindai Joseishi,* VI: 205.

39. Yasuda Tokutarō (1898–) was a medical doctor who supported leftist causes in the prewar years. Later he broke with the Communist party and turned to writing.

40. Matsuo Naoyoshi (1900–35) was active in the labor movement and was arrested in March 1928. See Beckmann, p. 373, for a biographical sketch.

41. Kazama Jōkichi (1901–68) studied in KUTV, returned to Japan in 1930

to revive the party. He was arrested in 1932 and defected in 1933. See Beckmann, p. 370.

42. Yamamoto Masami had just returned from Moscow in 1932 and set out to rebuild the party but was arrested in May 1933. M refers to Matsumoto Noboru, who was actually a government spy, Iizuka Michinobu. See Tsurumi Shunsuke et al., eds., *Nihon no Hyakunen* (Hundred Years of Japan), 10 vols. (Tokyo: Chikuma Shobō, 1961–64), IV: 159.

43. Ōizumi was suspected of being a government spy and was tortured by the Communist party members. He later confessed during his trial that he was working for the Special Higher Police (Beckmann, p. 244). Another person who was suspected of being a government spy was Obata Tatsuo, who was tortured to death by the party leaders.

44. Undoubtedly patterned after Stalin's slogan "Socialism in One Country," which was posited against Trotsky's call for a "Permanent Revolution," that is, support for revolutionary movements outside of Soviet Russia, for he believed that the Communist movement could not survive in Russia unless it became a worldwide movement.

45. Shiga Yoshio (1901–) was active in the Communist party in the prewar years. He was imprisoned in 1928 and remained in prison for eighteen years. In the postwar years he broke with the mainstream of the Communist party and formed a splinter group. Beckmann, p. 382.

46. Ryū Shintarō (1900–67) was a journalist and a political analyst.

47. See Beckmann, *The Japanese Communist Party*, p. 388, for a biographical sketch.

48. Esashi, *Sameyo Onna-tachi*, p. 132.

49. E. Patricia Tsurumi, "Feminism and Anarchism in Japan: Takamure Itsue, 1894–1964," in *Bulletin of Concerned Asian Scholars*, XVII, no. 2 (1985): 9–10. Takamure championed anarchism over Bolshevism. In 1931 she left the political arena and devoted her life to writing a massive history of Japanese women.

50. Yamakawa Kikue, *Onna Nidai no Ki* (Records of Two Generations of Women) (Tokyo: Heibonsha, 1972). Excerpts from pp. 157–58, 160–61, 224–25, 241–42, 260–65, 269–70, 294, 296–97, 302.

51. President Theodore Roosevelt invited Japan and Russia to send delegates to Portsmouth, New Hampshire, to settle the Russo-Japanese War of 1904–5. The concessions gained by the Japanese from the Russians were regarded as inadequate by the critics of the government. They staged massive rallies to protest the treaty.

52. Yasui Tetsuko (1870–1945) was president of Tokyo Women's College from 1923 to 1940.

53. Higuchi Ichiyō was a prominent poet and novelist. See Robert Lyons Danly, *In the Shade of Spring Leaves: The Life and Writings of Higuchi Ichiyo* (New Haven: Yale University Press, 1981).

54. A study made by the Ministry of Agriculture and Commerce of working conditions in the factories as groundwork for labor legislation. It was completed in 1903.

55. Baba Kochō (1869–1940) was a translator and essayist. He was a supporter of the Seitō group.

56. Iwanō Hōmei (1872–1920) was a poet and writer and ostensibly a supporter of women's rights, but he was abusive toward his wife, and when she challenged him in court over property rights following their divorce, he beat her with his cane. Nagabata Michiko, *Honoho no Onna* (Women in Flame) (Tokyo: Shinhyōron, 1980), p. 113.

57. Tanaka Shōzō (1841–1913) was a member of the Diet who devoted his life to fighting a major copper-mining company for polluting the waters and farmland of the Kantō Plain by pouring toxic mineral waste into the river.

58. She was the wife of Tadokoro Teruaki, who assisted the Yamakawas in publishing the *Zen'ei*. See Beckman, *The Japanese Communist Party*, p. 383, for biographical data.

Chapter 6

1. *Tanno Setsu, Kakumei Undō ni Ikiru* (Tanno Setsu, Living for the Revolutionary Movement), Yamashiro Tomoe and Makise Kikue, eds. (Tokyo: Keisō Shobō, 1970), p. 333. Subsequent references will be to *Tanno Setsu, Kakumei*.

2. *Ibid.*, p. 150.

3. George M. Beckmann and Okubo Genji, *The Japanese Communist Party, 1922–1945* (Stanford: Stanford University Press, 1969), pp. 121–24, 387–88.

4. Tanaka Sumiko, *Josei Kaihō no Shisō to Kōdō Senzen-hen* (Thought and Behavior in Women's Liberation, Prewar Years) (Tokyo: Jiji Tsūshinsha, 1975), p. 258.

5. *Tanno Setsu, Kakumei*, pp. 256–57.

6. Excerpts from *Tanno Setsu, Kakumei*, pp. 9–26, 87–97, 99–112, 152–69, 173–74, 178–80.

7. Fujinuma (1881–1952) was active in the labor movement and the Communist party. He was imprisoned during the mass arrests of March 15, 1928.

8. In late 1921 Takatsu and others distributed antiwar handbills to soldiers on maneuvers. See Sakai Magara in chapter 5.

9. Shirayanagi Shūko (1884–1950) was a proletarian writer and a social critic.

10. *Tane Maku Hito* was a journal founded to publish proletarian literature. The first issue appeared in February 1921. It ceased publication in April but was revived in October of that year. The last issue came out in October 1923.

11. Hirabayashi Taiko (1905–72) was a proletarian writer who avoided political dogmatism. In the postwar era she was critical of worshippers of Stalinism.

12. Takano Minoru (1901–74) was a left-wing labor leader.

13. Inomata Tsunao (1889–1942) was an economist educated in the United States. He received his Ph.D. from the University of Wisconsin. He was active in

the Communist party but left it and became an independent Marxist writer. See Beckmann, p. 566, for biographical data.

14. Vasily Yakovich Yaroshenko (1889-1952) was a blind Russian poet and anarchist. He arrived in Japan in 1919 and made many friends among socialists and communists. He was deported in 1921 as a "dangerous person."

15. The black flag was used in contrast to the red flag adopted by the Communists.

16. Nozaka (1892-) was active in the Communist party from its inception, and operated from the Soviet Union, the United States, and China during the war years. He played a key role in rebuilding the Communist party in the postwar years, serving as first secretary and central committee chairman till 1958. See Beckmann, pp. 379-80.

17. A month after the Kameido killings the Asashi newspaper headlined: "Again. Nine Socialists Killed by Army Swords. Mysterious Incident in the Kameido District. Kerosene Poured on Corpses and Burned." One eye-witness of the killings reported: "I was forcibly dragged to the Kameido police station. The place was crowded with men who had been arrested. They threw me in their midst. A little later a terrible shriek came from the open ground to the right of the military drill ground. I wondered what was going on and looked in that direction and saw a man about twenty years old lying on the ground. To the north some men were engaged in a violent scuffle. Horrible sounds came from the direction of the janitor's room. We all kept quiet. A series of desperate shrieks continued to be heard in the darkness. Afterward I found out that a number of people had been killed. I was released one week later. But I can still see the white blade flashing in the dark and hear the agonizing shrieks. Because of the physical pain caused by my arrest and the terrifying experience of that night I have been bedridden ever since." It was reported that over seven hundred socialists, labor leaders, and Koreans were arrested and detained in the Kameido police station alone. *Tanno Setsu, Kakumei,* p. 23.

18. Kawai Etsuzō (1903-66) was active in the Communist party. He went to the Comintern meeting of 1927 and accepted the 1927 thesis, but defected from the party in 1929 after his arrest. Kasuga (1903-76) was active in the Communist party and the Hyōgikai. He was arrested in 1938 and remained in prison till the end of the war. See Beckmann, pp. 368-69.

19. Hakamada Satomi (1904-) was active in the Communist party in the prewar and postwar years. He was sent to KUTV to study in 1925. He returned in 1928 and worked to rebuild the Communist party. He was arrested in 1935 and imprisoned till the end of the war. He became a key party official in the postwar years. See Beckmann, p. 365.

20. Kokuryō Goichirō (1902-43) was a member of the Communist party central committee, was arrested in 1928, refused to defect, and died in prison. See Beckmann, p. 371. Yamagata Tamezō, who led the political police in this arrest, claims that the police were not armed. *Bungei Shunjū,* special edition, October 1954, p. 40.

21. Another person testified to the fact that the police did beat women brutally. Terao Toshi, a member of the Communist party, was arrested in 1928 and was beaten all over her body with an iron bar during interrogation. She was arrested again in the April 16, 1929, roundup. She writes that the interrogator "hit me all over my face, grabbed my hair and threw me over his back, picked me up and threw me down again. Then he made me sit down on the floor and jumped on my knees with his shoes and ground his heels into my thighs. My skin was torn and began to bleed. Then he grabbed a bamboo fencing pole and hit me all over with all his might. I fainted and don't remember what happened after that. All I remember is being carried back to my cell. I did not become fully conscious until quite a while later." Terao Toshi, *Densetsu no Jidai* (Legendary Years) (Tokyo: Miraisha, 1960), pp. 14, 137.

22. Watanabe was killed by the police in Keelung in Taiwan. Although the police claimed that he shot himself when they were pursuing him, his friends are convinced that he was gunned down by the police.

23. Yoneda spent his youth in Japan during the Taishō years and was influenced by the socialist currents of that era. He returned to the United States and played an active role in the labor movement and in the Communist party. See Karl G. Yoneda, *Ganbatte* (Los Angeles: Asian American Studies Center, University of California, 1983).

24. Shimonaka Kunihiko, ed., *Nihon Zankoku Monogatari* (Tales of Japanese Inhumanity), 5 vols. (Tokyo: Heibonsha, 1960), V: 289–95.

25. Interviews excerpted from *Tanno Setsu, Kakumei,* pp. 126–40.

26. 1 chō equals 2.45 acres.

27. Kamimura Susumu (1883–1969) was a lawyer who supported the tenant movement.

28. Inamura Junzō (1900–55) was a Waseda student who helped to organize the Kisaki tenants.

29. Satō Satōji (1901–65) was an agrarian reformer and a member of the Communist party.

30. Mii's husband became a member of the Niigata City Council in the postwar years as a Communist party member.

31. Inamura Ryūichi (1898–) was an agrarian reformer and a member of the Diet in the postwar period.

32. May 5 is Boys' Festival when gigantic paper carps are flown on bamboo poles. The counterpart for girls is Girls' Festival, which comes on March 3. These days used to be holidays when people took time off to honor the children.

33. The affair involved the All Japan Peasants' Conference, which was tied to the Communist party, and the All Japan Peasants' Union's fission.

Chapter 7

1. The 1932 Thesis stressed the Japanese monarchy as an obstacle to the staging of a revolution. George M. Beckmann and Okubo Genji, *The Japanese Com-*

munist Party, 1922–1945 (Stanford: Stanford University Press, 1969), pp. 230–31.

2. *Tanno Setsu, Kakumei Undō ni Ikiru* (Tanno Setsu, Living for the Revolutionary Movement), Yamashiro Tomoe and Makise Kikue, eds. (Tokyo: Keisō Shobō, 1970), pp. 315–20.

3. Mitsuko is Tomoe and Tsuneo is Yoshimune.

4. *Tanno Setsu, Kakumei,* p. 331.

5. See Mikiso Hane, *Peasants, Rebels, and Outcastes* (New York: Pantheon Books, 1982), pp. 85 ff.

6. Usui Yoshimi et al., eds., *Tsuchi to Furusato* (The Earth and Home Villages), 15 vols. (Tokyo: Ie no Hikari Kyōkai, 1976), I: 236–37, 239–41, 243–61, 268–76. The first half of this "story" is in Hane, *Peasants, Rebels, and Outcastes,* pp. 85–101.

7. Asano Sōichirō (1848–1930) was a business tycoon who branched out into numerous industrial sectors after establishing his power base as the "cement king" of Japan.

8. This was actually a massive war launched against China by Japan in 1937, which the latter insisted on calling an "incident."

9. Kashima was Katō Yotsumi, a comrade in Yamashiro Yoshimune's circle. In 1933 he was arrested and sent to prison for five years for his activities in the tenants' movement in Ibaraki prefecture. After his release he visited the Yamashiros frequently. In May 1940 Katō, the Yamashiros, and another friend, Itatani Takashi, were arrested. Katō died the day he was arrested, while undergoing interrogation. Itatani died in prison in Yokohama in February 1945, and Yamashiro Yoshimune died in prison in Hiroshima the following month. Yamashiro Tomoe, "Yamashiro Yoshimune no Koto" (Concerning Yamashiro Yoshimune), in Ueno Hidenobu, ed., *Kindai Minshū no Kiroku, Kōfu* (Record of the Modern Masses, Miners) (Tokyo: Shinjimbutsu Ōraisha, 1971), p. 333.

10. Prisoner number 72 is the person whose story is reproduced in Hane, *Peasants, Rebels, and Outcastes,* pp. 85 ff.

INDEX

ABOUT THE AUTHOR

Mikiso Hane, Szold Distinguished Service Professor of History at Knox College, was born in California in 1922. He went to Japan in 1933 and grew up in a peasant village in Hiroshima prefecture. Returning to the United States in 1940, he was soon thereafter interned in a wartime detention camp. He has taught at Yale and is the translator of Maruyama Masao's *Studies in the Intellectual History of Tokugawa Japan*. He is also the author of numerous books, including *Japan, a Historical Survey* and *Peasants, Rebels, and Outcastes*.